Sew It Up

Sew It Up

a modern manual of practical and
decorative sewing techniques

Ruth Singer

First published in Great Britain in 2008 by
Kyle Cathie Ltd
122 Arlington Road, London NW1 7HP
general.enquiries@kyle-cathie.com
www.kylecathie.com

10 9 8 7 6 5 4 3 2 1

978-1-85626-810-3

Text © 2008 Ruth Singer
Photography © 2008 Jan Baldwin and Dominic Harris,
except for pages 134, 155, 171 and 251 © V&A Images,
Victoria and Albert Museum
Illustrations © 2008 Philip Haxell
Book design © 2008 Kyle Cathie Limited

Project manager: Kate Haxell
Designer: Louise Leffler
Photographers: Jan Baldwin and step photography by Dominic Harris
Illustrator: Philip Haxell
Editorial Director: Muna Reyal
Production Director: Sha Huxtable

A Cataloguing In Publication record for
this title is available from the British Library.

Colour reproduction by Sang Choy
Printed and bound in China by SNP Leefung Printers Ltd.

Contents

Introduction

Sewing for pleasure is getting the stylish revamp it deserves. Making clothes, accessories, presents and beautiful things for your home is a great way to express your creativity and personal style. Sewing shouldn't be a chore: making things for yourself and your friends and family should be a pleasure, a hobby, a distraction from real life, a creative outlet. Nothing beats the pleasure of saying 'I made it!' when asked where you got your lovely bag or skirt or cushion.

We all want gorgeous and original things for ourselves and our homes. We can buy nice cushions in big brand shops, but our friends will have the same ones, as will millions of other people. Our homes express part of our personalities and they should be as original and vibrant as ourselves, not carbon copies of a magazine shoot or our neighbour's house. And really, shouldn't we stop buying cheap and throwaway products and instead invest time, money and effort in real, handmade, ethical and unique things?

Unlike our grandmothers' generation, we don't have to sew to clothe our families. Sewing for ourselves is unlikely to be an economic choice for most of us now: clothes and homewares can be cheap, and time is money. You can spend almost infinite amounts on patterns, fancy fabrics, a sewing machine (or two), steam irons, a made-to-measure tailor's dummy – or you can choose to make sewing an affordable hobby, buying fabrics from markets, using remnants and recycling. You should buy the best you can afford – not necessarily the most fancy, but the best quality for your needs.

Plenty of people find sewing an odd to thing to want to do. I once caused consternation in a flatmate's boyfriend by sitting sewing in front of the TV. He had only ever seen his grandmother and mother sewing, and then only out of financial necessity. To do such a thing for pleasure, when clothes could be bought cheaply on the high street, was to him bizarre and somehow radical. Why would a young, professional woman, brought up to reject stereotypical female roles, choose to do a chore our mothers happily abandoned when feminism and changes in world trade made it unnecessary to sew clothes? The answer is, because I love fabric and clothes and always have. It seems to be in my blood. And I was brought up to do what I wanted, not what anyone else thought I ought to do.

Although I'm now a professional maker, I spent over 20 years sewing for myself, for fun. I made the over-ambitious mistake of starting with dressmaking, which wasn't perhaps the easiest way to learn. Clothes (for grown ups) are great to make, but actually quite hard projects, and it's harder still to get them to fit perfectly. Crafts and home projects – like cushions, shopping bags and pincushions – are a much easier way to learn sewing, but by all means use a complicated project as a way of learning lots of skills on the job.

I often work that way, and there is no reason why you shouldn't do, too, as long as you enjoy it!

Whether or not you can already sew, this book will be your guide to exploring what sewing can offer, from simple, practical techniques for the beginner through to complex patterns and decorative techniques for the more experienced. You can pick and choose from the techniques and projects that interest you, or start at the beginning and work your way through any techniques you want to learn. If you already know how to sew, you can enjoy the book as creative inspiration to develop your own ideas and individual designs. I hope you will find this book more inspirational and exciting than traditional sewing manuals, and more in-depth than the average book of projects. I'm a professional designer-maker working every day with fabric, but I'm mainly self-taught. This book is what I wanted when I started to sew, and what I needed when I got better at sewing and wanted to learn more. It's also the kind of book I still love now as an experienced stitcher, for inspiration, ideas, good reading and fabulous pictures.

I've tried to cover everything you need to start sewing, from threading a needle, setting up a sewing space and choosing fabric to how to use dress patterns. If you have more experience there are over 150 decorative and practical techniques to incorporate into your repertoire, with 20 masterclasses that cover useful and fascinating techniques such as trapunto quilting and couture hemming.

The 20 projects range from an easy T-shirt transformation to a complex handbag and include presents, accessories, garments and home textiles. The projects are cross-referenced to detailed and truly practical techniques, pointing out possible pitfalls and common mistakes and including personal tips I have developed to make sewing easier, more successful, and above all, fun.

I try to be an eco-friendly designer and with this in mind, I have made several of the projects using recycled or eco fabrics and vintage haberdashery. Almost anything can be made with eco fabrics if you try. I have also included advice on repairing and altering, as well as ideas for customising clothes using the techniques in the book.

I love exploring sewing shops and trying out new tools and equipment, so I have included a detailed guide to wonderful things available from sewing and craft shops. There is also an extensive fabric guide, including interfacing and stuffing as well as organic fabrics. The resource section includes a glossary of weird sewing words, plus lists of my favourite books, websites and shops. But don't just read – pick up your needle and get sewing!

RUTH SINGER

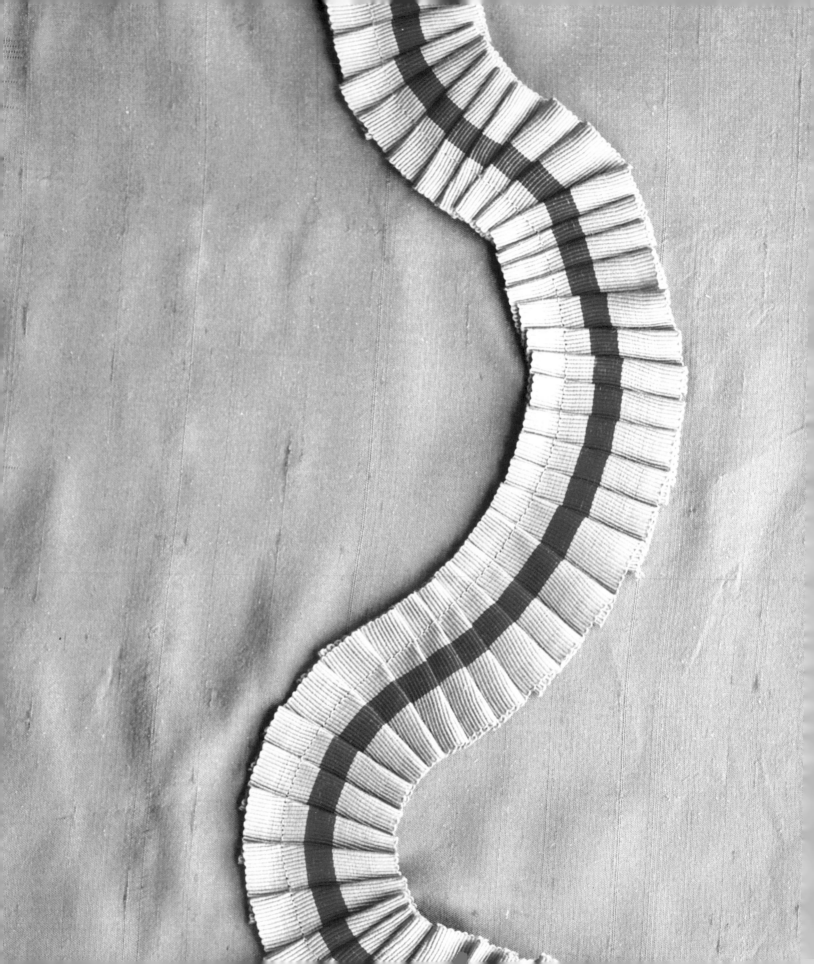

Practical Techniques

Setting up a sewing space

How much space do you need to start sewing? The easy answer is, how much have you got?

Lots of people think they haven't got the space in their home to get really into sewing. Maybe that's because they have seen other people with dedicated sewing rooms stuffed with machines, boxes of fabric and neatly (or otherwise) arranged jars of buttons, threads and other stuff filling miles of shelf-space. Most of us can quite easily manage to take up all the available space with things we like, and indeed I can quite easily take over unavailable space, like the dining table and the living room floor. Storing sewing paraphernalia compactly is possible, especially if you are tidy. Sewing itself though generally needs space.

Of course, the ideal is a dedicated sewing room with a large table for cutting, a smaller one with drawers and shelves around it for your sewing machine and tools, and an ironing board. You are much more likely to get into sewing if you don't have to set up the machine each time you use it, so if you can find a corner where it can live, so much the better. For years I kept my sewing machine on my bedroom desk and moved it only when I needed to do paperwork, which says a lot about my priorities!

Making the physical space is just one half of the battle. Making time is difficult, too. You may be able to squeeze in a few hours sewing one evening a week, or you may prefer to set aside a whole Sunday purely for sewing. Either way, remember that sewing is your relaxing, creative time, which is good for the soul – and so much more productive than lounging in the bath! If you like listening to music or the radio, make sure you can do so in your sewing room, otherwise it's awfully quiet. Better still, get together with like-minded friends for sewing and gossip. Share your skills, go out fabric hunting, browse through this book together. Make sewing an enjoyable part of your life.

Work surface

A table for cutting out and sewing on is essential for most people. I say most people, as I spent my teenage years cutting out fabric on the floor and many quilters keep agile by laying out their work on the floor. A small corner of a table is fine if all you make is little toys like Mr Mouse (page 124) or wee purses and pretty things. If you plan to make clothes, then give yourself the space to spread out at least 1.5m of fabric. If you are making curtains, take over the biggest table you can find or place two together. Many people use a dining table – protect the top from the sewing machine with a cutting mat or large placemat, or even thick, folded fabric. These protectors have the

added bonus of enabling you to slide the sewing machine around on the table if you need to make a rapid move to accommodate the arrival of dinner or a laptop.

Scissors and pins can also damage the surface of the table, so try using large cutting mats under the work, or even big sheets of cardboard. You can buy specially made cardboard cutting surfaces for this very purpose. They can also be used on a bed (take off the duvet first), so are particularly good for spare-bedroom sewing.

If you can have a dedicated table, I recommend an old-fashioned solid wood desk with drawers on both sides to hold all the bits and pieces to hand. Make sure the table is solid and doesn't wobble when the machine is running. If you use a drop-leaf table, try and sew at the side, not on the leaf-end as it will bounce up and down! Likewise with any table that folds – make sure it won't collapse under the weight and vibration of the sewing machine.

Ironing board

You must have somewhere close by to iron. It's tempting not to bother ironing a project until it's finished, but the best sewing tip I have ever learnt is to iron as you go along. If you are pushed for space, try a folded-up towel on the table, but make sure you don't leave it on there when you finish work, as the damp caused by steaming can damage varnish and paint. You can buy mini tabletop ironing boards and cloths designed for ironing on a table and there are some nice vintage wooden ironing boards around.

Chair

Watch out for your back and get a decent chair! A second-hand office chair will be just fine, as long as it supports your back and is adjustable so you can sit at the right height for the table and machine. A padded seat is pretty good, too, if you want to enjoy lengthy sewing sessions. If it's too ugly, re-cover the seat and back in nice fabric.

Armchair

This isn't a sewing room essential, but you will need somewhere comfy to curl up to do your hand sewing – hemming, binding, embroidery or whatever. There is no point doing this at a sewing table when you can be in front of a film or with your family. Choose a spot with good light – a window or a reading light – and a side table or wide chair arms to pile up the pins and thread. Settle in and enjoy hand sewing.

Lighting

Always sew under natural light or with good artificial task lighting. You can now get low-energy daylight bulbs that are perfect. Experiment with positioning the sewing table by a window so you get the best light at the time of day when you sew.

Storage

If you have to be a mobile sewer, then get a nice big toolbox to store everything in. You can buy cheap ones in a DIY shop, but they are often ugly and not quite right for the job. Sewing shops will have more useful ones, along with storage for bobbins, embroidery threads and all sorts of things you never knew you needed. You can even get sewing toolboxes on wheels.

Shelves can be useful around the sewing area to keep boxes and jars on, and even neatly folded fabric. If you can, screw cup-hooks along the edges of shelves or the sewing table to hang scissors, tape measures and rulers from.

If you are using a multi-purpose room that needs to look nice when you aren't sewing, store sewing bits in vintage hat boxes, decorative tins, baskets and glass jars, though you do need to be tidy for this to work. I like to store small pieces in shoe boxes covered with nice fabric or paper and labelled with luggage tags. Vintage hatboxes look lovely piled up and metal tins can be good for small items like buttons.

Drawers are useful for storing sewing materials and equipment. Small wooden drawers from office suppliers can be painted or covered in nice paper. Browse antique and junk shops for old tool drawers, which are perfect for buttons, trims and small things.

Fabric storage

Most people have to store fabrics in plastic crates under beds or in cupboards. I'm not a fan of sealed boxes as the fabric can't breathe and can get musty and damp. I prefer a deep cupboard or storing folded fabrics in wooden under-bed drawers, or even wicker baskets or hampers with old sheets over the top to protect from dust (or cats). This won't protect fabrics from moth attack though; see below.

Some people use a cataloguing system to keep track of their fabric stash. Cut a snippet of each fabric and stick it onto an index card and file in order of fabric type, noting the length and width of each piece and any other information. You might like to keep track of what you bought where and for how much, too.

If you have space, it's nice to keep fabrics folded on shelves in piles according to colour, type of material or size of piece. It's much easier to see what you have, and to select co-ordinating colours, when it's all out on display. If you get strong sunlight in your sewing room, use curtains or blinds to keep the sun off the shelves, as prolonged sunlight will eventually damage fabrics and other materials out on display. If you plan to hoard very precious things for a long time, it's worth doing a bit of research on textile conservation and wrapping precious things in acid-free tissue and archival boxes.

Moths

Moths and other fabric-eating creatures tend to go for animal-based fibres like wool and silk. If you think there is a risk of moths, keep animal fibres in sealed plastic zip-lock bags and put in a natural moth repellent like lavender or cedar. If you don't have moths, do your best to avoid getting them. Wash or dry-clean vintage fabrics immediately, or isolate them in sealed bags until you can launder them. Learn to identify insect damage and don't buy anything that has it.

You can get rid of moths and other insects by freezing the infested item in a zip-lock bag for a week or so. When you take it out, let it come to room temperature before you open the bag. Then brush off or wash out any remaining bits of insect or waste products – the black gritty stuff technically known as frass.

Basic tools

You don't need much to start sewing. Some of the projects in this book can be made with very little equipment and you can acquire more as you get into sewing.

It's always worth having good tools and like kitchen tools, sewing equipment varies in quality. Cheap tools are rarely up to the job – household scissors won't cut fabric properly, cheap needles and pins are too chunky and rough, and cheap polyester thread will break. It's worth buying the best you can afford, and this applies as much to needles as it does to fabric and sewing machines. These are items you need to get started; you'll find more detailed information on these and other tools on pages 280–285.

Needles

The thinner the needle, the more easily it will glide through the fabric and a too-thick needle will leave larger holes in the fabric. This applies to both hand and machine needles. There is more information on different types of needles on page 282.

Threads

The most common types of thread for both machine and hand sewing are cotton, polyester or a mix. Threads come on small spools, commonly 100m, which is usually enough for one small garment like a skirt. There is more about threads on page 19.

Scissors

The one thing you cannot skimp on is proper scissors. You MUST have decent fabric scissors and do not let anyone else near them or they will be used for opening packaging and stripping wires because they are the only sharp scissors in the house. Pinking shears have zigzag blades that stop fabrics from fraying. While not essential, they are very useful. There is more about scissors on page 280.

Pins

I use extra-long dressmaker's pins with glass heads. Good, long pins are sharper, easier to get in and out of thick fabrics, don't bend so much and make smaller holes in fabrics. Plastic heads will melt and stick to the iron. Correct pinning techniques are shown on page 22.

Chalk

Basic tailor's chalk is cheap and works fine, but I prefer to use old slivers of soap instead. It draws more smoothly and can be removed by steaming or washing. You can also buy special pens that either wash or fade out and chalk in the form of pencils. There is more about marking tools on page 281.

Measuring tape

A retractable metal tape measure for DIY is okay for measuring fabric and trims, but under no circumstances try to measure bodies with one. The measurements won't be accurate and you run risk of injury! A soft, plastic sewing tape measure is considerably easier to use. There is more about measuring tools on page 281.

Iron

If you do a lot of sewing you might want to think about a fancy iron, but to start with just have one in the same room as your sewing. My two favourite irons are a separate-tank steam iron and a small travel iron. Buy a cheap iron for techniques that risk getting sticky gunk on the soleplate, such as using fusible webbing, see page 188.

Sewing machine

You don't actually need a machine to sew anything, but it will save you masses of time if you want to make clothes, let alone curtains. Small projects can be easily hand-sewn. It takes time to sew well by hand, but it's worth the effort as it can be immensely enjoyable and rewarding. Advanced sewing and couture techniques usually require hand sewing, so be prepared.

It is hard to advise on buying a sewing machine as it will depend on what you want to do, how much you are going to sew and how much money you have to spend. I have only ever bought second-hand machines, all of which have been great. If you are trying out sewing, it's probably not worth buying a machine until you are sure you will get good use from it. If you can, borrow one for a few months to get an idea of whether you are really going to get into sewing. Repairs and servicing are pretty expensive, so make sure the one you borrow actually works.

Once you have decided to buy a machine then make friends with your local independent sewing machine shop. They will usually give you the best advice and help you find a machine that really suits your needs, rather than the most expensive one. Many small shops will sell second-hand machines that they have repaired and serviced, and this is by far the best way to start. New machines at the bottom end of the price range are clunky and unrefined. Start with a solid, fairly basic, old machine by one of the major brands, and you will get good value for money. I advise getting a major brand simply because it will be easier to get accessories. If and when you decide to upgrade, the shop may well do a trade-in for you.

Sewing machines do vary, but shown here are the features that most machines have.

1 Tension discs. These hold the upper thread tension to help form even stitches. There is a dial for changing the upper thread tension.

2 Stitch selector for a range of automated stitches, such as blind hemming stitch.

3 Spool pins for top thread. The second spool pin is for use with a twin needle. Thread both sets of sewing thread at the same time in the normal way.

4 Stitch width and length. The positions of these vary from machine to machine.

5 Needle position selector. This moves the needle to the left or right.

6 Reverse setting. This is used to set the machine to sew backwards.

7 Presser foot lever. This raises and lowers the presser foot and engages the top tension.

8 Thread guides. Keep the thread in place while you sew. It is important that the threads are in the guides at all times.

9 Bobbin winder. In most machines thread goes from the spool, round the thread guide and over to the winder.

10 Flywheel for starting the sewing by hand. In most machines you pull or turn the inner section to disengage the needle while you wind the bobbin.

11 Bobbin access. Some machines load the bobbin from the top.

12 Foot. Interchangeable feet snap on and off.

13 Feed dogs. These little teeth grab and move the fabric backwards as you sew.

14 Throat plate. This metal plate covers the workings of the machine and is usually marked with seam widths.

15 Free arm. Most machines have a removable plate that means you can easily place sleeves and other tubular pieces over the free arm to sew around them.

16 Needle clamp. This holds the needle in place and it is important to make sure this is done up properly with the needle in fully and the correct way around.

17 Presser foot. This helps keep the fabric in place as you sew.

18 Bobbin casing. Front-loading machines will have a separate bobbin case that clicks in and out.

19 Part of the bobbin case can usually be removed to extract fluff and threads.

Some machines also have a presser foot regulator. This adjusts the amount of pressure exerted by the presser foot onto the feed dogs.

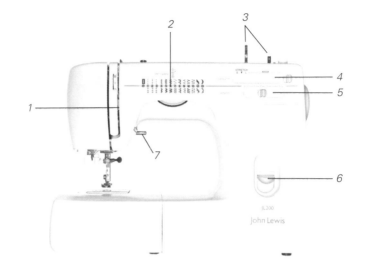

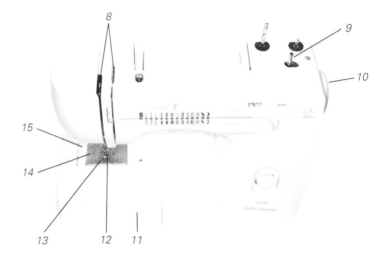

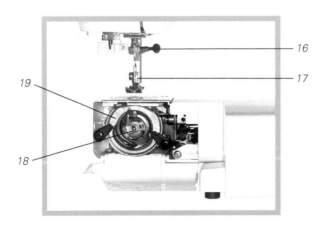

RUNNING A SEWING MACHINE

If you buy or borrow a machine that hasn't been serviced, get it looked at, even if it does seem expensive. Sitting in cupboards there must be thousands of machines that would run like a dream with a service and some care. The shop you buy from should be able to advise you on the right needles and bobbins and if you make friends with them, might even help you out with basic things for no charge – always buy a little something every time you go in. If you don't have a manual for your machine, hunt around on the Internet. You may be able to buy one or download a copy. Try a manual for a similar model if your particular one isn't available. Have the machine serviced every year or whenever you start to have problems you can't solve.

MACHINE CARE

The machine should come with a basic tool kit (see below) including:
- Small screwdriver for changing the needle and/or feet
- Tiny screwdriver for bobbin adjustments
- Stiff brush
- Tool for lifting the throat plate

Check what the manual says about regular maintenance that you can do at home. Oil the machine regularly with sewing machine oil as directed and remove dust and lint build up. The biggest lint problem always occurs in the bobbin casing and can snarl up the machine if you leave it. One of my second-hand machines had an extraordinary quantity of lint inside it.

Take out the bobbin and inspect the casing. You will see a build up of fluff. The tool kit should include a stiff brush for cleaning this out. If there is a lot of fluff you can also use a pair of pointed tweezers to remove it, but be careful you don't damage the delicate inner workings. In some machines you can also remove the bobbin casing to clean out more lint. Make sure you know how to put it back before you remove it! Most machines have a removable throat plate, too. Again, only remove if you need to and make sure you know how to put it back.

TROUBLESHOOTING

Most sewing snarl-ups are caused by needle, bobbin or top thread issues rather than a mechanical fault. Firstly, read through Using a Sewing Machine (see opposite) and ensure you are using the machine correctly.

If the machine really won't sew properly, start by looking carefully at these elements.

1 Make sure you have all the stitch settings correct with the right width and length for the stitch you are using. Zigzag and decorative stitches sometimes need a looser tension. Check what the sewing machine manual says.

2 Re-thread the top thread, making sure the thread itself isn't tangled or faulty. Check the top thread tension, it should be in the mid-range for ordinary sewing. Loops on the underside of the sewing indicate a top thread problem (page 35).

3 Take out the bobbin, check it's in the right way around and that the thread is wound properly. Loops on the top of the sewing indicate a bobbin thread problem (page 35). Change to a different bobbin in case the thread or bobbin is damaged.

4 Change the needle, making sure it is in the right way around and is pushed in fully. Check that you are using the right needle for the thread and for the type of fabric. Damaged needles can create uneven stitches and snags on fabric.

5 Make sure the presser foot pressure is correct. The manual will tell you how to do this. Thick fabrics require less than average pressure while thin fabrics need a bit more. If the pressure is wrong then the machine may slip stitches.

6 If none of these solve the problem, consult the manual.

Sew simple

If the threads catch at the end of sewing a line and you can't move the fabric, turn the fly wheel a few times and the threads will be released.

Using a sewing machine

The parts of a sewing machine are explained on page 13 and some care tips are given on page 14. Here, we are looking at how to use the sewing machine.

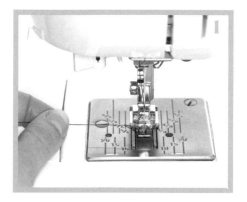

1 Start by pulling the bobbin thread up to the top. This avoids tangles at the start of the sewing. To do this, thread the bobbin and top thread, then turn the fly wheel to bring the needle down and back up again. It will bring the bobbin thread back up with it. Use a pin to catch it under the presser foot.

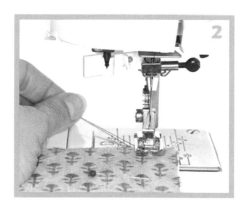

2 Pull both threads backwards behind the presser foot and try to hold them there when you start to sew.

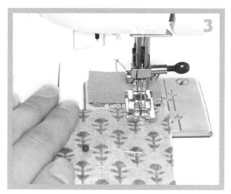

3 If you can't hold the threads, try sewing through a small square of fabric just before you start your actual sewing. This anchors the threads and stops them snarling up.

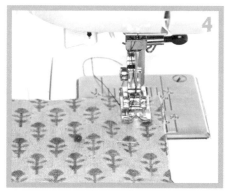

4 Position the fabric in the correct place. For seams, place the edge of the fabric on the marker on the throat plate for the width of seam you require – so 15mm for a 1.5cm seam allowance. Some machines will only show inches, or no markings at all. If so, measure the distance needed from the centre of the needle hole and put a piece of masking tape on the throat plate, or make marks with a permanent pen.

Start with the needle down. Turn the fly wheel to position the needle in the fabric, then put the presser foot down.

Press the pedal slowly at first and only build up the speed when you are confident and are working on a long, straight seam. Starting and finishing the thread are explained on page 34.

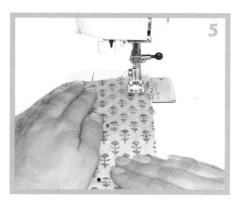

5 The position of your hands is important. Keep your hands away from the needle area to avoid the risk of sewing your fingers. Work with your hands flat, not grasping the fabric. The machine pulls the fabric through by itself, you don't need to push or pull – doing so will damage the machine. Unless there is a problem with the machine, it will feed the fabric through in a straight line, with just a little guidance from your hands.

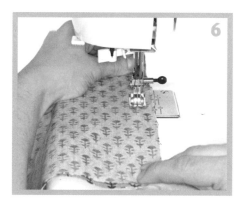

6 The only time you need to hold the fabric firmly is for slippery or very thin fabrics that get snarled up by the needle. Hold these fabrics gently in front and behind the presser foot, just tightly enough to create tension, but not tightly enough to pull the fabric in either direction.

Fabric

Sadly, it has got harder over the last few years to buy fabrics; fabric shops and department store sections have been closing down. However, at last the tide is turning and fabrics are creeping back into the shops as sewing becomes fashionable.

It's worth exploring local shops and markets as there are often gems among the polyester and cheap curtaining, particularly if there is any kind of clothing manufacture in your area. Learn to recognise the feel of different fabrics and assess their qualities so you can select the best. A good way to start is to go to a big fabric shop where everything is marked with the fabric content and name. Find out what silk dupion or cotton lawn looks and feels like and identify pure wool and linen. You could collect samples in a notebook for when you are choosing from unlabelled fabrics.

Don't always assume the seller is right about what the fabric is, particularly on markets. I've been told many times that 'it's pure silk' when it's clearly not! Don't be afraid to lift down the fabric bolts and unroll a couple of metres to drape and hold up to yourself in front of the mirror.

Many independent fabric shops offer a mail-order service where they will send you samples of new fabrics seasonally, or you can request particular fabrics or colours and they will send you whatever fits the bill. Some will charge for this and some will do it for free. Sewing magazines are the best place to find adverts for shops that offer this service, but if you have a favourite shop that's hard to get to, just ask them what they can do.

Shopping online

Online fabric shops are a great source of fabrics at both ends of the quality and price spectrum. Once you know about fabrics, buying online can be great, but it's hard to buy without seeing and touching and certainly isn't as much fun as browsing in the shop and handling all the fabrics. Some shops will send samples out for a small cost, so you can see what it feels like and check the colour. It's best to use online shopping for known brands or types where you can select the colours and prints you want without worrying about whether the fabric will be good quality.

Once you are confident in fabric buying, you can buy second-hand or vintage online. It will always be risky, as the fabric may be described wrongly (usually by accident) or just not feel right for the project you had in mind. If it isn't right you can always resell it, or just put it aside for a future project.

The language of fabric

Fabric specialists use all sorts of strange words to describe their goods. Mostly they refer to the behaviour of the fabric – the drape, the weight, the hand. The 'drape' is simply how the fabric hangs. Compare a light silk to a curtain fabric: the silky one flows and drapes and bunches up small. A heavy fabric is stiff, sticks out and doesn't bunch up. Drape is important for clothes, both in terms of comfort and how it looks on the body. Drapey fabrics hang straighter along the body and flow around your curves. Stiffer fabrics stick out at more of an angle.

The 'weight' of the fabric is usually to do with the thickness of the yarns that make up the weave. A lightweight fabric can be sheer and flimsy, but also could be a super-soft cotton. Heavy-weight fabrics are things like thick corduroy, denim and furnishing fabrics.

The 'hand' of a fabric means how it feels and relates to drape and weight. A soft hand is a drapey, flowing fabric, a firm hand is a crisper fabric that holds folds well.

Some fabrics have a special finish so they behave differently to the same fibre in its natural state. A good example of this is waterproofed or waxed cotton, or stain-resistant upholstery fabric. Ready-made clothes often use fabrics with special finishes to reduce the need for ironing or to make wool suitable for machine washing. Fabrics bought on the roll won't necessarily have these finishes, but will have some kind of treatment put on them during manufacturing. Wherever possible, wash out the finishing treatments before you sew. Some fabrics will change their character completely when you wash them, so beware of this if you want to keep the original crispness. Silk dupion becomes soft when washed, compared to the stiff fabric straight off the roll. Dry-cleaning usually preserves the original hand of the fabric. If in doubt, buy a small piece and test it. If you want to dye fabrics, you will always need to pre-wash them to remove the finish, which inhibits the dye penetration.

Fabrics in general are either woven or knitted. Some other fabrics, like felt and interfacing, are non-woven and are created using a different process. Woven fabrics are made with two sets of threads; the warp, which runs vertically along the loom, and the weft, which runs across, under and over the warps to make the fabric. In woven fabrics, the threads along the length are called the lengthwise grain, while the cross grain goes across the fabric from selvedge to selvedge. Both of these are a straight grain. The selvedge (or selvage) is the finished, woven edge of the fabric that doesn't unravel. The true bias runs diagonally at 45 degrees across the two straight grains. When pulled along the bias, fabric has more stretch than along the straight grain. Fabric cut on the bias clings to the body, and behaves quite differently to that cut on the straight grain. Unless bias-cutting is specified, always cut fabrics following the straight grain or they will twist and distort.

Different arrangements of warp and weft create textures and patterns in woven fabrics. Some types of fabric, such as velvet, are available in both woven and knit, which can be confusing. Make sure you buy the right type for your project.

Plain weave can usually be identified by the cross-threads running vertically and horizontally. Twill weaves have a different arrangement of threads and a diagonal effect on one side. Denim is a twill weave, as is satin. Satin refers to a type of twill weave, not the fibre content – it can be silk, polyester, cotton or even wool. Decorative weaves come in many different types but usually have the same basic properties of all woven fabrics and you should always cut them on the straight grain.

Knit fabrics are made by machine with one single yarn joined in a series of loops to make a stretchy fabric. They can be flat or tubular.

Many types of knit fabrics are available, from T-shirt jersey to chunky knit, and each has its own requirements for sewing. Knit fabrics don't have a grain in the same way as wovens, but still have a right and wrong direction. Normally the ribs in the knit should run vertically. Inspect jumpers and T-shirts to get an idea of how this works.

Non-woven fabrics include felt, polyester fleece and certain interfacings, plus fake suede, vinyl and other synthetics that usually don't fray when cut.

Net and lace are made using a unique process. Net doesn't have a grain and normally lace doesn't either, but it might well have a directional design that you need to be aware of when cutting out.

For more on fabric types turn to the Fabric Guide (pages 286–293) and the Glossary (pages 298–299).

Choosing the right fabrics for your project

Ask yourself these questions when choosing fabrics.
Is it easy to wash? Will the hand change if I wash it? Is it colourfast?
Is it wearable? Does it crease too much? Is it breathable?
How easy is it to sew?
Is it the right hand/weight for this project?
Have I worked with a fabric like this before?
Does it need any special handling?

When working with a tricky fabric for the first time, don't go straight into making a complicated dress with it. Start dressmaking with easy fabrics, like cotton, before you try working with slippery or stretchy ones.

Working with vintage fabrics

I have a hunter-gatherer attitude to buying vintage, second-hand and recycled fabrics. There is nothing I like more than a good flea market or junk shop with heaps of fabric piled up. Charity shops are good hunting grounds, though they do vary. Think about what you could use; sheets, curtains and duvet covers often yield yards of good-quality printed fabric and garments are a good source of fabrics for small projects.

Vintage fabrics can be wonderful and they can also be awful. You probably won't know exactly what the fibre content is, which makes it difficult to assess how to wash, iron and sew the fabric. If in doubt, treat it carefully. Hand-wash the fabric to make sure it's not harbouring any moths (page 11). I use a gentle biodegradable detergent. Drying on a washing line will help get rid of musty smells. Treat stains with caution using a gentle preparatory product and following the instructions. Or just avoid the stains, which is safer! I never use a tumble dryer and don't advise them. Iron on a cool to medium setting unless you are sure you are dealing with linen or cotton. Most vintage fabrics will be 92cm (36in) wide, which is much narrower than modern fabrics.

Haberdashery

I could spend hours exploring trimmings, thimbles and types of thread, but it can be overwhelming when you are faced with endless things you don't recognise and can't imagine the purpose of.

Bias tape or bias binding

Bias tape and bias binding are two terms for the same thing; bias-cut strips folded and pressed ready for covering an edge. See pages 68–77 for instructions on how to make and use bias tape or binding.

Dress shields

These hidden secrets are discussed in Dressmaking (page 253).

Elastic

Elastic comes in a range of widths, generally only in black or white. Specialist shops might have a wider range, including different colours. Bra elastic is less stretchy but more comfortable and can be used for waistbands and cuffs. Lingerie elastic comes in more colours, is soft and slightly stretchy, and some shops will have clear elastic. Round cord elastic is suitable for light gathering, such as for cuffs, hats, headbands and crafts. Shirring elastic is fine enough to go through the sewing machine and can be used for decorative effects (page 170).

Fastenings

Zips, poppers, hooks and eyes, skirt hooks and buttons are all discussed in Fastenings, (pages 84–105).

Fusible webbing

Fusible webbing is a dry fabric glue in a sheet that is activated when heat and steam are applied. At the haberdashery counter you will probably see this webbing in narrow strips that are designed for hemming (page 56). For appliqué (page 188), a similar product is available in large sheets with a paper backing.

Glue

Fabric glue is most useful for crafts projects, such as the Falling Blossom (page 114). I wouldn't recommend using glue for clothing as it usually makes the fabric stiffer, though it can be great for quick fancy-dress details. Follow the manufacturer's instructions for use, but as a general rule apply a thin layer of glue, allow it to nearly dry and go clear, then press the two pieces together.

Glue designed for leather is used for seams and hems (page 57). You can also buy wash-out glue that can be used like tacking during the making process to hold down seam allowances, hold zips in place and for awkward corners. Fray stop is a clear glue designed to be run along cut edges to stop fraying. It is useful on buttonholes and on tiny raw edges that are impossible to finish in any other way. I use it in crafts much more than in dressmaking.

Hook-and-loop

This is available by the metre in a long strip or as small dots. Either version can be sew-on or stick-on. Don't try and sew on the sticky version as your needle will get in a sticky mess. Sew-on is much better for clothing, while stick-on is useful for crafts.

Piping cord

Piping cord is like tiny cotton rope and is used to fill fabric tubes (page 79) to make a decorative edging. It is available in a range of thicknesses from thin to chunky. For some reason piping cord is not pre-shrunk, so make sure you shrink it before you use it in a washable project. To shrink cord, place it in a bowl of hot water and leave until cold, then air dry it. Because of the shrinkage, always buy more than you need.

Petersham

Petersham is a ribbed-weave ribbon used for waistbands and in tailoring. It is hard to get these days, so look out for vintage packages. You may find curved petersham that is designed specifically for skirt waistbands.

Hem or seam tape

This is used to finish seams and hems (page 59). The tape is made on the straight grain and is very like ribbon. It can be of natural or synthetic fibres in a narrow range of colours.

Weights

Dress weights are very hard to buy nowadays and are not used all that often. You will sometimes see them in vintage clothes, weighting down drapes or cowl-necks, and occasionally in jacket and dress hems. A small coin sewn into a tiny fabric pocket works very well instead. For a skirt hem that needs a little weight, you could try bathroom plug chain threaded into the hem.

Shoulder pads

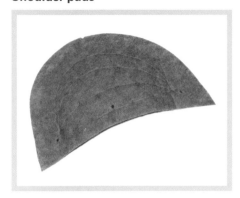

Don't dismiss shoulder pads as relics of 1980s power suits; they have their place. You can buy pads in a range of thicknesses to suit your particular garment and even to suit the slope of your own shoulders. If your sewing pattern requires them, use them or the garment won't hang well. Specialist tailoring suppliers are the best place to get them in many different styles.

Threads

Cheap threads are a waste of money. They break and tangle and are all round frustrating, and the spool may only have 20m of thread on it so you run out halfway through your project. When buying threads to match a fabric, undo the end of the thread and hold it over the fabric. Try several colours, even if they look wrong on the spool, and select the one that disappears the most, usually a darker colour than you initially expected. Don't try and guess the colour from memory. I have a fine memory for colours and still always guess wrongly when I go to the shop without the fabric.

The most common threads for general sewing are polyester, cotton or a mix of the two. I prefer cotton, though it's harder to get. Threads come in different weights, but cotton is often thicker than polyester. You are unlikely to get more than two different ranges in your local shop, so usually you will just have to choose the best colour match.

Polyester is much stronger, which is why it's recommended for seams that take a strain and things that need to stand up to a lot of wear or washing. Polyester thread is able to stretch, so it is good for stretchy fabrics and seams under strain. As a general rule, sew natural fabrics with natural fibres and synthetics with polyester. Leather should always be sewn with polyester because the processing chemicals in leather can rot cotton thread.

Silk thread is available in machine and hand-sewing versions. Silk thread is ideal for wool and silk garments, as it will disappear into the fabric. It can be used for tacking on special projects where other threads might leave marks in the fabric after pressing.

Hand-quilting thread is usually cotton and has a high twist that makes it easier to use in long lines of running stitch. Specialist threads for machine quilting and other quilting requirements are also available.

Invisible thread is a clear, plastic thread, usually made from nylon, which can be used on any fabric. However, it's quite shiny and too scratchy to use for dressmaking. It also comes in a grey-brown colour for use with dark fabrics.

Top stitch thread is a thicker thread, available in cotton or polyester, which stands out more than normal thread when you want a decorative effect. Use a bigger sewing machine needle when using thick thread.

Button thread is hard to get hold of. It is a thicker version of normal sewing thread.

Embroidery threads

The majority of hand embroidery threads are cotton, some shiny, some matt. Stranded cotton has six strands that can be separated to the right thickness for your needs. Perlé cotton is one thick strand.

Synthetic embroidery threads, silk and hand-dyed threads can be found in specialist shops, along with a huge array of fancy threads. Crewel wool is a fine thread suitable for embroidery, while tapestry wool is quite chunky, more like a knitting yarn.

Machine embroidery thread comes in different fibres, mostly synthetics. Cotton machine embroidery thread is very fine and is useful for sewing lightweight fabrics like chiffon. Variegated threads change colour along the length. Always use a fine machine needle with fine threads.

Left to right: Polyester (500m spool), cotton, upholstery or button, quilting, silk and embroidery threads.

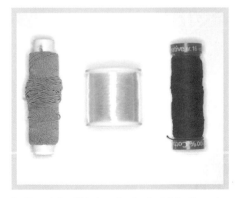

Left to right: Shirring elastic, invisible thread and top stitch thread.

Left to right: Hand-dyed rayon, crewel wool, perlé and stranded cotton embroidery threads.

Starting sewing

Before you actually put needle into fabric, there are some things you need to know.

Pre-washing

Most fabrics will need washing before you use them. New fabrics have treatments to keep them smooth and uncreased in the shop. If you are making something that won't be washed then you might want to leave the fabric unwashed to preserve the crispness of the finish. The other exception is, of course, dry-clean only fabrics. I don't really hold with dry-cleaning. It's expensive and not, on the whole, good for the environment. Most fabrics can be washed, but their character will change. Once a dry-clean only fabric has been washed, it will stay washable, so for dressmaking I always wash the fabrics first. Silks and wools should be hand-washed very gently, while sturdier fabrics can go through the machine on a 30° wash. This is of course a general rule – every fabric and every project will be different, so if you want to try pre-washing, TEST A SMALL PIECE FIRST! I suggest cutting a 30cm square and washing that in with another load, then see what it's like after the wash. Look for shrinkage, fluffing or felting of fibres, loss of dye, change in texture and hand. For more information, read Fabric (page 16), the Fabric Guide (pages 286–293), and for the care of vintage fabrics, turn to page 17.

Colourfastness

Pre-washing will also highlight problems with dyes bleeding from the fabrics. Some coloured fabrics will bleed colour for a number of washes, so be careful in mixed loads. You can test for colourfastness by hand-washing a small swatch of fabric and seeing what happens. Dyes generally bleed less in cold water than in hot, so hand-washing in cold water may be the answer for a problematic fabric. Be careful when you

mix fabrics in case a darker one bleeds into a lighter one when you wash it. I always use dye-catching cloths in my wash, which amazingly catch all the dye swirling out of fabrics in the washing machine. Some people swear by white vinegar as a dye-fixer.

Straightening the grain

Woven fabrics always have a grain, or direction of weave. One grain goes across the width of the fabric from edge to edge (cross-grain) and one grain running the length of the fabric (page 16). When cutting fabrics, particularly for clothes, you must cut in the direction of the grain otherwise the finished piece will be twisted and the seams will pucker.

Fabrics can get twisted off-grain during processing and while they are rolled on tubes in the shop. To make sure you are working with the grain straight, always check the grain before you cut the fabric.

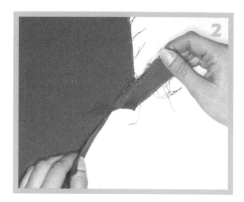

2 The best way to straighten up the cut end is to tear the fabric. Tears will run straight across the grain. Make a short snip a few centimetres from the cut end in the edge of the fabric and pull the two pieces. If it doesn't want to tear then don't force it and try another method. If it does tear, make sure the tear goes right across the fabric. If it doesn't do this, then cut a little further down and make another tear. This establishes the cross-grain.

1 First establish if the cut end is straight. With some fabrics you will see that there are lots of threads hanging off, which means the cut isn't straight on the grain.

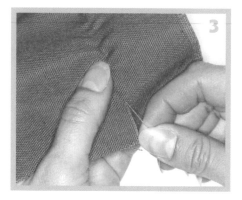

3 If the fabric won't tear, snip into the edge and try and remove one cross thread and pull it out. The pull should run across the width of the fabric and you can then cut it along the line of the pulled thread.

4 Once you have established the cross-grain, check to see if the cross-grain runs at right angles to the selvedges. If the cross grain runs off at a wonky angle, then the grain is twisted and the fabric needs to be straightened.

5 Work out which direction the grain skews in then pull on the opposite corners of the fabric to pull the threads back into alignment. This works best if you have pre-washed the fabric. Also try steaming it to soften the fibres before you pull, or work with the fabric slightly damp. Straightening the grain of a large piece of fabric may require the help of a friend.

Tearing

Tearing is recommended for finding the cross-grain of the fabric and is fine for separating large pieces of fabric. I don't recommend it for use on an actual cutting line; for example, tearing out a square of fabric for a cushion cover.

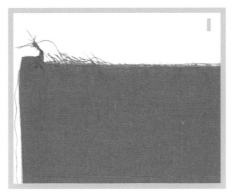

1 In some fabrics you will see wrinkles, pulled threads and marks along a tear line. Tearing compresses the weave and damages threads. Having said this, tearing can be used on some fabrics without too much damage; always test a bit first. Torn edges are useful for pressing cloths, as the threads are compressed enough not to need hemming, which avoids a lumpy edge that would leave marks on the pressed fabric.

Measuring and marking

Don't start measuring the fabric until you have pressed it (page 23). With the fabric flat on a table, smooth out ripples and make sure the selvedge and cross-grain edges are straight. If you have two layers of fabric to cut at once, make sure the edges are all aligned and there are no twists or ripples in the fabric.

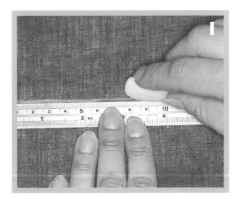

1 Use a ruler and chalk to mark cutting lines, making sure you don't shift the fabric around as you do so.

2 When cutting pattern pieces, arrange all the pieces on the fabric first to make sure they will fit, then pin as shown, with pins at corners and on curves, pointing outwards, but not sticking out over the cutting line.

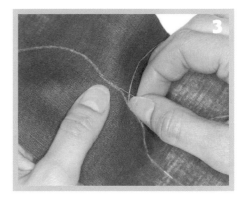

3 Marks can be made with thread tracing; make tacking stitches over chalk marks. This is useful for fabrics that are hard to mark or where marks need to show on the right side and chalk would be hard to remove.

Sew different

If the fabric is delicate, use weights to hold down pieces and draw around them instead of pinning. There are purpose-made sewing weights, but heavy, unbreakable objects work fine. Weights are also useful if you are working with large pieces of fabric that tend to slide off the table.

Careful cutting

When cutting out, always use proper sewing scissors with a bent handle. The handle is bent so you can run the scissors along the table surface and avoid lifting the fabric too much. When cutting dress pattern pieces from a large piece of fabric, try and move yourself around the table to cut out the pieces, rather than turning your hand at an awkward angle to reach.

Another tip is to cut each piece out roughly then cut it out again more carefully once the fabric is in smaller, more manageable pieces. For freehand cutting, always turn the fabric, not the scissors, to get around curves. Don't try and cut with your hand at an awkward angle.

1 For smooth cutting, always use the full length of the scissor blades, rather than chopping at the fabric with the tips of the scissors, which will give a jagged edge.

Pinning

Placing pins in fabric properly will make sewing it easier.

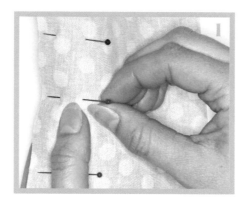

1 For machine sewing, try and put the pins in at right angles to the edge, normally with the heads pointing to the left so you can take them out with your left hand as you get to them. Sometimes it is easier to take them out with your right hand, but it depends on the shape of your sewing.

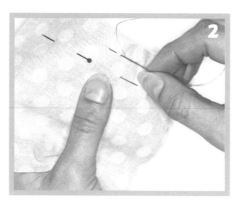

2 For hand sewing, place the pins at right angles to the seam if that works, but place them vertically along the seam if that makes the fabric easier to hold. Always put them in point up, so you don't stab yourself as you sew along the seam.

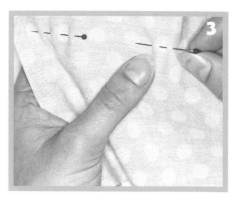

3 If the pins are staying in for some time, put them in and out of the fabric twice for security, and poke the points back into the fabric. This only works with long pins, which is why I always use them. There is more on pins on page 283.

There is more on pins on page 283.

Sew simple

Always keep pins handy. A wrist pincushion is great when fitting garments or checking curtains. A magnetic pin holder may seem a great way to keep pins tidy, but the pins get magnetised and then stick to scissors and sewing machines! I like to make and use my own pincushions (page 214) or keep pins in a small bowl.

Pressing and steaming masterclass

Pressing is a vital part of sewing. To sew properly, you need to spend as much time pressing as you do cutting and stitching. Proper pressing and the use of steam when appropriate will make your sewing work better, and it will look more professional.

THE BASICS

Pressing is not ironing. We iron clothes after washing them to get out the creases by moving the iron back and forth. We press fabrics to shape them by applying gentle pressure without moving the iron around. This is particularly important with iron-on interfacing and other layered fabrics – moving the iron around might dislodge or wrinkle the layers, while the lift and press technique keeps everything in place.

PRESSING SEAMS

In many of the techniques in this book you will see the instruction, 'Press the seam allowance open'.

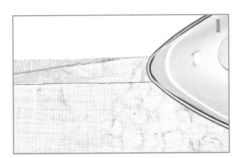

1 Before pressing the two seam allowances open, you should first press the seam flat along the line of stitching, which allows the stitches to blend into the fabric.

2 Then open up the seam, with the two allowances facing up, and press them open.

PRESSING CURVES

There is no point in going to the trouble of making smoothly curved seams, then just pressing them flat.

1 To create a curve, press the curved seam over a curved surface. The edge of an ironing board will do if there is nothing else, but a tailor's ham or sleeve roll is ideal (see making instructions, overleaf).

STEAM

Steam is just amazing. Steam helps remove unwanted creases, set wanted creases and form shapes. Steaming curved seams over a tailor's ham helps to set the curve in shape and will help shape and form unwieldy fabrics that do not want to sit flat. After steaming, always leave the fabric to cool on the ironing board or ham, as it can stretch or go out of shape while it is still warm.

ACHIEVING STEAM

Most irons have a steam setting. Make sure there is plenty of water in the iron and let it heat up properly before you start pressing. Always test the fabric in case the iron drips and leaves watermarks. Some fabrics are more susceptible to watermarking, usually dry-clean only ones, so beware.

I A more controllable way to create steam is to spray the fabric with water from the iron or ideally, from a spray bottle. You can buy spray guns in garden centres, but I prefer the smaller ones that hairdressers use; try a large chemist for one of these.

For very small areas that need steam, you can dampen the fabric itself with a damp cloth. The best way of doing this is to use a dampened pressing cloth, which creates steam and also protects the fabric at the same time.

A separate-tank steam iron is the best sewing tool I have ever acquired. The large tank heats up and creates endless steam at the touch of a button without spitting water.

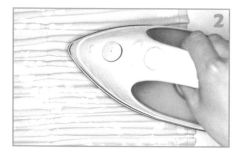

2 Steaming also works to set shapes and curves. Hold the iron slightly above the fabric and spray a burst of steam onto it. This is great for setting pleats and folds in the tops of curtains or in decorative pleating without actually flattening them. You can also pin fabric in place on the ironing board and then steam it to set the shapes. The shapes will hold until you wash the fabric. Synthetics will hold the shapes even more than natural fibres will.

PRESSING CLOTH

A pressing cloth is simply a plain piece of fabric, about 40 x 40cm, used between the iron and the fabric. It will protect the fabric from excessive heat and stop the shine that irons cause on some fabrics.

A pressing cloth can be as simple as a cotton tea-towel or other piece of plain, white cotton fabric. It needs to withstand plenty of heat, so cotton is good. Cut off the hems as they can leave imprints on the fabric. For a deluxe pressing cloth, use a piece of silk organza. Organza is very heat resistant and its transparency enables you to see what you are doing. If you hunt around you can buy low-grade organza very cheaply, but make sure it's silk because synthetic organza will melt!

I A Teflon cloth is useful for fusible webbing, (page 56 and page 188).

PRESSING MITT

A pressing mitt is a heat-resistant glove that you can use to press delicate fabrics without touching them with the iron.

I Hold the iron above the fabric and use the mitt to do the shaping. You can also use the glove like a tailor's ham, by pressing onto the glove on your hand. A silicone oven glove also works for this.

FINGER PRESSING

Finger pressing is simply using your fingers to press a crease in place, without the use of steam or heat.

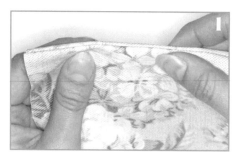

I Pressing in this way helps to get things in place before you use the iron and is good for awkward corners where the iron is unwieldy.

IRON STAND

When you are doing a lot of pressing, replacing the iron upright each time puts a strain on your wrist.

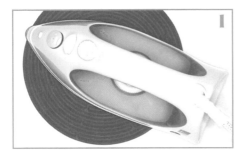

I A silicone iron rest or a kitchen trivet will work as a temporary rest for the iron during bouts of pressing.

IRONS

I have two favourite irons – a steam-generating iron and a small travel iron for fiddly work. Other people swear by mini-irons (which are like an electric soldering iron with interchangeable feet), for very tiny work and awkward corners.

I With care, you can just use the tip of an ordinary iron for awkward corners, or lift the piece up on a tailor's ham to make it easier to shape.

TAILOR'S HAM AND SLEEVE ROLL

A tailor's ham is a ham-shaped, stuffed fabric cushion used for pressing curves. A sleeve roll is much the same, but is more of a sausage shape and is used for pressing seams on sleeves without crushing the rest of the sleeve. Both are very useful and are easy to make. Once you have them, you will find loads of uses for them. Press wool on the wool side and cotton on the cotton side.

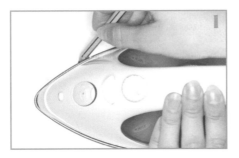

I To make a tailor's ham, draw around the plate of an average-sized iron. Add about 3cm all around and round off the corners.

Using this pattern, cut two pieces of calico, one piece of wool and one piece of pure cotton. Layer a piece of calico, the wool face up, the cotton face down, the other calico piece. Sew around, leaving a 10cm gap. Turn out and stuff with sawdust. Use a funnel to get it in and a ruler to poke it down. The ham must be stuffed really firmly. Sew up the gap. After a week or two the sawdust compacts, so unpick the gap and add more.

Make a sleeve roll in a similar way, using fabrics as above and a sausage-shaped pattern about 30cm long.

SLEEVE BOARD

This is a mini-ironing board designed for ironing sleeves. These can be useful for sewing in place of a sleeve roll and also as a small ironing surface on the table for tiny projects and small irons.

VELVET BOARD

This is a special cloth with teeth to protect the velvet from crushing when you iron it. Place the velvet face down and press or steam the back. Specialist sewing shops sell these boards.

Sew simple

It is really important to press sewing projects at every stage. Having an ironing board near where you are sewing really makes a difference as you don't have to leave the room to press. You could use a folded towel on the table or, if you have a small work surface, invest in a little ironing board and travel iron just for sewing.

Hand stitches

I love hand sewing; sitting down somewhere comfortable with my fabric and thread and working away in a meditative mood is one of my favourite things. For good hand sewing you must have a good needle, as fine as the thread you are using, and good quality thread suitable for sewing by hand. For more information on suitable needles and threads see pages 19 and 282.

Single or double thread

Needles can be threaded single or double. A single thread should be no more than 50cm long, including a 10–15cm tail. Knot the end or fasten it to fabric with a couple of stitches. A double thread should be about 80cm and have the two cut ends knotted together.

Sew simple

Take the thread in the direction it comes off the spool; use the already cut end in the needle and knot the freshly-cut end. This reduces the chance of the thread tangling.

Tying a knot

Knot the thread properly so it doesn't come undone or pull through the fabric.

Threading a needle

Cut the thread at an angle, moisten the end if you want, then flatten it between your thumb and finger. Leave about 1cm sticking out between your fingers. With the eye of the needle facing you, thread the flat end through the eye (right), then hold the needle and thread with your right hand, and pull the thread through with your left.

Most of the time you will want to work with the thread single, not doubled, even if it does mean you sometimes pull the needle right off the thread and have to re-thread. Start with a length of thread about 50cm long and pull about one third of the length through the needle as a tail – a thread longer than this will get tangled and you will get frustrated; too short and you will have to start a new thread all too quickly.

A knotted double thread is best used for gathering and pulling up, where a strong thread and firm knot is needed.

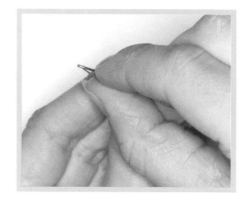

Freeing a knot

If the thread does snarl and you get a loop-like knot in it, don't just pull; you'll tighten the knot. Put the tip of the needle into the loop and pull gently on one end of the thread below the knot. If that doesn't work, pull the other end. Most knots can be freed this way. If yours can't, then cut the thread and unpick.

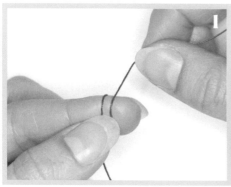

1 Moisten your left thumb and index finger. Loop the thread twice around the tip of your left index finger.

2 Use your thumb to roll the knot off your finger and catch the knot with the tips of your finger and thumb.

3 Pull on either end of the thread to tighten the knot. This technique works with both singe and double thread.

Stitching in two directions

It is helpful to have a longer thread if you don't want a break in stitching or a knot in the middle of something like quilting.

1 Cut thread about 1m long and pull it through to the middle. Put a pin in the fabric then wrap half the thread in a figure of eight around the pin. Sew to the left and then come back and sew the rest of the thread to the right.

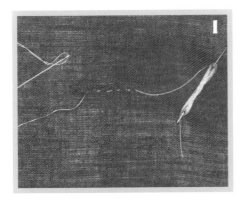

Waxing the thread

Traditionally, tailors would run threads through beeswax to strengthen and make them less inclined to tangle as they run through the fabric. This certainly helps with long, hand-sewn seams. After waxing the thread, run over it with a warm iron to melt the wax into the thread, or a residue will be left on the surface of the fabric.

Hand positions for hand sewing

Most stitches are made from right to left. Follow the photographs to see how to hold your hands when sewing particular stitches.

Starting and stopping

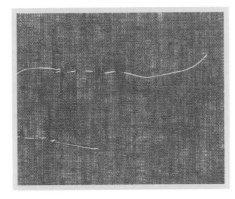

The best way to secure the start and end of the thread is to make two tiny stitches in the same place.

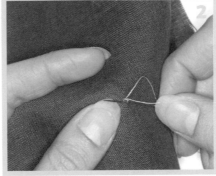

1 Make one stitch.

2 Make the second stitch over the first.

Tacking stitch

Tacking (or basting) is making quick, large stitches to hold pieces of fabric together. It is usually made with a single thread. Use silk thread to tack delicate fabrics as it leaves smaller holes and less indentations when you press the fabric.

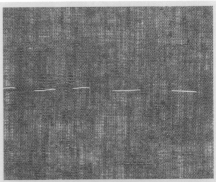

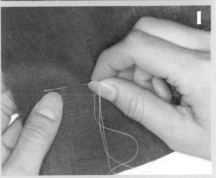

1 Take the needle in and out of the fabric with stitches up to 1cm long. You can make several stitches on the needle before you pull it through. Don't pull the thread too tight.

Sew different

Thread tracing is simply the use of tacking to make semi-permanent markings where a guide is required, such as for hemlines or dart placements.

Running stitch

Running stitch is a basic sewing stitch for joining pieces of fabric together or for gathering. It does not make a strong seam. It is made in the same way as tacking, but with smaller stitches.

I Take the needle in and out of the fabric with small stitches about 3–6mm long. You can make several stitches on the needle before you pull it through.

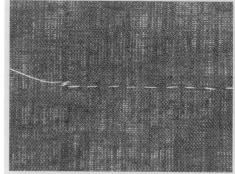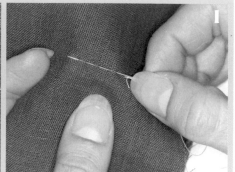

Backstitch

Backstitch is the main hand sewing stitch for making a firm join or seam. On the front side the stitches should lie neatly next to each other in a straight line, while on the back they will overlap. Make sure you sew the right way up to get a neat line on the front.

I Bring the needle out to the front. Insert the needle one stitch length (about 3–6mm) to the right of where the thread emerges. Push the needle through to come out one stitch length to the left of where the thread first emerged, and pull through. Insert the needle right next to the previous stitch and under the emerging thread, coming out one stitch length to the left, as before.

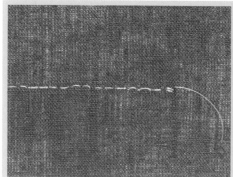

Pick stitch

Pick stitch is a very neat stitch, similar to backstitch but with shorter stitches on the front side. It has reasonable strength and is often used for zips (page 85).

I Bring the needle out to the front. Insert the needle 2–3mm to the right of where the thread emerges. Push the needle to come out 6–8mm to the left of where the thread first emerged and pull through. Insert the needle 2–3mm to the right again and under the emerging thread, coming out 6–8mm to the left, as before.

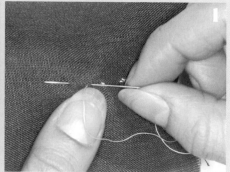

Overcasting

Overcasting is simply a thread stitched over a raw edge to stop the edge fraying and is most commonly used on seam allowances (page 37).

I With the thread at the front of the work, insert the needle from the back through to the front on a diagonal, about 5mm from the raw edge. Work the stitches close together for fabric that frays easily, or more widely spaced for non-fraying fabric.

Whipstitch

Whipstitch is similar to overcasting, but is used to join two edges together, either on the right side or the wrong side, without a seam allowance (Mr Mouse, page 124).

I Hold or pin the two edges together. With the thread at the front, insert the needle from back to front on a diagonal, so the thread emerges 3–5mm from the previous stitch. Make the stitches about 2mm from the edge on non-fraying fabric or 4–6mm on raw or fraying edges.

Slip stitch

Slip stitch is very useful for quickly joining layers of fabric together. It is used for attaching binding (page 75), appliqué (page 189) and for attaching the sleeves in the jacket project (page 265).

I With the thread coming out of the front of the top fabric, make a very short stitch to the right and into the lower fabric, taking only a couple of threads of the lower fabric. Bring the needle diagonally into the top fabric, from back to front.

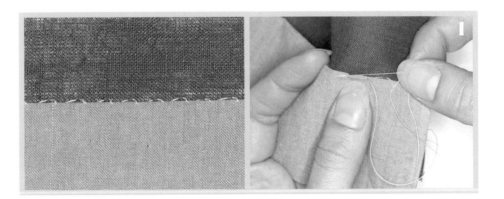

Herringbone stitch

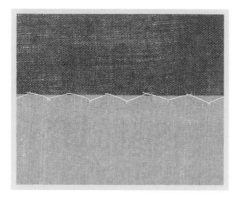
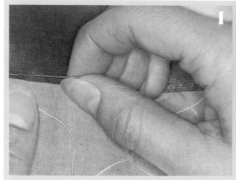
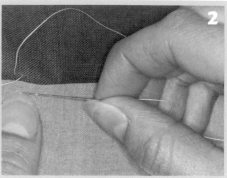

This is used for hemming (page 53) and attaching interfacing (page 255). It allows movement without pulling out stitches.

1 This stitch is worked from left to right. Fasten the thread in the hem, then take a small stitch from right to left in the upper fabric, catching only a couple of threads.

2 Bring the needle to the lower fabric and make the same stitch again. Continue taking alternate stitches in the upper and lower fabric, about 1cm apart.

Hem stitch

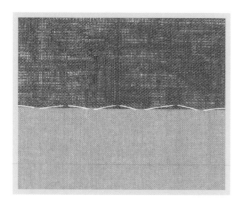
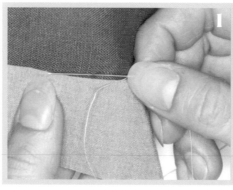
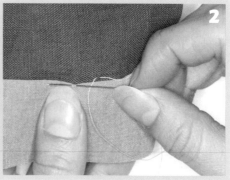

Hem stitch is similar to slip stitch, but the stitches are worked wider apart. It is a quick and basic way to hem fabrics.

1 Bring the needle up through the hem and stitch diagonally to the left, picking up a few threads of the main fabric.

2 Stitching diagonally again, pick up a couple of threads close to the edge of the hem.

Blanket stitch

This is used as an edging, for appliqué (page 191) and for decorative stitching.

1 Bring the needle out on the fold or edge. Front to back, insert the needle about 5mm from the edge. Bring it out over the trailing thread to form the first upright stitch. Front to back, insert the needle about 5mm to the right of the first stitch, with the trailing thread under the needle to form the horizontal bar.

Catch stitch

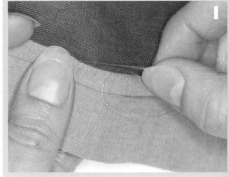
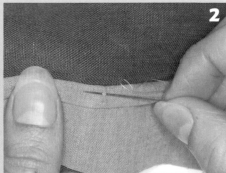

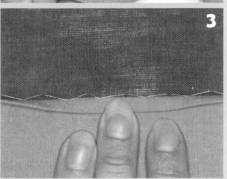

Catch stitch is a great stitch for creating hems that are invisible from the inside. It is the same as hem stitch, but is worked underneath the folded-back hem, so when the hem is flat no stitches are visible. It is great for unlined jackets where the insides show. Fold the top of the hem back by about 1cm before you start stitching.

1 With the thread coming out to the back of the hem, pick up a few threads of the main fabric about 8–10mm to the left of where the thread emerges.

2 Insert the needle diagonally close to the edge of the folded-back hem, picking up only a few threads.

3 This shows the hem held back so you can see the stitching.

Lock stitch

Lock stitch, or loop stitch, is a fast and efficient way to hem, but it has less give than herringbone stitch (opposite). It is useful for attaching facings to seam allowances (pages 252–253). It can be worked on the edge of the fabric to produce a visible stitch, or with the hem folded back like catch stitch (above).

1 This stitch is worked from left to right. Secure the thread in the lining or seam allowance, then stitch through the hem, two or three threads in from the edge.

2 Insert the needle horizontally through the lining and into the hem, picking up only a few threads on each. Make sure the needle goes OVER the trailing thread to produce the locking loop.

3 Pull the thread through to secure the loop and continue.

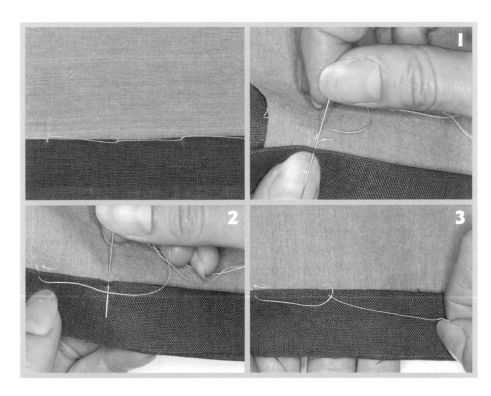

Buttonhole stitch

Buttonhole stitch looks similar to blanket stitch but has a firmer edge. It should be worked in a thick thread or waxed embroidery thread (page 27). Mark the stitching lines to ensure it stays even. (See page 93 for making a buttonhole.)

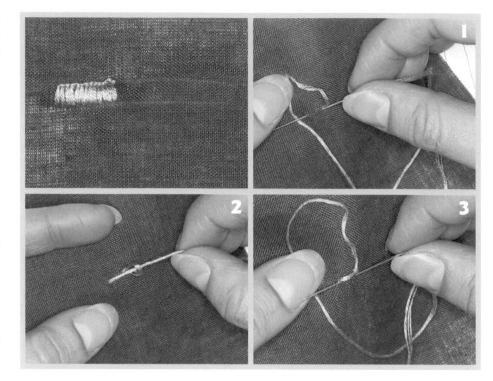

1 Working from left to right, bring the needle out on the top or cut edge, and put it back in right next to where the thread first emerged. Bring the needle out at the bottom edge of the buttonhole, making sure that the trailing thread is looped UNDER the needle.

2 Pull up the stitch so the loop is formed on the cut or top edge.

3 Make the next stitch very close to the first, inserting the needle at the top edge or under the cut edge and out at the bottom, making sure the trailing thread is looped as before. Keep the stitches close and even.

Bar tack

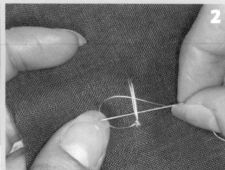

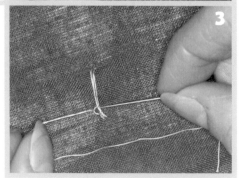

A bar tack is a small chain of detached stitches used for fastening skirt hooks (page 105) or for joining lining hems to the main fabric in coats and curtains.

1 Mark the required length of the tack and make three long stitches. If you want to make a curved bar tack, make these long stitches over a pencil. Continue working with the same thread.

2 Work blanket stitch over long stitches by inserting the needle under the threads from right to left, ensuring the trailing thread is looped under the needle.

3 Pull the stitch tight and use the needle to slide each stitch along the threads so it lies close to the previous one. At the end of the tack, take the needle through to the back of the work and fasten the thread.

Machine stitches

All sewing machines are different and it's important to familiarise yourself with your machine's capabilities. Start by reading the manual and trying out the stitches – all but very old machines will have zigzag stitch and many have a selection of practical and decorative stitches. Together with some general machine sewing tips, I have explained several machine stitches in this section. (See also page 13 for more information about sewing machines.)

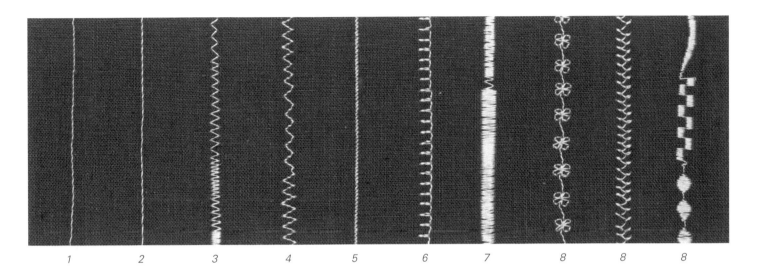

| 1 | 2 | 3 | 4 | 5 | 6 | 7 | 8 | 8 | 8 |

Selection of machine stitches, from left to right:

1 Straight stitch. Small stitches are normally used for fine fabrics, while larger stitches are best for thick fabrics or lots of layers.

2 Machine tacking is simply sewing using the longest stitch length. You can also loosen the top tension (page 35) slightly to make the stitches easier to remove. Some sewing machines will have a machine tacking setting.

3 Zigzag stitch. Most machines will have a zigzag feature though you may need to manually set the stitch width and length. A short stitch length creates a satin stitch effect that can be different widths – experiment with your machine. Zigzag is used to neaten raw edges (page 37), for decorative stitching and to attach binding (page 74) or ribbon (page 149).

4 Three-step zigzag or overcasting. This stitch uses three stitches to create zigzags. It is a very secure stitch and is used where zigzag isn't strong enough to join pieces and for finishing raw edges (page 37).

5 Stretch stitch. This stitch is a very small zigzag that creates a slightly stretchy stitch suitable for seams on stretch fabrics. Make sure you don't pull the fabric as you sew but let the feed dogs (page 13) move it through as required.

6 Machine blanket or seam and overcast stitch. This stitch looks like blanket stitch and can be used as a decorative stitch. It is also a very useful practical stitch that forms a seam and finishes the raw edges at the same time. To use this stitch as a seam and overcast stitch, the straight part of the stitch needs to be on the seam line, while the legs cover the raw edge. You will need to trim the seam allowance down to about 5mm before stitching.

7 Satin stitch. This is created using zigzag stitch set very wide with a short stitch length. Some machines will have an automatic setting for satin stitch. Satin stitching often puckers the fabric, so use a stabiliser underneath (page 194).

8 Decorative stitch patterns are generated automatically by some machines.

Feather stitch can be used to join butted seams. Refer to your sewing machine manual for more information.

The satin-stitched scalloped stitch can be used as a decorative edge by trimming close to the edge of the stitching.

Stay stitching

Stay stitching is a technique used to stop pieces of fabric cut on a curve from stretching while they are being worked on. Simply sew a machine tacking stitch (page 33) just inside the seam line (within the seam allowance). In some cases the stay stitching stays in permanently, otherwise it is removed once the pieces have been sewn up. Follow the pattern instructions.

Ease stitching

Where two pieces of fabric of different lengths have to be joined, the longer one has to be eased into place. The easiest way to ease the fabric is to run a line of machine tacking stitches (page 33) along the seam allowance and pull up the threads just enough to make the edge the right length to match the other piece. This technique is used in the circular skirt project (page 270).

Starting and finishing machine sewing

There are several ways to secure the thread at the start and finish of a line of machine sewing. The most common is to sew a few stitches in reverse at the start and end of a seam. This works well in most situations but can lead to an uneven seam if you don't straighten up properly, or extra bulk when you turn the fabric the right way out. Don't reverse over the raw edge or the fabric will get snarled in the machine.

A very neat way to finish ends is to reduce the stitch length to as small as possible (1mm) and sew a couple of stitches. This is used on buttonholes (page 92) and in very tight corners.

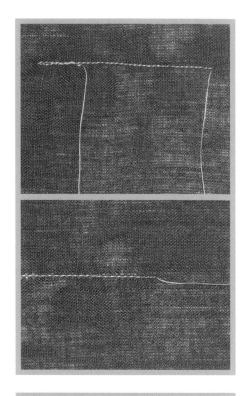

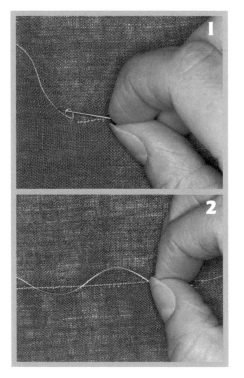

Knotting threads

Where the stitching is visible, such as top stitching, quilting or embroidery, try this method of knotting threads on the back. Do not reverse or reduce stitch length at the start and end of sewing and leave long top and bobbin threads.

1 On the back, use the tip of a needle to pull a loop of thread through from the front side.

2 Tie the ends in a double knot and trim off the excess thread.

Unpicking

However careful you are, there are always times when you will need to unpick stitches. You can use a stitch ripper (page 283) or try these two methods, which I prefer. For both methods, you need to carefully unpick where you have fastened off the seam.

Cutting surface thread

This is ideal for delicate fabrics but not suitable for very short stitches.

1 Cut either the bobbin or top thread every two or three stitches.

2 Pull out the thread on the other side.

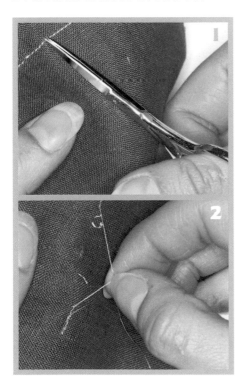

Scissor unpicking

Do this very carefully on delicate fabrics.

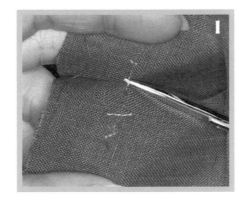

1 Hold the seam open and cut through the threads with small, sharp scissors. Make sure you only cut the threads, not the fabric. Pull the seam apart as you go.

Eliminating holes

After unpicking, there are often small needle holes left in the fabric, particularly in close-weave fabrics.

1 Ironing and steaming will reduce the holes, but another method is to lay the fabric flat on the table and scrape over the holes with your thumbnail or fingernail.

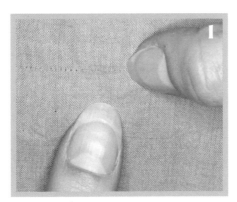

Tension tips

One of the most common issues with machine sewing is incorrect tension.

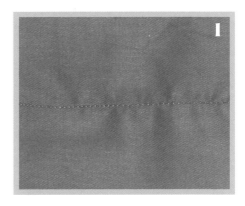

1 If the thread is sitting on the top layer, the tension is too tight. Turn the tension dial to a lower number or in the minus direction.

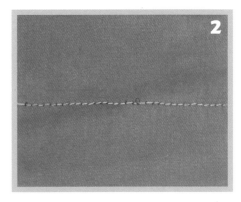

2 If the thread is sitting on the bottom layer, the tension is too loose. Turn the tension dial up to higher number or in the plus direction. If altering the top tension doesn't fix the problem, the bobbin tension may need adjusting. Turn the screw clockwise to increase the tension and anti-clockwise to decrease it. Turn it only a quarter turn then test the stitching. If the machine allows it, make the adjustments with the bobbin inserted into the bobbin case.

Seams

Seams are the fundamentals of sewing and there is a lot more to them than you might expect, but don't be put off by the many different types. The basic seams work well for most purposes, but those who sew a lot might like to try some of the fancier seams for a more professional finish. This section also includes related techniques, such as trimming seam allowances, making darts, turning and intersecting corners as well as sewing bias-cut seams. Read the basics of machine sewing (pages 12–15) before you sew your first seam.

What is a seam allowance?

The seam allowance is the amount of fabric between where you sew and the raw edges. If the pattern states a 1.5cm seam allowance then the seam should be sewn 1.5cm in from the raw edge. Most patterns use 1.5cm seam allowances, or ⅝in if the pattern uses imperial measurements. Either use metric or imperial in your sewing, don't mix the two.

Some patterns only need 1cm seam allowances, while occasionally you will need 2cm allowances. In most cases, the seam allowances can be trimmed down after sewing so they are not so bulky. Follow the pattern instructions.

Seam width markings

The machine throat plate (page 13) will have markings in millimetres or fractions of inches. By lining up the raw edge of the fabric with these markings, you can sew the seam a consistent distance from the edge.

Sewing a seam

Make sure that the raw edges of the two layers align. Pin the layers together with pins horizontal and the heads to the left. Align the raw edges with the correct markings on the throat plate. You can mark the sewing line on the fabric with chalk as well. Let the machine feed the fabric through, don't pull or push. If the fabric is very slippery or the seam is awkward, hand tack it first.

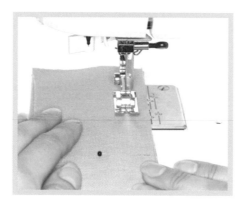

Pressing seam allowances open

First press the seam flat, pressing along the line of stitching. Then open up the seam allowances and press from the wrong side (page 23). The edges of seam allowances need to be finished to stop them fraying and there are various ways of doing this, depending on the fabric you are using and the finish you want.

Pinked

Pinking shears are scissors with zigzag teeth (page 280) and cutting with them will stop the fabric from fraying. Pinked seams are good for dressmaking when the fabric doesn't fray too readily.

1 If the fabric is thin, pink the two layers together before pressing the seam allowances open. If it is thick, press the allowances open first then pink each side separately. Pinking also reduces the imprint of the seam allowances showing through when you iron from the right side.

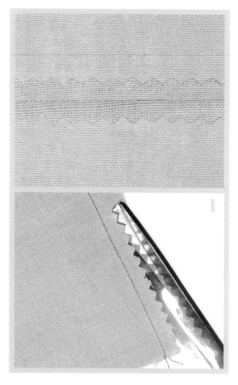

Stitched and pinked

For a more anti-fray finish, stitch each seam allowance about 6–7mm from the raw edge.

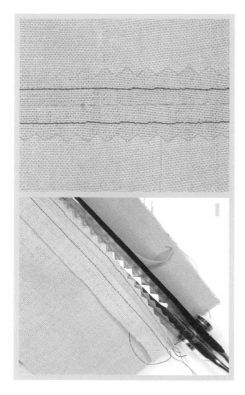

I Cut close to the line of stitching with pinking shears.

Overcasting

A traditional way to neatly finish edges is to use hand overcasting (see page 29).

I Stitch each seam allowance separately.

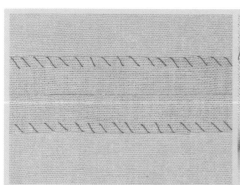

Zigzag seams

Zigzag stitch can be used to finish seam allowances and is good for medium-weight fabrics. On light fabrics the zigzag can show when you iron the item.

I Set the machine to a medium zigzag and sew each seam allowance about 5mm in from the edge. Trim close to the stitching, making sure you don't cut the stitches.

Zigzagging allowances together

In instances where the seam allowances really don't need to be pressed open, both seam allowances can be zigzag-stitched together. As it makes a bulky seam, this finish isn't suitable for clothes but it is great for cushions where the seams aren't going to be ironed.

Press the seam allowance flat, trim if required then zigzag along the raw edge. If the fabric frays a lot, zigzag first then trim close to the stitching.

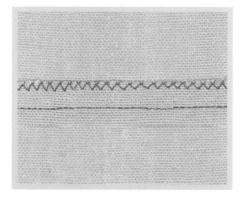

Sew different

If your machine has an overcast or three-step zigzag (page 33), it is better to use this than plain zigzag stitch.

Bound seams

Binding seam allowances stops all fraying and looks very smart on the inside. It is ideal for unlined coats or jackets or for fabrics that fray readily.

1 Bias binding is used to enclose the raw edges of each seam allowance separately. Use the double-fold method (page 74) and zigzag stitch to attach the binding.

Sew simple

When top stitching it is hard to keep in a straight line as there is no raw edge to follow. Use the edge of the foot as a guide, or mark the sewing line with chalk or a sliver of soap (page 12).

Top stitch

Top stitch is a seam finish that shows on the right side. Use a top stitch thread if required and set a longer stitch length than usual.

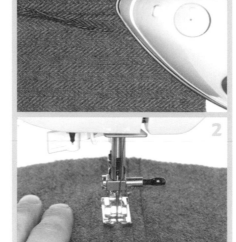

1 Press the seam allowances open. Finish the raw edges as required using one of the methods above.

2 From the right side, top stitch close to the seam on one or both sides of it. Stitch through the allowances underneath.

Layering and trimming seam allowances

When several layers of fabric are joined in a seam, the seam allowances can get very bulky. Trimming and layering the seam allowances reduces the bulk and creates a smarter finish.

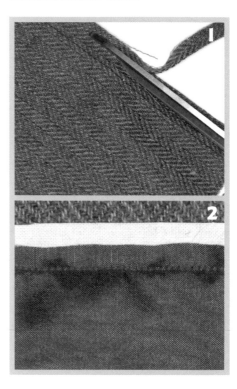

1 To reduce the amount of seam allowance, trim one or both allowances.

2 When there are more than two layers, layer the seam allowances in sequence by cutting the allowance of the uppermost layer narrowest. Interfacing can be trimmed right up to the stitching.

Self-bound seam

The self-bound seam is a good choice for lightweight fabrics and straight seams.

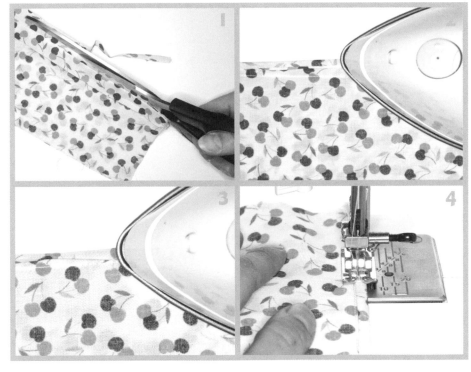

1 Make a plain seam (page 36) and press the seam allowances open. Then press one seam allowance up and trim it down to half its width.

2 Fold over the wider seam allowance and press it in half.

3 Fold the folded edge over the trimmed edge to meet the line of stitching.

4 Sew along the folded edge very close to the fold, making sure that the line of stitching does not stray over the original seam line.

Sew simple

Covered and bound seams are incredibly useful for fabrics that fray a lot or for garments where the seams will show. Self-enclosed seams, like the French seam or self-bound seam, are ideal for transparent or thin fabrics, or anywhere where seams are visible inside. However, as the seam allowance sticks out, they are not good for tight-fitting clothes as they can create a ridge that will show on the outside. Flat-fell seams (page 42) are a better choice in this instance as they are completely flat and are very comfortable to wear.

French seam

French seams are a classic seam finish for professional garments and are ideal for sheer fabrics. French seams work best on fairly straight seams. The first seam is sewn with the wrong sides together, which is counter-intuitive and can be confusing. Take it slowly, concentrate and check it's right before you sew. Practise before starting on a project to make sure you can get the seam allowances fully enclosed without any stray threads poking out of the stitching.

These measurements are based on a 1.5cm seam allowance. It is useful to mark the actual seam line so you know where to sew on the last step.

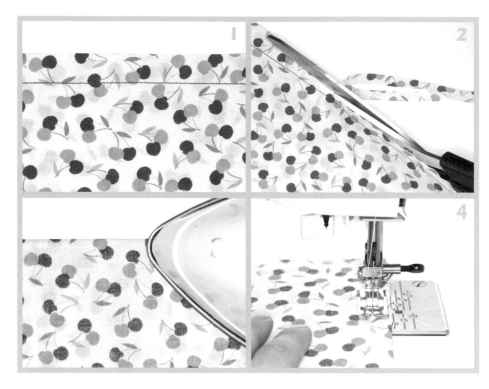

1 Sew a plain seam with the pieces WRONG sides together and using a 1cm seam allowance. Press the seam flat.

2 Trim both seam allowances to 3mm. Press the seam allowances to one side.

3 Fold the piece right sides together so the seam allowances are enclosed and press the seam flat.

4 Sew along the actual seam line, which should be 5mm from the fold.

The right side of a French seam.

The wrong side of a French seam.

Mock French seam

This is a simpler version of the French seam that looks very similar. It is better than the French seam for sewing curves.

1 Make a plain seam. Press the seam allowances open and fold the first seam allowance to the centre so that the raw edge is against the stitching line. Press.

2 Fold the second seam allowance to the centre and press.

3 Fold the fabric right sides together and press with folded seam allowance edges together.

4 Sew the folded seam allowances together, very close to the fold.

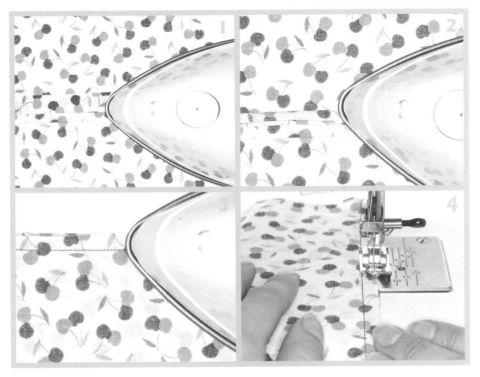

Flat-fell seam

The flat-fell seam is very strong and is used for garments that get heavy wear. It is also used on jeans. Because the stitching will show on the right side, make sure the widths are very even and the stitching neat. The seam is worked with the wrong sides together, which is counter-intuitive and can be confusing. Take it slowly, concentrate and check it's right before you sew. Make sure you sew all seams so they face in the same direction. An edge guide foot can be useful for the final seam (page 285).

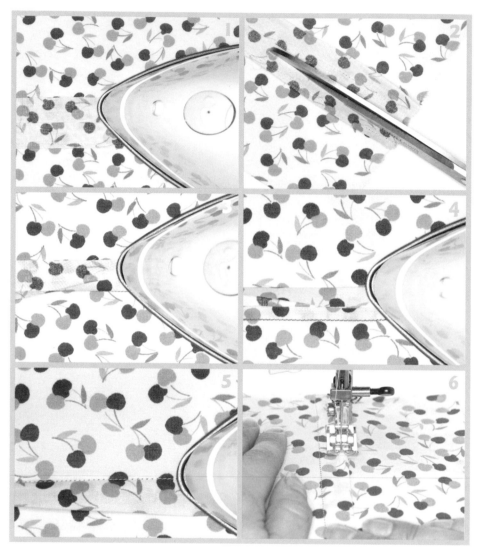

1 Sew a plain seam along the seam line with WRONG sides together. Press open.

2 Trim one seam allowance to about 3mm.

3 Press the trimmed seam allowance up.

4 Press the raw edge of the other allowance over to touch the raw edge of the trimmed seam allowance.

5 Fold the whole lot over so the raw edges are enclosed, and press flat.

6 Top stitch (page 38) on the right side about 2mm from the folded edge.

Intersecting seams

Where seams cross, the seam allowances need to be trimmed to reduce bulk. Matching the seams carefully will make the end result look very professional. Sew the seams of each section to be joined in the usual way.

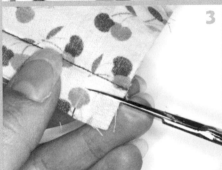

I Press the seam allowances open on both sections that are to be joined.

2 Trim the ends of the seam allowances.

3 Trim from the other direction to cut out squares from the seam allowances.

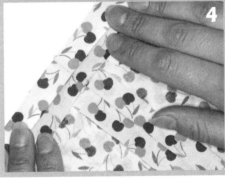

Sew different

This technique is very useful when you are making patchwork (page 195) with thick fabrics. It can also be used to join garment pieces together. Don't trim the seam allowances very close to the stitching if the fabric frays a lot.

4 With the seam allowance on the upper piece folded back, position the pieces right sides together so the seams match. Pin in place with the seam allowance flat.

5 Sew the seam. When you come to the seam allowances, make sure they stay open and sew over them.

6 Press the new seam open. Here, the seam is shown before pressing so that you can see how the seams intersect.

Sewing a curved seam

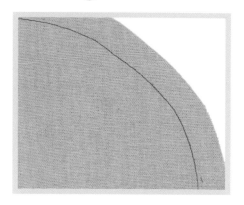

Curved seams are sewn in much the same way as straight seams, but there are a few things to bear in mind. Keep the raw edge of the fabric against the correct marking on the throat plate, or use a separate seam guide attached to the machine (page 285). Keep your hands in front of the needle and gently guide the fabric in the right direction. Use a short stitch length and go slowly and make small adjustments as the fabric moves through. For very tight or small curves, use the pivot method for turning a corner (page 49) and turn the fabric very slightly.

Clipping an inward curved seam

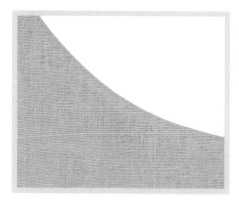

Inward curved seams need to have the seam allowances clipped to help them lie flat. This is because the seam allowance will be stretched once the piece is turned the right way out and the clips allow the seam allowance to spread. If you don't clip a curved seam, the curved edge will have puckers in it and won't lie flat even when it is pressed.

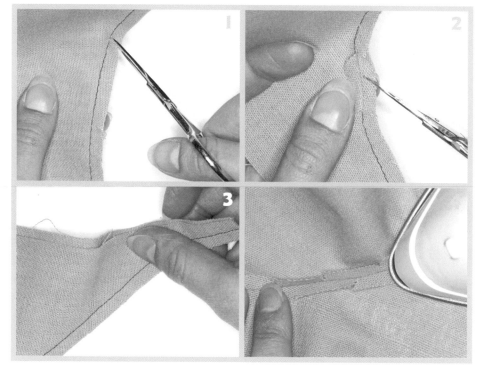

1 Trim the seam allowances to 7–10mm. Clip one seam allowance, clipping at an angle (so you cut on the bias) and about 2cm apart. Use only the tips of small scissors so you don't cut too far. The clips should be about two-thirds the depth of the seam allowance, so not too close to the stitching.

2 Turn the piece over and clip the other seam allowance. Clip at the same angle but make the clips between those on the other seam allowance so they are staggered.

3 The seam can now be straightened out.

4 Press the seam allowances open before folding right sides out.

Notching a curved seam masterclass

Outward curved seams need notches cut in the seam allowances to help them lie flat and avoid any puckering along the curved edge when the piece is turned right sides out. The notches remove excess fabric to allow the seam allowance to lie flat. Each seam allowance needs to be notched separately and the clips should be staggered so the seam isn't weakened.

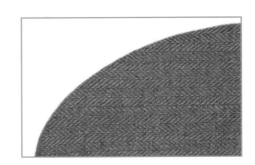

1 Trim the seam allowances to 7–10mm.

2 On one seam allowance, clip at an angle, all the way along the seam. Use only the tips of small scissors so you don't cut too far. The clips should be about two-thirds the width of the seam allowance, not too close to the stitching.

3 Clip in the other direction to cut out notches. It is quicker to cut one side of all the notches, then the other side, than to cut each notch individually. Cut the notches about 1.5cm apart unless the curve is very tight, in which case you should make the notches closer together.

4 Fold the notched allowance back and notch the other seam allowance in the same way, but stagger the notches so that they do not meet at the seam line.

5 Turn the piece right sides out and finger-press the seam (page 24), making sure that it is right on the edge. You should be able to see if the seam allowance is lying flat on the inside.

6 Press the seam. If it won't lie flat, then more notches are needed.

Princess seam masterclass

A princess seam runs over the bust in dresses and blouses. It is made from an inward curved piece joined to an outward curved piece. This technique also applies to any seam when a straight seam is joined to a curved seam. The seam allowances can be trimmed if required, but in this sample they are not.

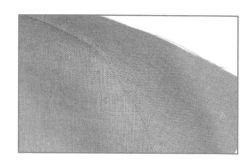

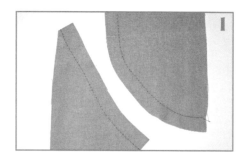

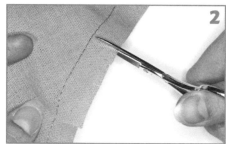

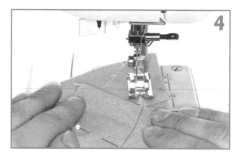

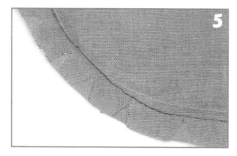

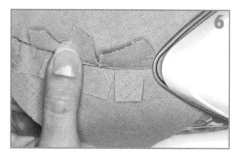

1 Stay stitch both edges, just inside the seam line (see page 34).

2 Clip the edge of the straighter or inward curving piece (page 44).

3 Pin the pieces together, curving the straighter piece into place as you pin. The clips will allow the seam allowance to stretch to fit.

4 Sew the seam.

5 Notch the other seam allowance (page 45), making sure that the notches are staggered between the clips on the other seam allowance.

6 Press the finished seam over a tailor's ham (page 25). This allows the piece to curve to the required shape.

Sew simple

Where appropriate, trim seam allowances and overcast or zigzag them before notching. Princess seams are the exception, though edges can be zigzagged before seaming.

Bias seams

Working with fabric cut on the bias does take some care, as bias edges will stretch and pucker. There are three schools of thought on how to sew bias seams.

I find that fabrics behave differently, and it will depend on what you are sewing as to how you proceed. Long, vertical bias seams on skirts and dresses will continue to stretch for some time, so pre-stretching before you sew is probably a good move. For small projects and minor bias seams, you can probably sew as normal and leave them to stretch, or stretch as you sew.

When joining a bias edge to a straight grain edge, have the straight grain on top. Areas where fastenings will be need to be stabilised with a piece of woven interfacing. Buttonholes are very liable to stretch, so make sure the interfacing is cut on the straight-grain so it doesn't stretch, too.

Technique A
Here, you sew as normal, being careful not to stretch the fabric, and then leave the item to hang for at least 24 hours to allow the bias to stretch naturally.

1 Tack loosely but do not stretch the fabric as you sew.

2 Sew using a medium to large stitch length and polyester thread. Let the machine pull the fabric through, don't stretch it.

Technique B
The second technique is to stretch the bias before sewing. Press and stretch along the direction of the bias. This may stretch the fabric into a different shape, so it is best to cut the pattern pieces extra large, stretch the fabric, then re-cut.

1 Pull the fabric along the direction of the true bias and iron as you go. Make sure you stretch all of the fabric evenly. Then sew the seam as normal.

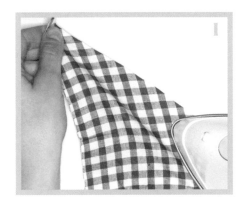

Technique C
You can stretch bias seams as you sew. This will pucker the fabric, but the puckers will press out. Sew without tacking or pinning if you can, or tack with very loose long stitches that allow you to stretch the fabric.

1 Pull the fabric with even tension from in front and behind the presser foot. Sew the seam, making sure you are only stretching the fabric, not pulling it through the machine.

2 Press the allowance open, using a tailor's ham (page 25) if it is a very curved seam.

Darts

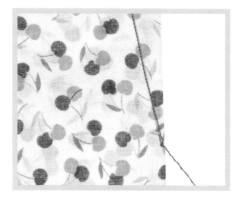

Darts are used to create curves and fitting in flat fabric. Your pattern will show the width and depth of the dart.

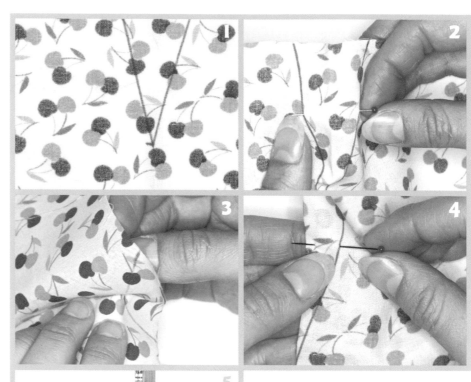

1 Transfer the pattern marks (page 246) for the dart onto the fabric .

2 Next, match up the dart legs neatly. My technique is to put a pin through one leg marking and then through the other leg.

3 Make sure the pin is horizontal so the marked lines meet accurately.

4 Pin the dart ready to sew it.

5 Start at the widest end of the dart and sew slowly and carefully. Angle the fabric so you are sewing in the right direction. Sew off the end of the dart, do not backstitch. Leave long tails of thread and knot them twice before cutting them off close to the end of the dart.

Sew different

There are other ways of sewing darts. Some people prefer to sew from the pointed end to the wide end as it is easier to be more precise, particularly for narrow darts. To avoid a dimple at the point of the finished dart, cut a small square of the same fabric with pinking shears and place this over the point of the dart. Sew the dart through all layers. The extra fabric fills up the end of the dart for a smooth finish.

Turning a corner

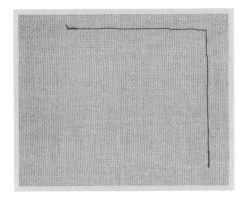

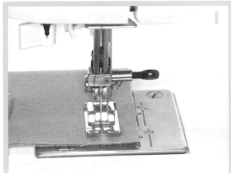

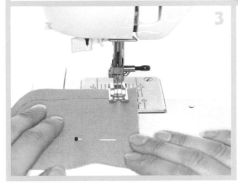

This method of turning corners is ideal for cushions where there is no strain on the corners. The same technique is used to pivot the fabric just a small amount when sewing curved seams. For corners that will take a strain, such as the corners of bags, sew right across to the edge, then sew the right angle seam, sewing that to the edge, too.

1 Sew as normal up to the corner. Either mark the seam line so that you know when you have reached the end of this seam or judge it by eye. You need to stop 1.5cm from the end of this seam in order to have a 1.5cm seam allowance on the second side. I use the presser foot as a guide as the legs of the foot are usually 1cm long, so I can judge when they are about 5mm from the raw edge.

2 At the corner point, leave the needle down and lift the presser foot up. Pivot the fabric around the needle.

3 With the fabric in the right position, put the presser foot down again and sew the seam on the second side.

Inward corner

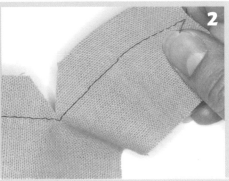

Inward corners are used to make square necklines. A clip allows the corner to sit flat when pressed.

1 Sew the corner, pivoting as described above. Snip into the seam allowance close to, but not into, the stitching.

2 Turn the piece right sides out and press.

Outward corners and points

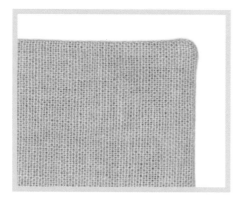

Corners and points need careful trimming to make sure they are neat. Don't cut too close to the stitching.

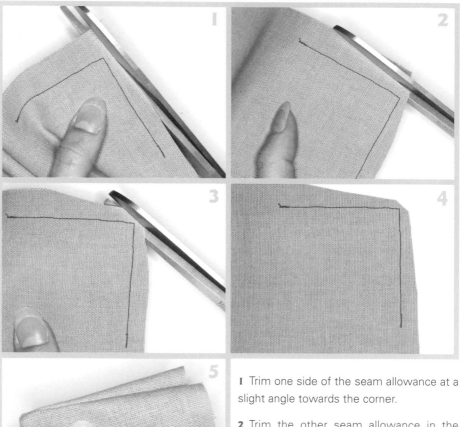

1 Trim one side of the seam allowance at a slight angle towards the corner.

2 Trim the other seam allowance in the same way.

3 Cut the corner off, but do not cut too close to the stitching.

4 Zigzag or overcast the edges if required to prevent fraying.

5 Turn the piece right sides out and gently push the corner out with the blunt end of a knitting needle or chopstick. Press the corner flat.

Sew different

For very long points, trim the side seam allowances at a very sharp angle, starting further along the seam allowance. This ensures that there is very little fabric to create bulk when the point is turned out. Finger-press points to make sure that the seams are sitting neatly before pressing.

Inset corner masterclass

Inset corners are used in complex dressmaking and in patchwork, where two different fabrics can be joined. The corner is reinforced with small squares of silk organza. Lightweight interfacing could also be used.

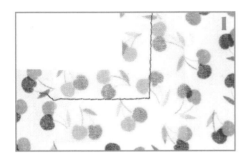

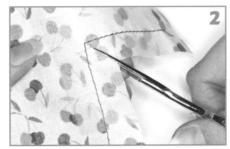

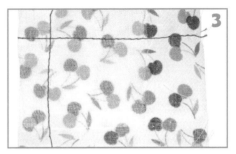

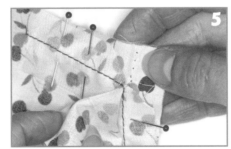

1 Position a square of reinforcing fabric over the L-shaped inward corner. Stay stitch just inside the seam lines (page 34). Trim away the excess organza.

2 Clip into the corner (page 49).

3 Pin and stay stitch the organza to the square as before.

4 Spread the clipped L-shaped section to fit over the square, making sure the corners match. Pin in place on the first side.

5 Pin the other side in place.

6 Sew the first seam up to the clipped corner. Pivot the needle (page 49) and move the excess fabric out of the way.

7 Turn the corner and sew the other seam.

8 Press the seam allowances towards the L-shaped piece.

Hems

There are many different types of hem, from the super-simple to time-consuming couture methods. The more complicated hems may seem like a lot of hard work, but they are worth it, particularly on special projects or difficult fabrics. If you are spending hours and hours making something, it's worth spending the time to make a really smart and hard-wearing hem.

What is a hem allowance?

This is the amount of extra fabric allowed for turning up a hem. The hem allowance will be shown on the pattern; a 5cm hem allowance is common on skirts.

Single hem

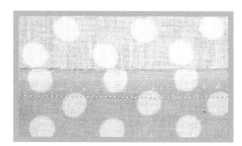

A single hem is just one fold of fabric, stitched down by machine. Use this when the hem is a selvedge (pages 16–17) or if the raw edge has already been finished (page 37). A single hem works well on straight and slightly curved hems. Simply turn over and press along the hem line and then sew with a medium straight machine stitch. Sew on the wrong side, quite close to the top edge. Make sure the threads match the fabric as the stitching will show on the right side.

Double hem

A double hem encloses the raw edge and makes a durable basic hem suitable for children's clothes, aprons and simple garments. As the stitching shows on the right side, make sure the top and bobbin thread both match the main fabric. A double hem works well on trousers and any tops with straight hems. This hem can be very narrow and so suitable for curved hems, or quite deep, which is best used on straight hems only.

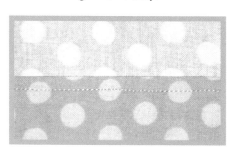

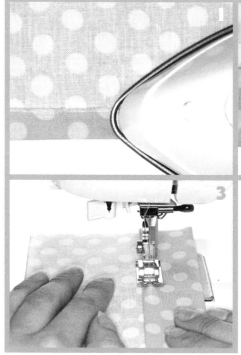

1 Press under the raw edge, usually by about 1cm.

2 Press under the remainder of the hem allowance (about 4cm), making sure the fold is on the required finished hem line.

3 Sew in place with the wrong side facing, following the folded edge. Use an edge guide foot if required (page 285).

Slip-stitched hem

A slip-stitched hem is fast and effective, and only small stitch marks show on the front. Overcast or zigzag the raw edge (page 37).

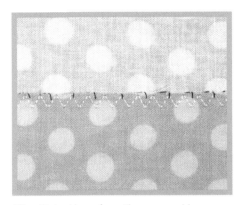

Slip-stitched hem from the wrong side.

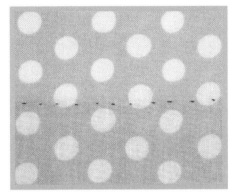

Slip-stitched hem from the right side. Contrast thread has been used for clarity.

1 Fold over the raw edge, making sure the fold is on the hem line. Use slip stitch (page 29) to attach the hem to the main fabric. Pick up only a couple of threads of the main fabric, so the stitches barely show on the right side.

Herringbone hem

Herringbone stitch is a traditional hemming stitch. It has quite a lot of give in it, so the hem can move and stretch. Herringbone stitch is very fast to work so this is a surprisingly quick hem.

Sew different

You can also make a double hem (opposite) and sew with slip stitch, herringbone stitch, hem stitch or catch stitch (pages 29–31).

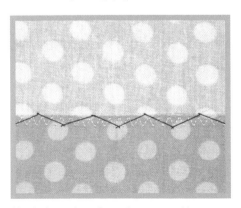

Herringbone hem from the wrong side.

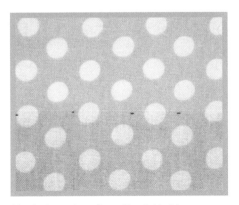

Herringbone hem from the right side.

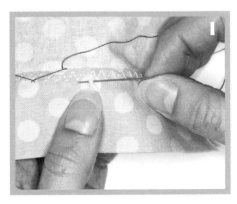

1 Fold over the raw edge, making sure the fold is on the hem line. Stitch the hem down using herringbone stitch (page 30). The stitching should cover the overcast edge. Pick up only a couple of threads of the main fabric, so the stitches barely show on the right side.

Couture hem masterclass

Couture techniques aren't always difficult. This hem is actually very simple and is completely invisible on the right side. It is best on thicker fabrics and is ideal for wool jackets and coats. The strip of interfacing inside the hem supports the fold and creates a slightly rounded edge rather than a sharp crease. Traditionally, a hem like this would be interfaced with a woven fabric sewn lightly to the inside. I have used woven iron-on interfacing, which is quicker and easier. This hem is great for satin and other fabrics that show every tiny stitch.

The hem line is thread traced, which makes it easy to make sure the fold is in the right place. Don't thread trace before you iron on the interfacing as it will be hard to remove the stitches. Hem line thread tracing means you can interface the hem, continue constructing the garment and come back to finish the hem later, without the marks wearing off, as chalk would.

Finish the raw edge if required, but this hem is designed to be covered with a lining, so it isn't essential. If you do want to finish the edge, the best method would be hand overcasting (page 37) as that doesn't leave any bulk that will create imprints on the front when you press the seam.

For more information on interfacing, turn to pages 255 and 292.

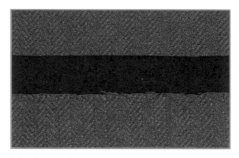

The finished hem from the wrong side.

The finished hem from the right side.

For a 5cm hem allowance, cut a strip of woven interfacing on the bias, 10cm wide and long enough for the whole hem. If the hem has seam allowances in it, cut strips of interfacing long enough to fit between the seams; do not interface over the seam allowances. Join the interfacing (page 255). Test the interfacing on a scrap of the project fabric, and if the edge shows up on the right side, pink the edges (page 36).

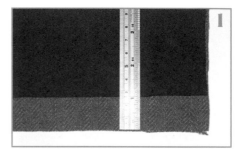

1 Position the interfacing 2.5cm up from the raw edge.

2 Attach the interfacing (page 255), using a slightly damp pressing cloth.

3 Thread trace the hem line (page 21).

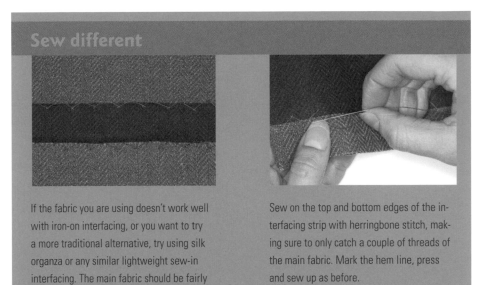

If the fabric you are using doesn't work well with iron-on interfacing, or you want to try a more traditional alternative, try using silk organza or any similar lightweight sew-in interfacing. The main fabric should be fairly thick or the stitches will show through. Cut the interfacing 10cm wide and on the bias.

Sew on the top and bottom edges of the interfacing strip with herringbone stitch, making sure to only catch a couple of threads of the main fabric. Mark the hem line, press and sew up as before.

4 Fold the hem along the thread tracing line.

5 Press the hem, covering it with a barely damp pressing cloth.

6 Sew the hem with herringbone stitch (page 53), catching only the interfacing, not the main fabric. Remove the thread tracing.

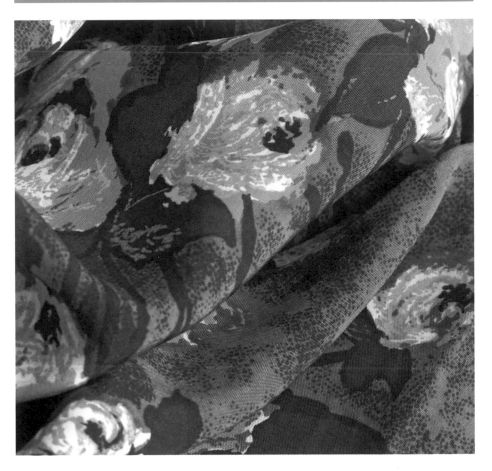

Fusible webbing

Fusible webbing is a type of fabric glue in the form of a dry ribbon that is activated by heat. It is a quick way to hem without sewing and is commonly used to hem trousers or skirts after shortening. It makes the hem quite stiff, which isn't ideal for most garments, though this could be used as a feature in a wide skirt where a stiff hem would be desirable. The hem is invisible from the front.

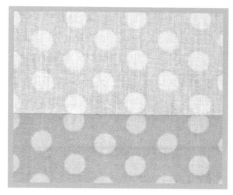

The hem from the wrong side.

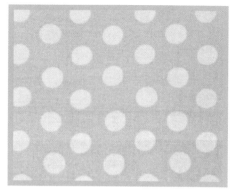

The hem is invisible on the right side.

1 Make a double hem (page 52). Draw a line above the top of the fold with a vanishing fabric marker.

2 Unfold the hem and lay the webbing 2–3mm below the line. If the hem is curved then you will need to cut the webbing into smaller sections and overlap them very slightly to go around the curve.

3 Fold the hem allowance back over the webbing. Without moving the fabric, cover it with a pressing cloth and press it for a few seconds, following the manufacturer's instructions on the pack.

Sew simple

Fusible webbing is nasty, sticky stuff if it gets on the iron. Always use a pressing cloth to avoid accidently melting it onto your iron; a Teflon cloth or baking paper is recommended (page 284). If you do get it on your iron, then use a preparatory iron cleaner or scrub the plate of the cool iron with a plastic scouring pad. If you use fusible webbing a lot, you might find it useful to buy a cheap iron just for this potentially sticky work.

Glued hem

Hems on leather and suede can be machine sewn, but glue creates an invisible hem. Use a glue specially designed for leather and follow the manufacturer's instructions.

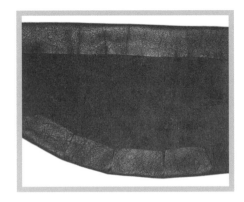

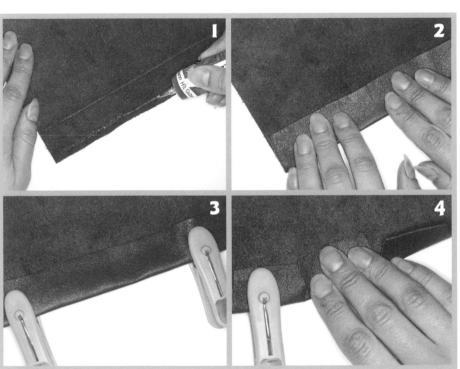

1 Mark the hem fold line on the back of the leather. Run a thin line of glue close to the raw edge.

2 Fold over the hem. Mop up any glue leaks with kitchen paper.

3 Use rubber-tipped clothes pegs to hold the hem in place until the glue dries.

4 For a curved hem, notch the hem allowance (page 45) and put a line of glue along the raw edge. Fold over and secure each notch with a peg, as before.

Rolled hem

Soft and very fine fabrics are difficult to work with so a rolled hem is a good option. Some fine fabrics will roll very easily and you can miss Steps 1–4 and just roll and stitch. Others that don't behave can be stitched along the hem line to make the rolling easier. The fabric is stitched over tissue to stop it puckering and becoming snarled in the machine.

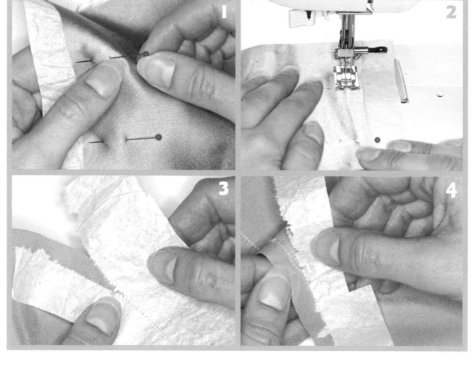

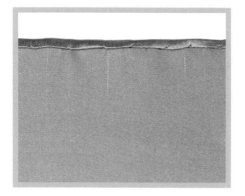

Sew simple

Use leftover scraps of tissue from the edges of dress patterns.

1 Pin the edge of the fabric to strips of tissue paper.

2 Machine-sew 1cm from the edge, using a short stitch length.

3 Tear off the tissue along one side of the line of stitching, taking care not to strain the stitches.

4 Remove the rest of the tissue and trim the fabric close to the stitching.

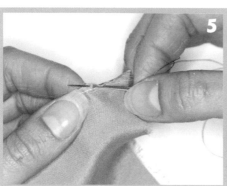

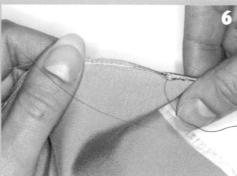

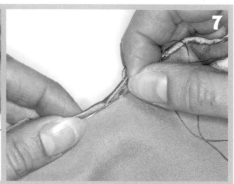

5 Make tiny securing stitches in the seam allowance (page 34).

6 Dampen your right forefinger and thumb and start the roll by rolling one end of the hem to cover the machine stitching line.

7 Continue rolling the hem with your left forefinger and thumb, and slip stitch (page 29) the hem as you roll. Press if required.

Hem or seam tape

Hem tape is designed to conceal the raw edge of the hem and make a neat finish on the inside. It is good for unlined garments, but not for fabrics that fray very readily.

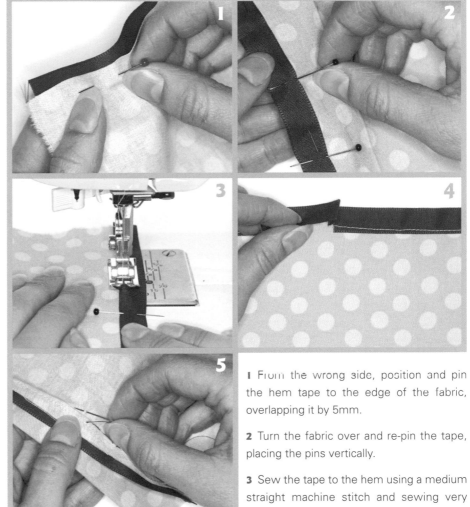

1 From the wrong side, position and pin the hem tape to the edge of the fabric, overlapping it by 5mm.

2 Turn the fabric over and re-pin the tape, placing the pins vertically.

3 Sew the tape to the hem using a medium straight machine stitch and sewing very close to the edge.

4 Join the ends of the tape by folding under one raw end, overlapping it over the other raw end and sewing over all layers.

5 Fold back the tape and catch stitch (page 31) below the line of machine stitching.

Sew different

You can also use slip stitch (page 29) or herringbone stitch (page 30) to attach the hemming tape to the garment.

Bound hem

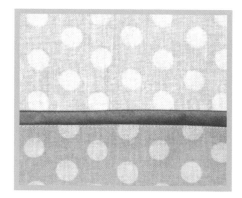

This hem is good for heavy fabrics that fray, such as wool tweed, and is suitable for gently-curved hems. The binding completely covers the raw edge and gives a very professional finish.

Cut strips of bias fabric (page 68) to match the garment and 2.5cm wide, or use unfolded bias binding that is the correct width.

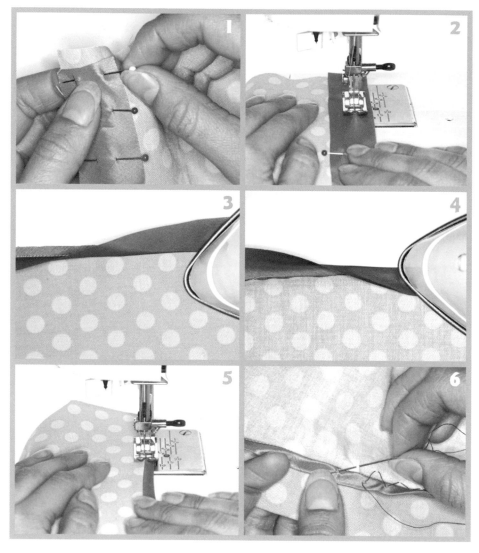

1 Right sides together, pin the bias strip to the edge of the fabric, placing the pins close together.

2 Sew the fabric and bias together, 5mm from the edge.

3 From the right side, press the bias strip up, over the raw edges.

4 Fold the bias strip over to the back to enclose the raw edge and press.

5 From the right side, machine-sew just below the join, sewing on the main fabric not the bias strip. This is called stitching in the ditch.

6 Fold and press the hem as required. Fold back the bound edge and catch stitch (page 31) the hem in place.

Sew different

Use this hemming technique for velvet and satin, but use strips of soft tulle or net instead of bias tape.

Bias-bound hem

Purchased bias binding can be used to cover the raw edge of a hem. Unlike the technique opposite, this version does not completely enclose the raw edge, but it is quicker. It is suitable for lightweight to medium-weight fabrics. Use 12–15mm (unfolded width) bias binding.

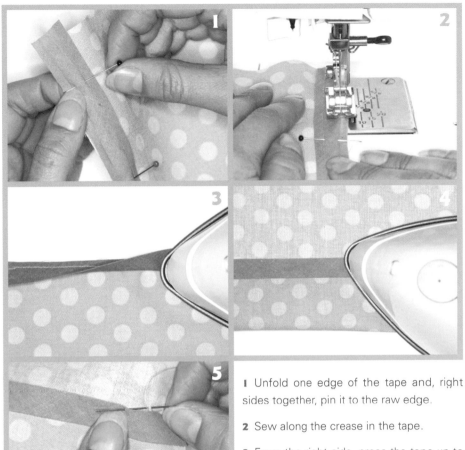

1 Unfold one edge of the tape and, right sides together, pin it to the raw edge.

2 Sew along the crease in the tape.

3 From the right side, press the tape up to cover the seam and raw edges.

4 Press the hem up as required, allowing the bias binding to curve as you go.

5 Slip stitch (page 29) the top edge of the tape to the main fabric.

Sew different

Either of these bound hems could be made using bias binding cut from patterned or contrasting fabrics (pages 68–73). Some specialist shops sell ready-made bias binding made from fancy fabrics, which would look very smart on an unlined jacket where the inside shows when it is open. You could also use herringbone stitch (page 30) to sew the bias binding in place.

Mitred corner hem

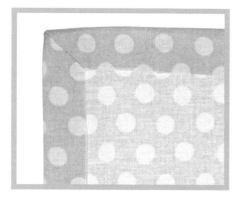

This hem is for sharp corners, such as the edges of jackets. Finish the raw edges as required and sew down the hem as appropriate using one of the techniques in this chapter.

1 Press under the seam allowances on both raw edges.

2 Open out the pressed seam allowances and fold the corner over, using the crossing points of the creases as the edge of the corner fold.

3 Unfold the corner again, turn the fabric right sides together. Aligning the edges, pin the layers together.

4 Machine-sew along the corner fold line.

5 Cut off the corner about 3mm from the line of stitching.

6 Turn the corner right side out and gently push out the corner with a knitting needle.

7 Press the corner flat and continue hemming as required.

Curved hem

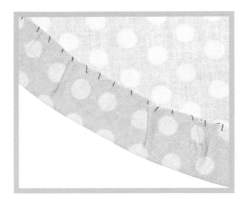

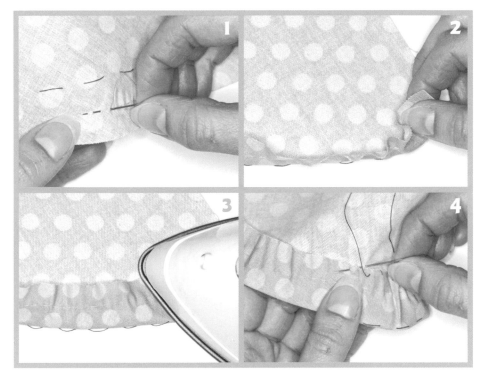

For very curved hems, like the Circular Skirt (page 270), try this quick method. Because the skirt hem is curved, most of it is on the bias and so will not fray. If fraying is a problem, finish the raw edge first or use a bound hem (page 60).

1 Thread trace the hem line (page 21). Run a line of ease stitches (page 34) in the seam allowance, either by hand or by machine.

2 Pull up the ease stitches.

3 Fold up the hem, easing the stitching to fit, and press it.

4 Sew the hem using slip stitch (page 29) or herringbone stitch (page 30). Remove the thread tracing.

Faced hem

A facing provides a hard-wearing edge to a garment and adds some weight to the hem. It is good for unusual or curved shapes that would be hard to hem in any other way. Faced hems are useful when a skirt has been lengthened and there is no fabric left to make a hem.

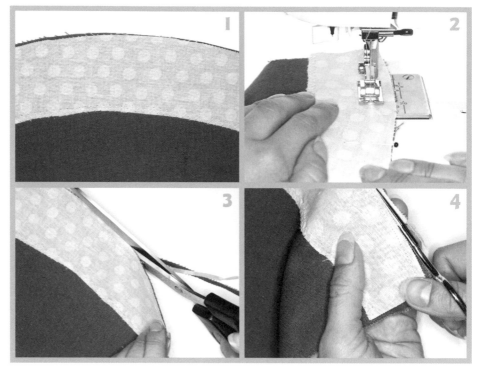

1 Cut the facing the same shape as the hem and overcast or bind the inner edge. Join facing pieces if required. Place the facing on the hem, with right sides together and raw edges matching.

2 Sew the facing to the fabric using a 1cm seam allowance.

3 Trim the seam allowance.

4 Layer the seam allowance of the facing (page 38).

5 Cut notches in the seam allowances (page 45), making sure you don't cut too close to the stitching.

6 Using a tailor's ham (page 25) to support the curve, press the seam allowances open.

7 Press both seam allowances towards the facing, again using the tailor's ham to support the curve.

8 Sew the seam allowance to the facing by sewing 3mm from the first line of stitching, through the seam allowance and facing.

9 Turn the facing to the inside of the garment. Finger press the hem to ensure that about 2mm of the main fabric is turned to the inside, then press it. Slip stitch (page 29) or herringbone stitch (page 30) the edge to the main fabric.

Sew different

The technique is the same for applying facing to any part of a garment. For more on facings see pages 252–253.

Blind hemming masterclass

This is a quick and effective method of finishing straight hems that is almost invisible on the right side. It is best used for curtains, but can be used for straight-leg trouser hems. Refer to your machine manual to see if you have a blind hemming stitch.

Blind hemming barely shows on the right side when matching thread is used.

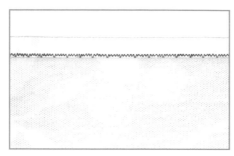

The finished stitch. The main part of the stitching is in the seam allowance and the long stitches catch the fold.

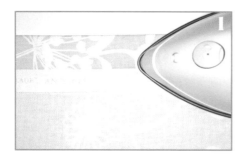

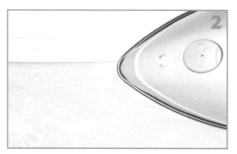

Sew different

To use this technique for trouser hems, turn the leg inside out and place the cuff over the free arm of the machine (page 13).

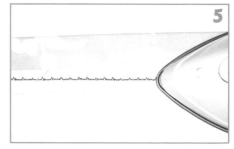

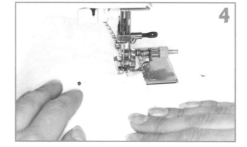

1 Turn under the hem and press it.

2 Turn the folded edge under so that about 1cm of the hem allowance shows.

3 Pin the hem allowance in place.

4 Use the blind hemming foot and set the machine to blind hemming stitch. Sew the length of the hem, ensuring that the longer stitches just catch the folded edge.

5 Unfold the edge and press the hem flat.

Sheer fabric machined hem and corners

This hemming technique is good for stiffer, sheer fabrics that need a folded rather than a rolled hem and it is all done by machine. Sew in matching thread.

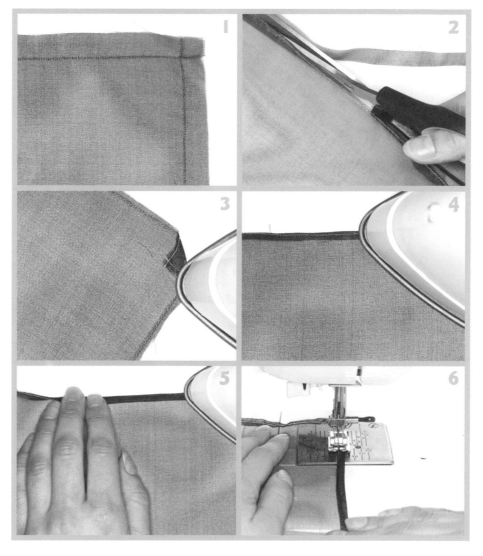

Sew different

A hemming foot attachment (page 285) for the sewing machine can be very useful when doing a long hem on stiffer fabrics. Start by turning the hem under by hand and finger-press it, then feed the hem into the foot and sew the whole hem in one go.

1 Sew a line of stitching 5mm inside the hem line (this will be 1cm from the raw edge if the hem allowance is 1.5cm).

2 Trim the fabric to 5mm from the stitching.

3 Fold the corner in and press.

4 Fold the fabric on the line of stitching and press it.

5 Fold the fabric over again to make a double hem and press.

6 Sew close to the inside fold and pivot at the corner (page 49).

Edgings, bindings and piping

Good edgings, bindings and piping will make a real difference to the quality of your finished project. A well-made binding is very satisfying. I've include lots of different options, so experiment and find which one suits you.

Bias binding

Bias strips are lengths of fabric cut on the diagonal grain (the bias) (pages 16–17). Bias binding is lengths of bias strip folded and pressed ready to apply to a raw edge. Bias binding is sometimes called bias tape.

Making your own bias strips and binding is surprisingly easy. You can make it to match your project, in a contrasting fabric or in something really special. If you only need a short piece of bias strip or binding, then you can cut single strips. If you need a larger quantity, try the masterclass on continuous bias strip (page 70). This section also includes turning the flat bias strip into bias binding, making bias binding fit curves and several ways of attaching it.

Sew simple

To calculate the width of bias strip you need to make bias binding, multiply the finished width by two. For example, for a binding that is 2cm wide, cut a strip 4cm wide. This will be 1cm wide when folded in half for the double-fold binding technique (page 73).

Bias strip

Use this method if you need a small amount of bias strip, bearing in mind that you can easily join pieces to make a longer piece. The pieces of strip will have diagonal ends that you need to keep to join them together.

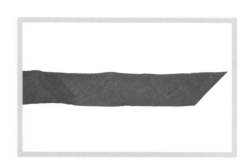

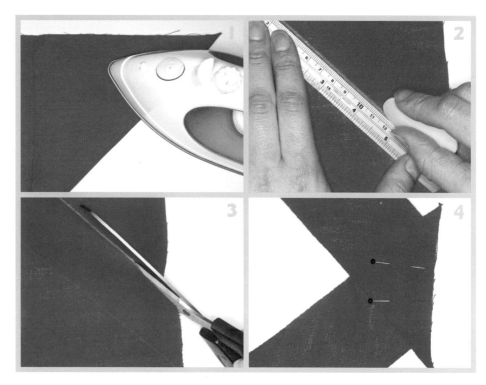

1 Cut a square or rectangle of fabric on the straight grain. Fold it diagonally, matching the edges to ensure that you have folded along the bias grain perfectly. Press the fold.

2 Draw along the fold line with a fabric marker and use this line to measure the width of strip you need. Draw a line parallel to the fold line and continue to draw as many strips as required, all the same width.

3 Cut the strips along the diagonal lines.

4 To join two pieces, pin as shown, making sure you overlap the edges by 5mm for a seam allowance.

5 Machine-sew the seam using a 5mm seam allowance.

6 Press the seam allowances open.

7 Trim the overlapping seam allowances.

Continuous bias strip masterclass

This method is perfect when you need lots of bias strip. Although it may appear to be thoroughly confusing and will look totally bizarre halfway through, persevere and it will work. Then you can really impress your sewing friends.

First, work out how much fabric you need. With a calculator, work out the total length, plus 10% (for seam allowances and wastage). Multiply the total length by the width of strip required. For example, for 2m of 5cm tape, you need 210 x 5cm = 1,100cm total area of fabric. To make that into a square, press the square root key ($\sqrt{\ }$) on the calculator, to give you the required measurement for each side of your square. 2m of 5cm bias strip needs a 33.1cm square. Round it up a little to give you some slack.

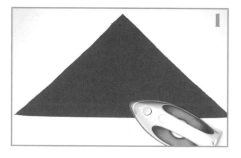

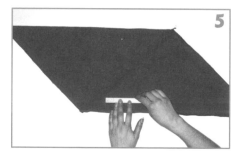

1 Cut the required size of square, making sure it is exactly on the straight grain. Press the square in half diagonally.

2 Cut along the pressed line.

3 Place two straight edges together so the bias edges cross. If you are using a single-sided fabric, place the right sides together. Pin along the straight edges.

4 Machine-sew the seam, using a 1cm seam allowance. Then press the seam allowances open.

5 Place the resulting parallelogram face down. From the bottom edge, measure and mark the width of the strips you need (don't worry if you have a little left over at the top).

6 Turn the piece over. Bring the edges together, matching the drawn lines, but offset the lines so the edges overlap by one marked width. This makes a strange shape, but persevere and it will work.

7 Pin the edges together. This makes the piece into a tube.

8 Machine-sew the seam, using a 1cm seam allowance.

9 Press the seam allowances open.

10 Starting where the edges overlap, cut along the marked lines, turning the piece over and over as you go.

Making bias binding with a bias-binding maker

This simple tool allows you to fold and press the raw edges under to make bias strip into bias binding in one simple step. Bias-binding makers come in various widths and you can only make one width of binding with each size of maker. Check the pattern instructions to find out the width of tape required. First, make the bias strip (pages 68 or 70).

Sew different

You can use binding makers to put folds in straight binding, too (pages 74–75).

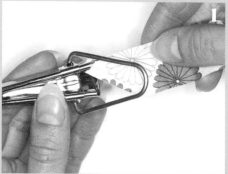

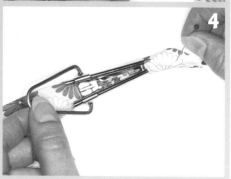

1 Feed the diagonal end of the bias strip into the maker, making sure you have the wrong side of the fabric facing up.

2 Use a pin to help push the fabric through if it is tricky.

3 Pull the strip through far enough to just catch the end of it.

4 Firmly pin this end of the fabric to the ironing board.

5 Pull the maker with your left hand, and press the binding with your right as it comes out of the maker.

Making bias binding by hand

If you don't have a bias-binding maker, then you can just turn under the fold allowances by hand and press them. You can buy special heatproof plastic strips over which to press the tape (page 284), so that the width is always consistent. Thin cardboard will also work. You can do it by eye, but this takes a bit of practice.

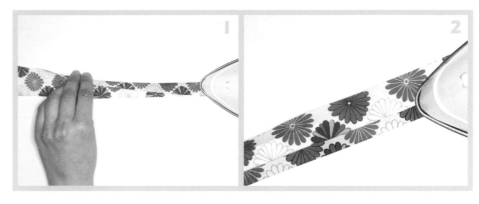

1 Fold the tape in half and press lightly then unfold it.

2 Press one edge to the centre fold, then turn the tape around and press the other edge to the centre.

Double-fold bias binding

Double-fold binding means you need the bias binding folded in half. This is usually used for the raw-edge binding technique. The two folded halves are not completely equal – the back of the binding should be slightly longer, which makes it easier to apply. You can do this with purchased binding or with binding that you have made yourself.

1 Fold the binding in half with the top edge not quite meeting the bottom edge. Press it as you fold.

Shaping bias binding

When bias binding has to fit around a curved edge, you can steam and press the binding to make it curve. This makes it much easier to sew on.

1 Pull the folded binding around with your left hand as you press it with your right. Use a template for the curve if required.

Double-fold binding

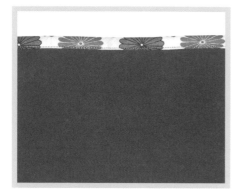

Straight-stitched binding.

Straight-stitched binding around a curve.

Zigzag-stitched binding.

This simple technique uses double-fold bias binding (page 73) and it is sewn entirely by machine. It is perfect for single pieces of fabric with straight or curved edges. I have used it on the pocket and neckline of the apron project (page 106).

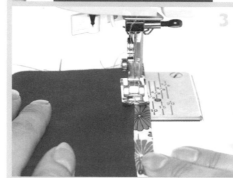

1 Press the binding in half (page 73). Place the binding, longer-side underneath, over the raw edge, ensuring the raw edge is right up against the fold.

2 Pin the binding in place.

3 Sew the binding on the machine, just inside the edge if using straight stitch, or nearer the middle if using zigzag stitch.

Sew simple

To use this binding on a curved edge, shape the bias first (page 73). Don't try this with very narrow double-fold bias binding, it is far too fiddly. With broad binding, keep the stitching close to the edge of the binding, not by the fold.

Single-fold binding

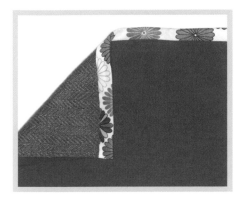

This type of edging is useful for finishing several layers, such as the edges of quilts, and is used to finish the edges of the Patchwork Needlebook (page 211). It also works well for curved edges. Sew corners following the mitred corner masterclass (page 78). In this sample, the pink side is the right side and the turquoise is the wrong side.

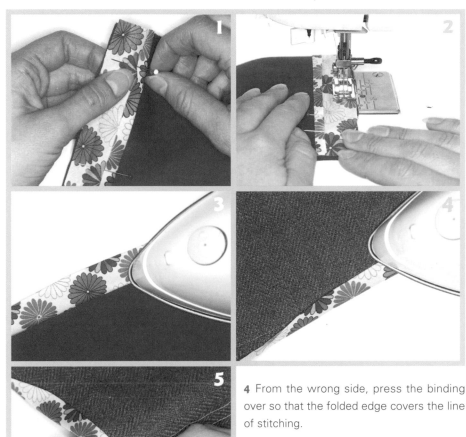

4 From the wrong side, press the binding over so that the folded edge covers the line of stitching.

5 Slip stitch (page 29) the binding in place, catching only the lower layer of fabric so the stitches don't show on the front. Use thread to match the binding, not the main fabric.

1 Unfold one edge of the bias binding. Pin the binding to the right side of the fabric, raw edges together.

2 Sew the binding to the edge of the fabric, sewing along the crease in the binding.

3 From the right side, press the binding up to cover the seam allowance.

Sew different

This binding can be sewn entirely by machine. At Step 5, machine-sew through all the layers, close to the edge of the binding.

Single-fold straight grain binding

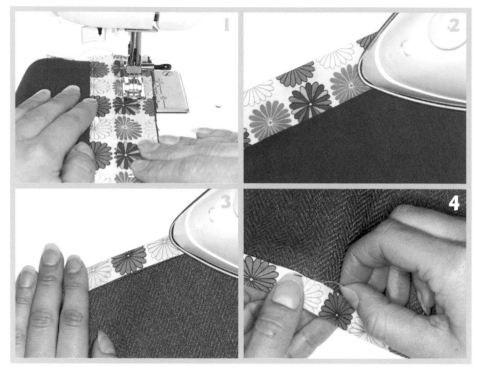

This technique is almost the same as single-fold binding, but instead of cutting the binding on the bias, the strips are cut on the straight grain, which is easier. This type of binding is useful for edging an item made from several layers. This technique works well for straight edges and is used to make the edges of the blanket project (page 201). Cut sufficient strips for the length required (plus a little extra), join them together to make one long strip and press the seam allowances open. The strip should be four times the required finished width (which is usually 1.5cm).

Prepare the folds in the bias strip following the instructions for making bias binding (pages 72–73). In this sample, the pink side is the right side and the turquoise is the wrong side.

1 Unfold one end of the binding and pin it to the right side of the piece. Sew along the crease in the binding. The seam allowance should be the same as the desired finished width (1.5cm in this sample).

2 From the right side, press the binding up to cover the seam allowance.

3 From the wrong side, press the binding over so the folded edge covers the stitching.

4 Slip stitch (page 29) the binding in place, catching only the lower layer of fabric so that the stitches don't show on the right side. Use thread to match the binding, not the main fabric.

Double-fold straight grain binding

This technique is very similar to the single-fold binding (opposite), but is more durable. As the binding is twice as thick over the raw edge, it is hard-wearing and is ideal for sheer fabrics as it hides the raw edges and stitching. Cut the strips six times the required final width of the binding (usually 1.5cm), then join them to make a strip long enough for the project, plus a little extra, and press the seam allowances open. In this sample, the pink side is the right side and the turquoise is the wrong side.

1 Fold the binding strip in half, right side out, and press it. Match the raw edges of the binding to the raw edge of the fabric on the right side. Sew, using a seam allowance the same as your desired finished width (1.5cm in this sample).

2 Follow Steps 2–4 of Single-fold Straight Grain Binding (opposite).

Sew different

You can sew this binding by machine instead of slip stitching. Fold the binding over as directed, press and pin. Machine close to the fold, through all the layers. This works well for sheer fabrics.

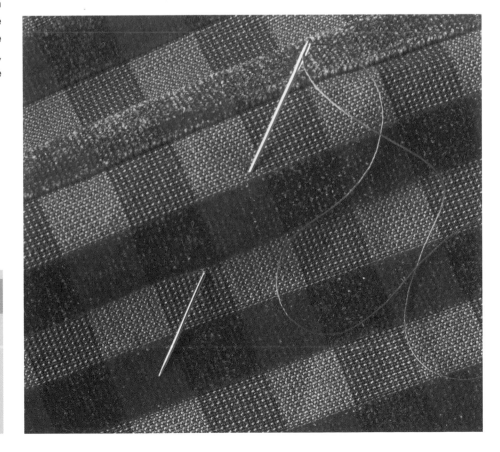

Mitred corner masterclass

This technique works for single-fold and double-fold binding, either straight grain or bias. The stitching line is marked on the binding to make it easier to see where to sew. If you are sewing along the crease line, then just keep to this line. Accuracy is important to get a neat mitre on both sides. In this sample, the right and wrong sides are the same colour.

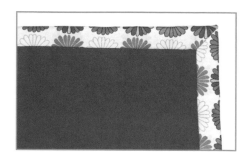

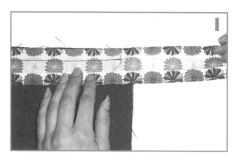

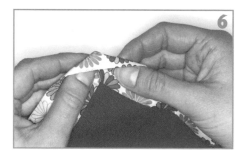

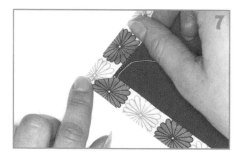

1 Sew along the first edge to the corner, stopping before you sew into the seam allowance for the next side (1.5cm from the end in this sample).

2 Fold the binding up at an angle where the stitching ends.

3 Keeping the top edge straight by placing a ruler over it, fold the binding back down along the second side.

4 Pin the binding along the second edge.

5 Start sewing the second side from the top edge, sewing over the fold and the corner. Continue machine-sewing the binding and come back to finish all the corners when you are slip stitching the back of the binding in place.

6 Fold the corner over to the wrong side.

7 Slip stitch (page 29) up to the corner, fold the corner flat and it will make a neat mitre, as long as your machine stitching and measuring were accurate.

8 Continue slip stitching, leaving the corner unstitched unless it's a very wide edging, in which case slip stitch the corner, too.

Piping

Piping is often used on cushion edgings and sometimes on clothes. What we normally call piping, with a cord inside, is actually corded piping, while standard piping is unfilled and flat.

A similar technique is used to make narrow fabric tubes, again either flat or filled with cord.

Corded piping

Corded piping is made from bias tape and piping cord. Wrap the cord in scraps of fabric to work out the required width of bias tape. Add seam allowances of 3cm to the width. Cut and join the bias tape (page 70). Pre-shrink the piping cord if the project will be washed (page 18).

Flat piping

Flat piping is simply a folded strip of bias fabric inserted in the seam allowance. Flat piping is very effective as a feature where facings and linings join.

Make the piping from narrow bias strip (pages 68–71), which will stretch nicely around curves. Fold the tape in half, right side out.

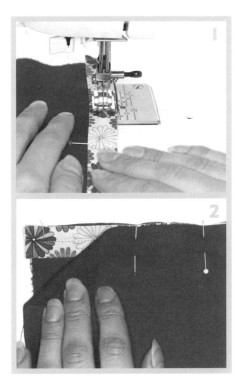

1 Place the folded tape with the raw edge to the raw edge of the right side of the fabric. Pin then machine tack in place.

2 Place the top fabric over the piping, right sides together. Pin in place. Sew the seam as usual, following the tacking line on the lower piece of fabric.

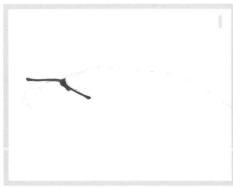

1 Tie the cut ends of piping cord with thread to stop them unravelling.

2 Wrap the fabric around the cord, right side out, and tack by hand.

3 Using a zip foot (page 84), machine-sew close to the cord.

Applying piping

This technique can be used with either purchased piping or piping that you have made yourself. Because piping is made with fabric cut on the bias, it will bend nicely around curves, but it won't make sharp corners.

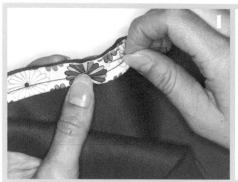 

1 Tack the piping to the right side of the fabric, raw edges together.

2 Pin the other fabric on top. Machine-sew through all layers, using a zip foot (page 84) to get the stitching very close to the piping.

Piping around a corner.

Piping along a curved edge.

Clip the seam allowance on the piping to help it go around corners and curves smoothly.

Joining piping

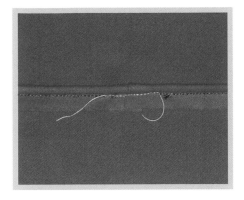

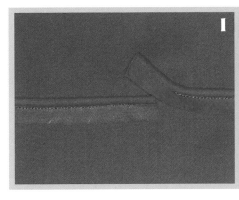

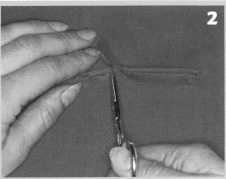

A neat join in piping will look very professional. This join can be done on purchased piping or piping that you have made yourself. Make the join in the centre of a straight seam, not on a curve or near a corner.

1 Sew the piping in place using machine or hand tacking. Leave about 2cm unstitched at one end and 1cm at the other end.

2 On the longer end (on the right in the sample), unpick the stitching holding the cord in place. Roll back the fabric to expose the cord and cut the cord so it is exactly the right length to butt up to the other end of the cord without a gap or overlap.

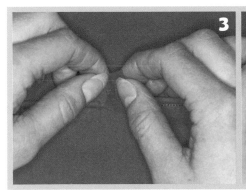

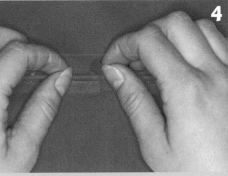

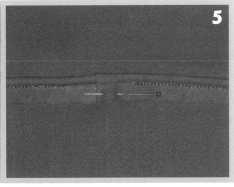

3 Fold under the end of the piping fabric by about 1cm.

4 Place the folded end over the other end of the piping.

5 Pin in place and sew over the join, using a zip foot as before.

Sew different

Decorative piping can be sewn into the seams of a garment to give a very smart and professional finish. Piping is great for emphasising curved seams that run along the front of the body, like princess seams or front panel seams on a fitted pencil skirt.

Bias tube

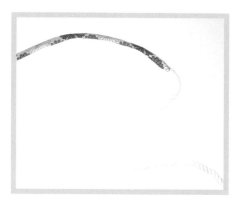

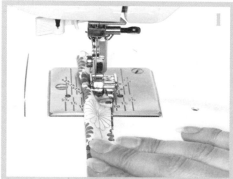

Tiny, narrow tubes of bias-cut fabric can be used to make button loops, fastenings and thin straps. Cut the required length of bias strip (pages 68–71). The tubes are made using piping cord to get the thickness consistent all the way along the length. Select piping cord of the right thickness and make sure that the bias tape will wrap around it with at least 1cm seam allowances on both edges. Use a length of piping cord 5cm longer than the bias strip. The piping cord is removed, so there is no need to pre-shrink it.

1 Wrap the bias fabric, wrong side out, around the cord and pin then tack as for corded piping (page 79). Make sure there is about 2cm of cord sticking out of one end.

2 Zigzag stitch over the other end of the cord, so the cord is firmly held in place. Sew along the side of the cord with a zip foot (page 84), in the same way as corded piping (Step 3, page 79).

3 Turn the tube inside out. To start the turning, hold the seam allowance and pull the end of the cord that sticks out.

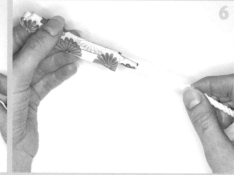

4 Hold the cord and ease the fabric over the end of it.

5 Pull the cord all the way through.

6 As the turned tube appears, pull it through. Snip off the end where the cord is sewn in.

Covered cord

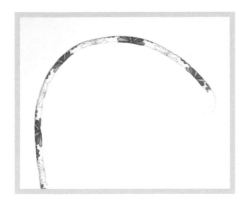

This is the same technique as making bias tubes (opposite), but by using twice the length of piping cord, when the tube is turned more piping fills the tube.

Cut the piping cord to twice the length of the required filled tube. Wrap the fabric around the piping cord as in Steps 1–2 (opposite), but start in the middle of the length of piping, so only the right-hand half is covered with fabric.

Machine over the end of the fabric in the middle of the cord to secure it, then sew along the side with a zip foot, as before.

1 Turn the tube by pulling the cord while holding the seam allowance, as before. The fabric tube will cover the previously bare half of the cord. Cut off the excess piping cord.

Folded fabric tube

Fabric tubes are ideal for making tab-top curtains, ties on clothes, bag handles and many other items. If you need lots of tabs, make one long tube then cut it into pieces. To make it easier to turn out long tubes, sew them up with a piece of cord inside like bias tube (opposite). Sew across the end of the cord before you sew up the length of the tube. Pull on the end of the cord to help pull the tube through.

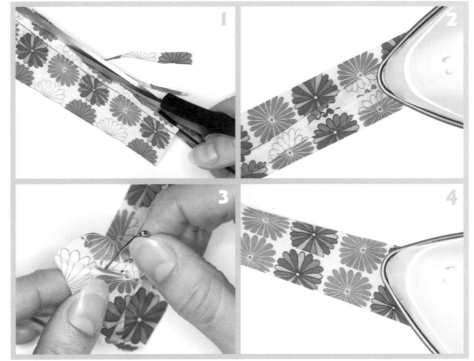

1 Cut strips twice the required width plus seam allowances. Fold the strips in half lengthways, right sides together. Sew the seam and trim the seam allowances.

2 Turn the seam to the centre back and press the seam allowances open.

3 Turn the tube right sides out with a loop turner (page 283) or a safety pin. Put the pin into and through one end of the tube.

4 Flatten out the tube, so the seam is at the centre back, and press it.

Fastenings

This section includes all the basics, from sewing on buttons to inserting a zip, as well as more specialist techniques such as invisible zips and bound buttonholes. The more complicated techniques are perfect for expanding your dressmaking repertoire and adding a professional finish.

Buying the right zip

There are lots of different zips available. A standard plastic zip can vary in price – and the price usually reflects the quality. A cheap zip will be perfectly suitable for a quick and simple purse, but if you are spending many hours making yourself a fantastic dress, don't be let down by a cheap zip that will soon need replacing.

Plastic zips are fine for most projects. Metal zips are generally only used for jeans or hard-wearing garments. Invisible zips are well worth learning to use for special garments or where another insertion method would show. Open-ended zips are used for jackets and cardigans, and are inserted in a similar way to a purse zip (page 91). Double-ended zips are usually used for coats or bags. They can be either open-ended or closed. Closed double-ended zips on bags can be inserted like an inset zip (page 88).

Zip foot

Many machines have a special narrow foot for sewing zips. It isn't possible to sew a zip in by machine without one, as an ordinary foot is too wide to be able to sew close enough to the zip teeth. There are some zip feet shown on page 285.

Shortening a plastic zip

You may not be able to buy the right colour zip in the length you need, so buy a longer one and shorten it. Oversew metal zips by hand before cutting them.

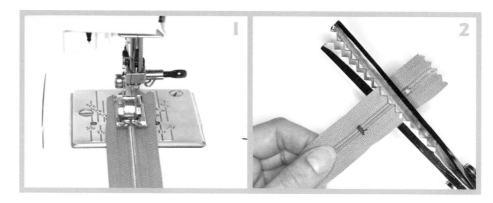

1 Set the machine to a 3–5mm zigzag and a short stitch length, or satin stitch if your machine has an automatic setting (page 33). Place the plastic zip under the foot with the teeth centred. Stitch over the zip a few times.

2 Using pinking shears (page 36), cut off the excess zip about 2cm from the stitching.

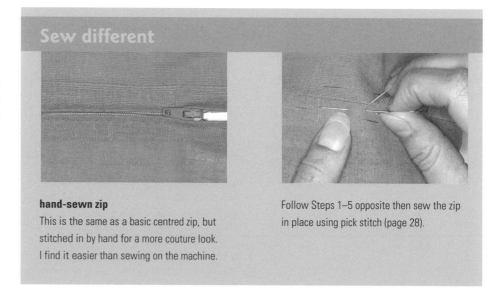

Sew different

hand-sewn zip
This is the same as a basic centred zip, but stitched in by hand for a more couture look. I find it easier than sewing on the machine.

Follow Steps 1–5 opposite then sew the zip in place using pick stitch (page 28).

Basic centred zip

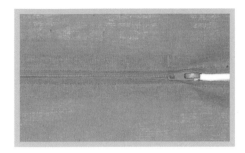

This is the most straightforward zip insertion technique and is ideal for skirts. It needs 1.5cm seam allowances. I use quilter's masking tape, which is 5mm wide, as a guide to sew around on the outside. If you don't have tape, draw in the sewing line or keep the edge of the zip foot close to the zip teeth.

1 Sew the seam up to where the zip will be inserted. Machine or hand tack along the seam line where the zip will be placed.

2 Snip the tacking (if done by machine) to make it easier to take out later.

3 Press the seam allowances open.

4 With the zip closed and the pull-tag sticking up, place the zip face down on the tacked seam, with the teeth centred on the seam line. Pin then hand tack the zip in position. The top of the zip should be 1.5cm from the edge of the fabric.

5 On the right side, stick narrow quilter's masking tape over the seam line. This provides a guide line for the top stitching in the next step.

6 Put a zip foot (opposite) on the machine. Open the zip part way, then starting at the top left, sew around the quilting tape, across the bottom and back up the other side.

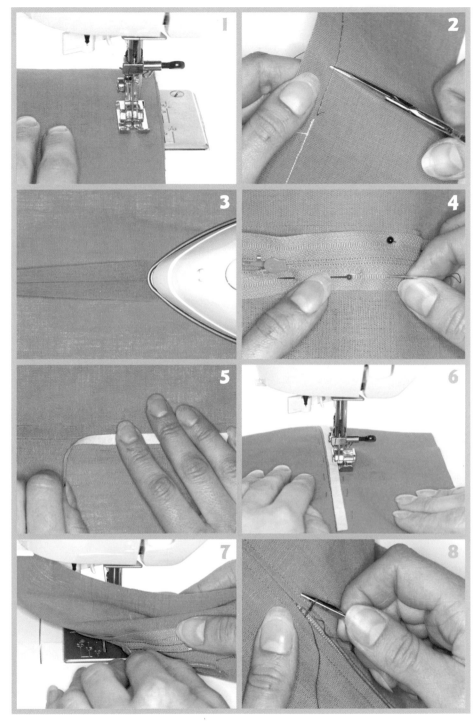

7 Stitch as far as you can before the zip pull gets in the way. Leave the needle down and lift the presser foot. Manoeuvre the zip pull out of the way, either up or down. Put the presser foot down then continue sewing.

8 Use the tips of small scissors to pull out the tacking. Don't just cut it, as it will leave lots of irritating little ends that are very hard to get out.

Lapped zip

A lapped zip has the seam allowance extended to completely cover the zip, which looks much smarter than the basic zip technique (page 85). It isn't very difficult, but requires an extra seam allowance for the zip opening. If your garment has a 1.5cm seam allowance, make the zip area slightly wider or cut the whole section with 2cm seam allowances and trim off what isn't needed. The seam allowances must be accurately measured for this technique to work.

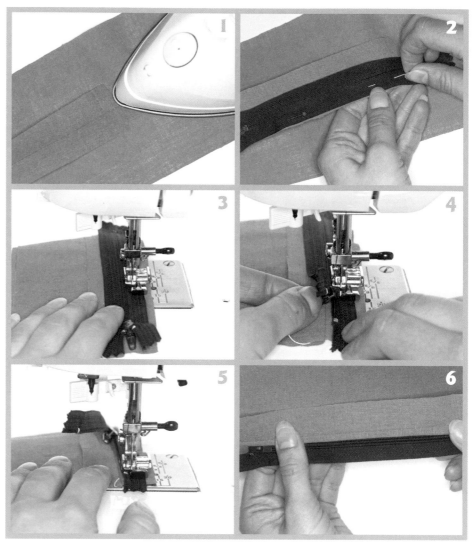

I Follow Steps 1–3 of Basic Centred Zip (page 85).

2 With the zip face down, pin the left side of the zip to the left seam allowance. The zip teeth are NOT over the tacked seam.

3 With a zip foot (page 84) and the zip face down, machine tack along the zip tape, close to the zip teeth.

4 To get around the zip pull, leave the needle down, lift the presser foot and slide the zip pull tag out of the way.

5 Complete the stitching.

6 Fold the zip back so that the folded edge of the fabric lies right up against the edge of the zip teeth.

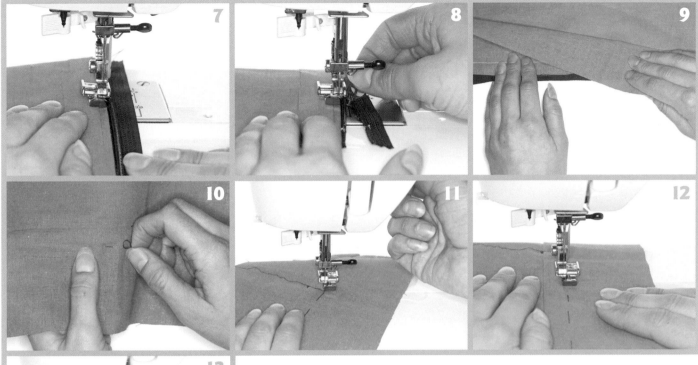

7 Change the zip foot to the other side. From the right side, sew as close as possible to the zip teeth, stitching through the folded edge of the fabric.

8 Work around the zip pull by leaving the needle down and opening the zip as before. Continue sewing close to the teeth.

9 Lay the zip face up and fold the other side of the fabric back over the zip.

10 Finger press the seam flat, then hand tack along the other side of the zip tape. Make sure you tack in a straight line as you will use this tacking as a guide when sewing with the machine.

11 Swap the zip foot to the other side again. Start at the lower end of the zip, on the seam line and sew across the bottom, then pivot the needle to turn the corner.

12 Sew up the other side of the zip, using the tacking as a guide.

13 Open the zip to move the zip pull out of the way and complete the stitching. Remove all the tacking.

Inset zip

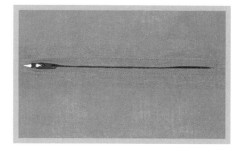

This type of zip insertion is useful for cushions and side-openings on dresses where the seam is sewn above and below the zip.

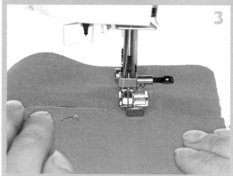

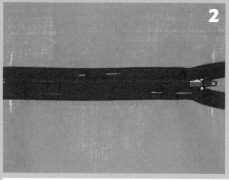

1 Sew the seams to the beginning and end of the zip placement. Machine tack the zip opening, snip the tacking threads and press the seam allowances open (Steps 1–3, Basic Centred Zip, page 85).

2 On the wrong side, mark where the tacking starts and stops. Place the zip face down, with teeth centred on the seam. machine-sew around the zip (Steps 4–8, Basic Centred Zip, page 85).

3 Sew across the short ends of the zip when sewing around it.

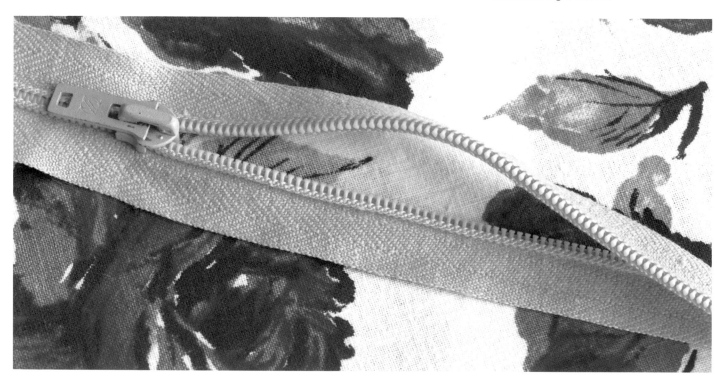

Invisible zip masterclass

Invisible zips aren't as hard as they look, but they do take some getting used to. They are a different type of zip – you won't get an invisible finish with an ordinary zip. An invisible zip might look the same as an ordinary zip at first glance, but look closely and you will see that the zip pull is on what appears to be the wrong side. The way the zip is made means you can sew right up to the zip teeth so that from the right side, it looks just like a seam. Ideally, you need a special invisible zip foot on your machine, but it is possible to use an ordinary zip foot or sew by hand if you are careful. Mark the seam line on the fabric, but do not sew up the seam or tack the zip section of it.

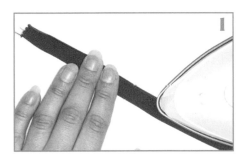

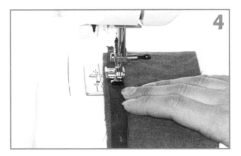

1 First, unzip the zip and use the tip of a warm iron to press the teeth flat (they will be sticking up almost vertically) to make it easier to sew.

2 Keeping the zip undone, place it on the right side of the fabric with the zip tape towards the raw edge and the teeth just over the seam line. Pin the zip in place then tack it if required.

3 Put the invisible zip foot on the machine and adjust the needle (page 15) to be as near to the zip teeth as possible. The needle should be right over to the edge of the needle hole in the foot. Turn the flywheel by hand to see if the needle hits close to, but not on the teeth. Sew the length of the zip and repeat for the other side, moving the needle to the other side of the foot.

4 If you are using an ordinary zip foot, make sure the zip teeth are folded flat out of the way, and that the needle is as far over as possible, and sew very close to the teeth. Sew the length of the zip and repeat for the other side, moving the zip foot to the other side and moving the needle as far across as it will go.

5 Alternatively, backstitch (page 28) the zip in place by hand, sewing very close to the teeth. Once the zip is sewn to the fabric, sew the seam below the zip.

Zipped pocket

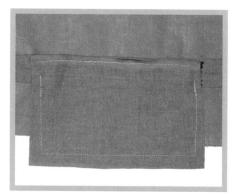

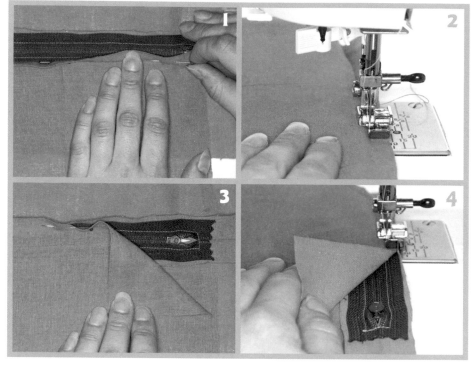

A zipped pocket in a bag or a garment is much simpler than it might first appear, as it is just a variation on the inset zip (page 88). You can also put in a pocket zip using the invisible or lapped zip techniques. The pieces that make the pocket are called the upper and lower pocket bags. Cut two pocket bag pieces the same length as the zip tape and as deep as required; the upper pocket bag needs to be 2.5cm deeper than the lower pocket bag.

To insert a zipped pocket into a bag lining, you will need to cut the lining pattern into two pieces and add seam allowances to both pieces; add 1.5cm for an inset or invisible zip and 2cm for a lapped zip.

1 Put in the zip as for an inset zip (page 88). On the wrong side, pin the lower (shorter) pocket bag to the lower seam allowance along the edge of the zip.

2 Fold the zip under the pocket bag piece and sew the pocket bag to the zip tape using a zip foot and using a 1cm seam allowance.

3 Pin the upper pocket bag to the top edge of the zip tape.

4 Fold the top part of the main fabric out of the way. Sew along the top of the pocket bag, sewing through the zip tape and upper pocket bag.

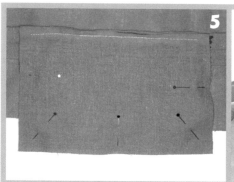

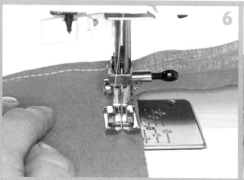

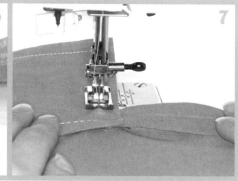

5 Fold the pocket bag pieces flat on top of one another and pin the sides of the upper and lower pocket bags together.

6 Starting at the lower edge of the zip tape, sew down the side of the pocket bag.

7 Pivot at the corners (page 49) and then sew back up the other side. Stop sewing just as you reach the zip tape. Finish the edges of the pocket bag if required.

Purse zip

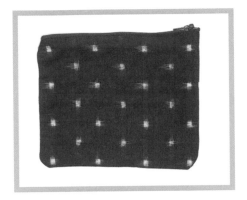

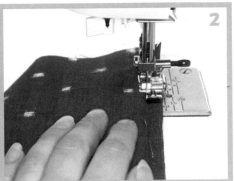

Putting a zip into a purse requires a completely different technique. Cut the two fabric purse pieces and shorten the zip if required (page 84).

1 With the zip face up, lay one fabric purse piece face down, matching the fabric raw edge to the top of the zip tape. Pin and tack if required.

2 Using a zip foot, sew the purse piece to the zip, close to the zip teeth. Sew the other purse piece to the zip tape on the other side of the zip, again with the zip closed.

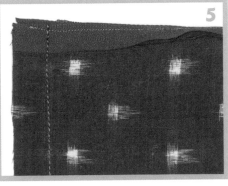

3 Open the zip halfway. Fold the zip ends in half, then sew across the end and around the purse.

4 Sew over the other end of the zip, with it again folded in half.

5 This shows the zip folded in half and sewn.

Sew different

This technique has been used to make the purse project (page 218). If you want the zip to be less visible in a purse, then stop after Step 2 and top stitch the fabric close to the zip, as in Steps 6–7 of the Lapped Zip (page 86). Then sew up the sides of the purse.

Machine buttonhole

Many machines will have a setting that sets the direction and width of stitching for making buttonholes. Check your manual for specific directions. If your machine doesn't have this function, then follow the instructions below. Mark the positions of the buttonholes on the fabric before you start. Buttonholes are worked on the front of the fabric.

In this sample we start at the left, near-side and work backwards, as this is how many machine auto buttonhole settings work. Before you start work on the project, always make a few test buttonholes using the same fabric in the same number of layers as the actual project. For lightweight fabrics, always interface (page 255) the buttonhole area before making the buttonholes.

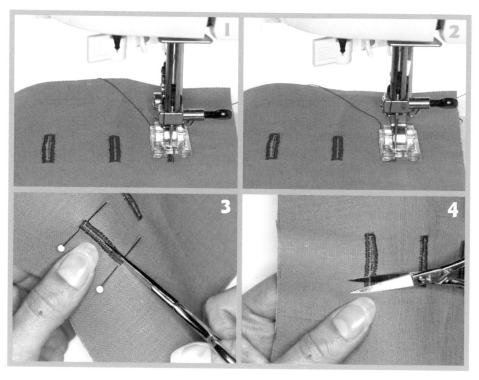

1 Set the machine to reverse stitching. Position the needle at the near end of the buttonhole markings, on the left-hand side. With the needle to the left, use a narrow zigzag and short stitch length to work backwards until you see the end markings appearing under the needle. This is auto setting 1 on most auto buttonhole settings. Change to a wide zigzag and very short stitch length (or satin stitch) and make 4 or 5 stitches to make the end bar. This is auto setting 2 on most machines.

2 Set the needle far over to the right, at the edge of the end bar and change back to narrow zigzag. Sewing forwards this time, sew down the other side of the buttonhole. This is auto setting 3 on most machines. Make the bar as before (auto setting 4). Fasten the threads by pulling the top thread through to the back (page 34).

3 To cut the buttonhole, put pins in the bars to stop you accidentally cutting through them. Stab a hole in the fabric near the middle of the buttonhole and snip carefully with a stitch unpicker or very small, sharp scissors, which give you more control.

4 Trim off any stray threads, and apply a fray stop glue (page 18) if required.

Sew simple

To work out the required size of buttonhole, add the diameter (across the middle) of the button to the thickness. This is the length for bound buttonholes. For sewn button-holes, add 3mm to the total.

Handmade buttonhole

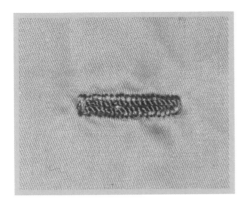

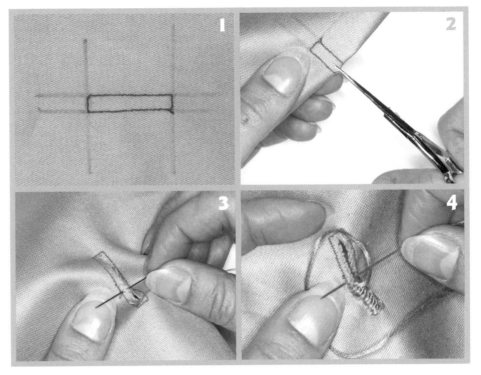

Handmade buttonholes can be time consuming but thay do look impressive. Practise several buttonholes before you start on the finished garment, making sure you practise with the same layers of fabric as there are in the garment. Interface the buttonhole area if the fabric is fine. Buttonholes are worked from the front of the fabric.

1 Mark the buttonhole position with lines about 6mm apart (this gives a buttonhole stitch length of about 3mm on each edge). Use a very short stitch length and starting in the middle of one of the long sides, machine-sew a box on the lines. Don't reverse to start and end the thread, pull the threads to the back and knot (page 34).

2 Fold the sewn box in half and cut down the centre of it.

3 Overcast the cut edges in a thread that matches the main fabric.

4 Work buttonhole stitch (page 32) to just cover the machine-stitched line.

Bound buttonhole masterclass

Bound buttonholes look very professional on a jacket or coat and are worth the extra effort involved. Be very careful when you mark and sew the buttonholes as it's hard to change anything once you have started. Check and double-check the markings and work slowly. Always do a couple of test buttonholes on the garment fabric before you start. When you are making several buttonholes, work each step on all of them before moving on to the next step. This helps keep the buttonholes consistent.

There are several different ways of making bound buttonholes; this is one of the more complicated, but it produces the most consistent results. I use a clear plastic foot for bound buttonholes so I can see what I am doing, as accuracy is vital.

The width of the buttonhole should be the diameter of the button plus its thickness. The height of the buttonhole should be 6mm unless it is a very heavy fabric, in which case make it slightly taller. The marked box should have a centre line, which will be the opening, then lines 3mm above and 3mm below this centre line.

The opening is patched with a piece of silk organza. If possible, use a colour that blends with the main fabric. Dye a small quantity to match the fabric, or colour it with fabric paints or pens, and make sure the colour is fixed. I have used white in this sample for clarity.

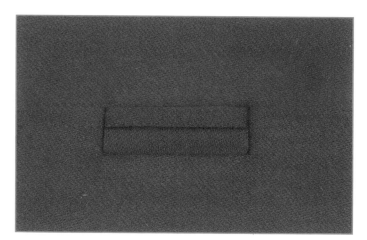

Buttonhole from the front, with the lips completely centred.

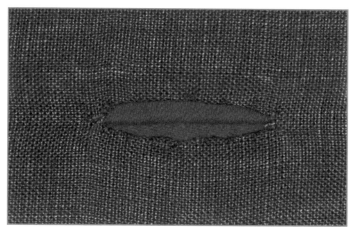

Buttonhole from the back showing facing / lining sewn in place.

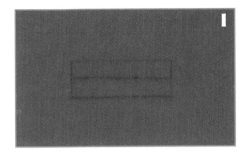

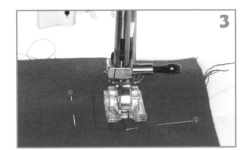

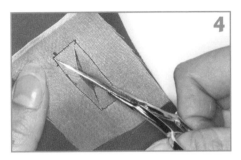

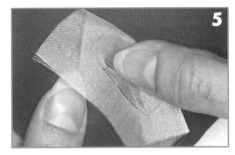

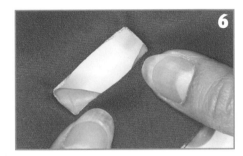

1 Draw the buttonhole box on the wrong side of the fabric, using a pencil if possible, or a fabric marking pen.

2 Cut a piece of organza 5cm wide and 2.5cm longer than the buttonhole. Pin this to the RIGHT SIDE of the fabric, centred over the buttonhole box. Push pins through the ends of the box markings to show the placement on the right side.

3 Working on the wrong side, using a very short stitch length and starting in the middle of one of the long sides, sew a box on the marked lines. Don't reverse to start and end the thread, instead pull the threads to the back and knot (page 34). Make sure you turn the corner in exactly the right place. Count the number of stitches you take on each short side and do the same number on the other short side.

4 Cut an X-shaped opening in the box, taking care not to cut right up to the stitches, but not into them.

5 Push the organza through the opening to the back.

6 Finger press (page 24) the edges so that no organza shows on the front. If the corners don't turn out properly, you may not have cut right to the stitching, or the stitching may be inaccurate.

7 Press the opening on the right side, using an organza pressing cloth (page 24).

Sew simple

A jacket or top with a single button would look very elegant with a bound buttonhole feature and an interesting vintage or hand-made button. Don't try to make these buttonholes on thin fabrics as the allowances on the back will show through.

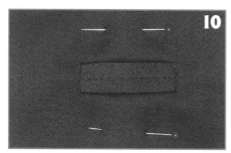

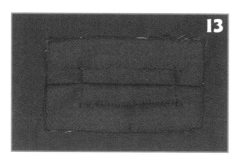

8 Cut the lips in matching fabric, on the straight grain. Cut two pieces each 4cm wide and 2.5cm longer than the buttonhole. Place the pieces right sides together and machine tack them together lengthways down the centre.

9 Fold the stitched lips open so that the right side of the fabric shows on both sides of the lips and the stitching is exposed down the centre seam. Press the lips flat under a pressing cloth.

10 Place the box over the lips and, from the front, pin the pieces together.

11 Fold back the main fabric on one side to reveal the cut triangle at the end of the box. Using small stitches, very carefully machine-sew across the triangle, sewing through the triangle, the organza and the ends of the lips. Only sew within the triangle, not over the edges. Don't reverse or knot the threads. Repeat with the other end.

12 Remove the pins. Fold back the main fabric on the bottom of the buttonhole and sew the longer triangle in the same way as in Step 11. Again, repeat for the top side of the buttonhole.

13 Trim stray threads from the edges of the lips and layer the seam allowances underneath if the fabric is bulky (page 38).

14 The facing or lining of the garment should be slit for the buttonhole. Turn under the cut edge and slip stitch (page 29) the facing or lining in place around the lips of the buttonhole.

15 Finally, once the whole garment is complete, carefully cut the tacking holding the lips together.

In-seam buttonhole

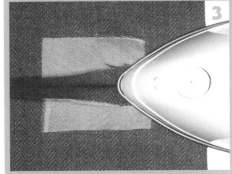

In-seam buttonholes are simply gaps in the seam, finished on the inside. They are a very effective way of adding visual interest to a garment, or they can be included in a bag as a design feature. The buttonholes are reinforced with patches of silk organza or any lightweight sew-in interfacing. The organza patches should be 2.5cm longer than the buttonhole and 3–5cm wide.

1 Mark the seam line on the wrong side of the fabric. Cut two patches of silk organza and mark the buttonhole length on both pieces. Pin the patches to the wrong side of the main fabric, matching the markings.

2 Sew the seam up to the marks on either side of the buttonhole.

3 Press the seam allowances open. Slip stitch (page 29) the edges of the seam allowances down if required.

Button loops

Single button loops can be made with narrow bias tubes (page 82) and sewn into seams. These loops work very well with buttons with a shank (pages 98–99). Make a sample tube and test the length required for the buttons you want to use.

1 Mark the seam line on the right side of the fabric. Fold the length of bias loop in half, making a neat fold at the end, or make the loop rounded. If you are using several loops together, mark on the fabric where the tips of the loops need to be to keep them consistent in length. Pin, then machine tack along the seam line.

2 With the fabric with the loops attached face up, place and pin the second piece of fabric face down on top of them, matching the raw edges. Sew with the tacked line uppermost, following the line of stitching.

Button with a thread shank

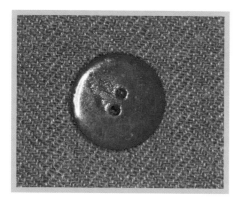

Buttons on jackets and coats, and anything made with thick fabric, should be sewn with a thread shank so that the button stands slightly proud from the fabric and doesn't pull when the button is done up. Only shirt buttons should be sewn flat to the fabric.

Sew different

You can make the shank even smarter by using buttonhole stitch in the same way as for a bar tack (page 32).

1 Start by fastening the thread on the wrong side by making two or three tiny stitches close together (page 27).

2 Come through the fabric and put the needle through a hole in the button. Place a thick tapestry needle or matchstick over the button and make the stitches over it.

3 After sewing three or four times through the buttonholes and fabric, bring the needle up between the fabric and button ready to make the shank.

4 Remove the tapestry needle or matchstick and push the button up to the ends of the stitches. Wrap the working thread around and around the threads attaching the button to the fabric.

5 Bring the needle through to the back, make one tiny securing stitch, then make a loop of thread and pass the needle through it to make a knot.

6 With the needle in the loop, slide the loop down to the fabric and pull it tight around the needle to make a knot. Cut the thread close to the knot.

Button with a shank

Buttons that have ready-made shanks are easy to sew on.

1 Fasten the thread on the wrong side by making two or three tiny stitches close together (page 27). Bring the needle through the fabric and pick up the button shank. Hold the button to one side then sew through the fabric and shank in one stitch.

2 Pass the needle through to the back, then fasten off as in Steps 5–6 of Button With A Thread Shank (opposite).

Buttons with decorative stitches

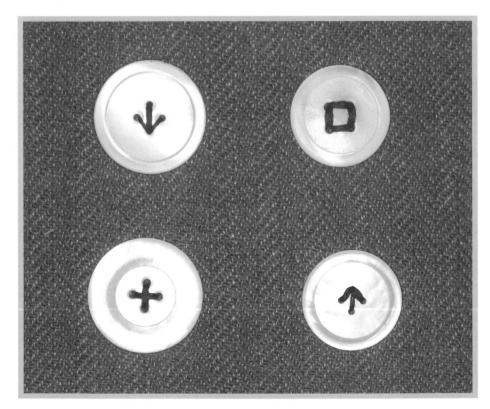

Four-hole buttons can be sewn on with decorative stitching patterns. Start and finish the thread as Step 1 and Steps 5–6 of Button With A Thread Shank (opposite).

Top left: Hold the button with the four holes on the diagonal. Make three vertical stitches first, then from the bottom to each side, take two stitches only.

Top right: Hold the button with the four holes square then take three or four stitches through each pair of holes, going clockwise around the sets of holes.

Bottom left: Hold the button with the four holes on the diagonal. Make three or four stitches vertically, then make the same number of stitches horizontally.

Bottom right: Hold the button with the four holes on the diagonal. Make two stitches vertically then three or four stitches from the top to each of the side holes in turn.

Button with a reinforcing button

A reinforcing button is an extra, plain button sewn on the inside of a garment at the same time as the main button. It adds strength and stops the button from pulling on the fabric if it is under strain. Reinforcing buttons are useful in coats and any garment where a single button is the only closure. They are also useful for delicate fabrics that might tear, but you should also use interfacing (page 255) on the back of the button area of fabric.

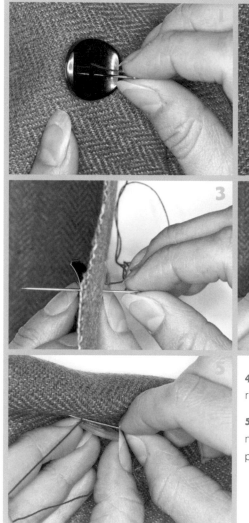

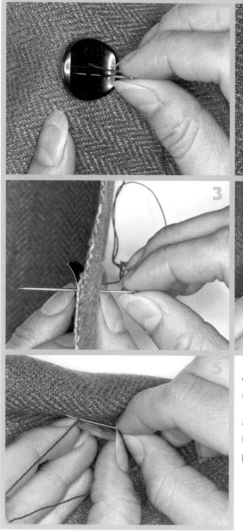

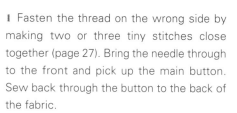

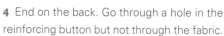

4 End on the back. Go through a hole in the reinforcing button but not through the fabric.

5 Make a couple of securing stitches then make a loop knot in the thread (Steps 5–6, page 98).

1 Fasten the thread on the wrong side by making two or three tiny stitches close together (page 27). Bring the needle through to the front and pick up the main button. Sew back through the button to the back of the fabric.

2 Thread the reinforcing button onto the needle and thread.

3 Sew through the reinforcing button, through the fabric and through the main button. Make three or four stitches in this way.

Sew simple

Sew buttons with a strong thread, either buttonhole twist if you can find it, or top stitch thread. Alternatively you could use a double thread (page 26). It is important to start and knot the thread securely.

Covered buttons

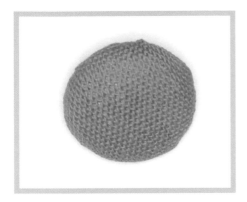

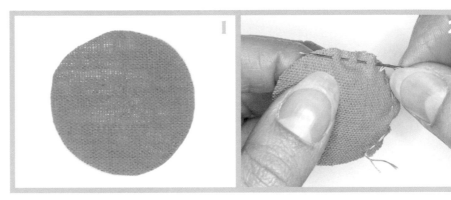

There are various sorts of covered button kits available. Experiment to find the one that works best for your needs. Each type of button kit will be slightly different, so follow the manufacturer's instructions for your kit.

1 Cut out a circle of fabric that is the recommended size; usually this is twice the diameter of the button.

2 Using doubled thread (page 26), knot the end firmly then sew small running stitches around the edge. If the fabric frays easily, don't sew too near the edge or the stitches will tear out. Leave the needle attached.

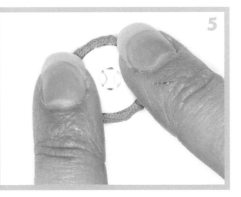

3 Start to pull up the thread and place the button face down in the fabric circle. Pull up on the threads to tighten the fabric around the button, making sure the button shank sticks out.

4 Use the tip of the needle to push down excess fabric around the shank.

5 Snap the button back on.

Sew simple

Always make the buttonholes in a garment first, then mark the placement for the buttons when the sewing is complete.

Fabric buttons

It is very easy to make your own fabric-covered buttons using cheap plastic or brass curtain rings. The one used in this sample are about 2.5cm in diameter, but you could use larger ones.

1 Cut a circle of fabric slightly smaller than twice the diameter of the ring. Gather the edge (Step 2, page 101). Insert the ring as you start to pull up the stitches.

2 Pull the stitches up tight and then make stitches across the gathered area to strengthen it. Trim stray threads if required and if necessary, use a little fray stop glue (page 18) to prevent the fabric fraying.

3 Sew around the inside of the ring using small running stitches, with the thread knotted on the back.

Using vintage and handmade buttons

Vintage and handmade buttons should be used as features in special garments, not as everyday buttons. Often they are delicate and shouldn't be machine-washed or dry-cleaned. Some, such as bone buttons, may not even be suitable for hand-washing and need to be removed each time you launder.

New handmade ceramic buttons can be remarkably tough, but check the washing instructions when you buy. Ceramic buttons can sometimes cut threads, so sew them on securely using a very strong thread, such as waxed upholstery thread (page 27).

Some vintage buttons have peculiar arrangements of holes, so experiment with how to sew them on most effectively. The yellow button (top picture, bottom left), would be best sewn with a contrasting thread stitched very neatly, or in a near-invisible matching thread. The large art-deco button (top picture, top right), should be sewn through the holes vertically, not horizontally as that would spoil the lines.

Other buttons may have strange fittings on the back, so use a thread shank (page 98) if required. Some buttons have a very long shank and are designed for thick fabric. Ball buttons should be sewn on like those with a shank. Fabric buttons without a shank or holes should be sewn on by catching the threads on the back of the button, not going all the way through. Covered buttons with metal shanks can sometimes cut the threads, so use strong thread, as before.

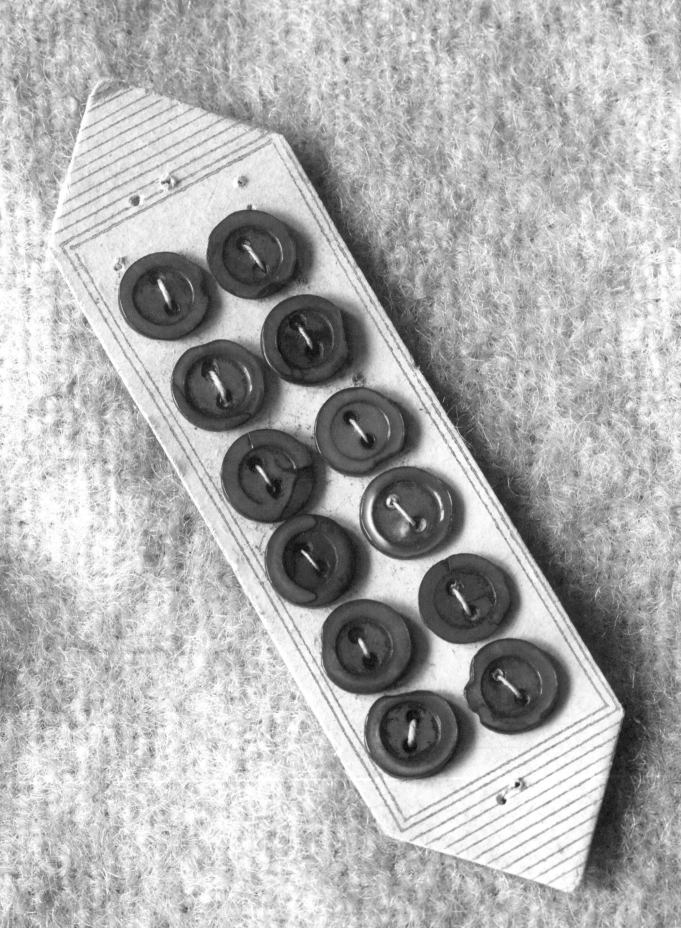

Poppers

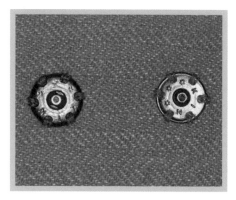

Poppers can be tiny, clear and almost invisible, or big chunky features. Either way, sew them on well in the first place.

1 Fasten the thread underneath where the popper will be placed, on the right side of the fabric. Sew three or four neat stitches through each hole in the popper. Fasten off with a couple of securing stitches then make a loop knot (Steps 5–6, page 98).

2 To position the second half, push a needle through the hole in the centre of the sewn-on popper. Thread the other half onto the needle and arrange the garment edges correctly. Use the needle to pinpoint the correct placement of the centre of the second half of the popper then sew that on.

Hooks and eyes

Hooks and eyes look much better if sewn on with blanket stitch (page 30). The extra holding stitches around the hook and eye help to stop them pulling.

Sew different

Instead of sewing on an eye or bar, you can use a bar tack (page 32).

Skirt hooks

Skirt hooks (and trouser hooks) are flat hooks and eyes that are more secure and less likely to snag. They can be sewn on with blanket stitch, or with three or four straight stitches through each hole.

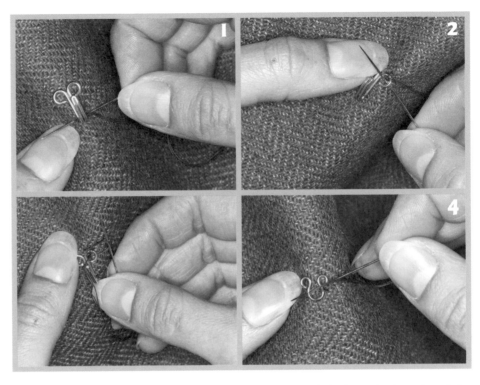

1 Fasten the thread on the underside then make two stitches over the bent end of the hook to hold it in place.

2 Sew the hook on using blanket stitch. Bring the needle under and up through the hole.

3 Pull the stitch through, then thread the needle through the thread loop.

4 Make two holding stitches on the eye, as in Step 1, then work blanket stitch around the holes in the same way as Steps 2–3.

The finished sample (left) shows the bar sewn on with stitches made between the two pairs of holes. This is neater, but maybe a little less secure than stitching over the edge, as above.

Stripy apron

This pretty yet practical design has a simple shape with bodice and waist darts for a flattering fit. Two different striped fabrics are used, both recycled from men's shirts. However, you could make the apron all in one fabric if you prefer.

You will need

Two men's long-sleeved striped shirts, in a large size to get the most fabric. Choose shirts that are in good condition and made from washable fabrics.

Scissors

Iron

Bodice and pocket patterns on page 294

Sewing machine

Sewing threads to match the shirts

70cm of 2.5-cm wide bias binding to match one shirt

Hand-sewing needle

Techniques

Pressing and steaming, page 23

Pattern markings, page 246

Double hems, page 52

Darts, page 48

Folded fabric tubes, page 83

Double-fold bias binding, page 73

Shaping bias binding, page 73

Sewing a seam, page 36

Top stitch, page 38

Zigzagging allowances together, page 37

Cutting list

Cut the shirts up by cutting along the side seams, removing the sleeves and cutting off the yoke (the shoulder and collar area, which is usually a double thickness). Slit open the sleeves along the seam. Iron all the fabric pieces.

Apron skirt: from the largest shirt back, cut a piece 50 x 50cm with the stripes running vertically. Leave the curved bottom hem of the shirt in place to become the bottom hem of the apron.

Apron bodice: fold the second shirt back in half, the stripes running vertically. Place the pattern on the fold (page 246) as shown on the pattern and cut out the bodice.

Pockets: using the pattern piece, cut two pockets from the second shirt, with the stripes running vertically. If the fabric has a right and a wrong side, make sure you flip over the pattern piece so you get a right and a left pocket. You should be able to cut both pieces from a single shirt sleeve. Turn to pages 244–245 for more about cutting pattern pieces.

Waistband: cut a 45 x 10cm strip from the remaining sleeve of the second shirt.

Ties and strap: cut strips from the sleeves or fronts of the first shirt and join them to make two 75 x 5cm strips for the waist ties and one 50 x 9cm strip for the neck strap.

1 Turn under and machine-sew a narrow double hem along each side edge of the apron skirt.

2 Fold the top (un-hemmed) edge of the skirt in half widthways to establish the centre point and mark this point with a pin. Measure out 7cm on either side of the pin and at that point make a dart that is 2cm wide and 10cm long.

3 For the waist ties, make flat tubes from the 75cm strips and sew across one end of each. Turn right side out and press both ties. Place the raw end of a tie on one short edge of the right side of the waistband piece.

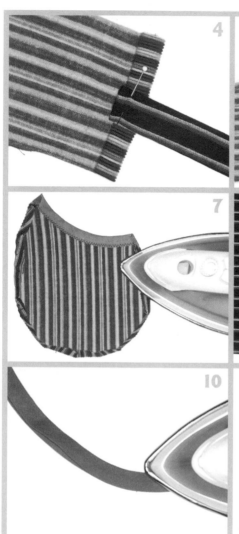

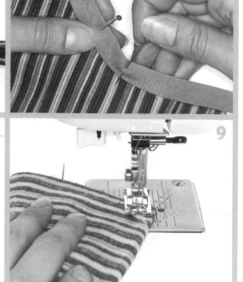
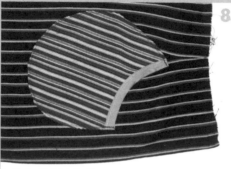

4 Fold both pieces over to the back by 1cm and then another 1cm, so the raw edges are enclosed in the fold.

5 Sew along the inner and outer folds, stitching over the tie. Repeat on the other end of the waistband with the other tie.

6 Cut 15cm of bias binding and shape it to fit the top curve of a pocket. Place the shaped binding over the curved edge, and pin in position. Sew through all layers slowly and carefully using a machine or by hand. Trim off any excess bias binding.

7 Fold the seam allowances under and press in place. Repeat Steps 6–7 for the other pocket, making sure you have a left and a right pocket!

8 Place the pockets on to the skirt piece covering the darts, as shown. The top point of the pocket should be about 5cm from the top of the skirt and the side should be about 4cm from the skirt edge. Top stitch the pockets in place around the sides, but not along the bound edge! Reinforce the corners with zigzag stitching.

9 Transfer the dart markings on the bodice pattern onto the fabric. Sew the darts and then hem the side edges of the bodice with a narrow double hem.

10 Cut 40cm of bias binding and press it to match the curve of the bodice neckline. Apply the binding to the top curve of the bodice in the same way as for the pockets (Step 6).

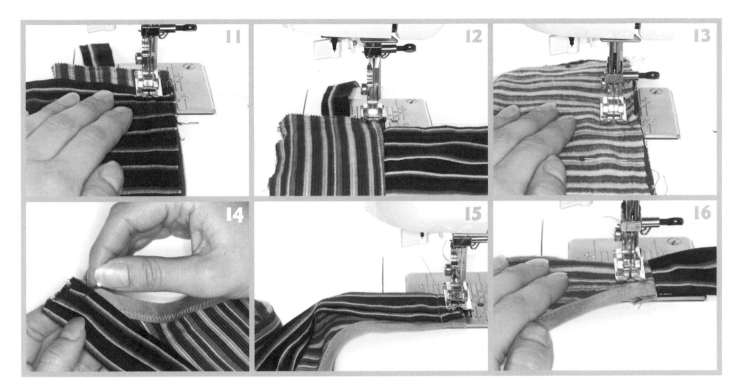

11 With the right-sides together, pin the skirt to the waistband, matching the centre points. Using a 1.5cm seam allowance, sew the pieces together. Zigzag the raw edges.

12 Press the seam allowances up to the back of the waistband, then top stitch along the whole length of the waistband.

13 Repeat Steps 11–12 to join the bodice to the waistband.

14 Make the neck strap in the same way as the waist ties (see Step 3), but don't sew across one short end. With the bodice face up, place one end of the neck strap on the raw edge at the shoulder.

15 Using a 1.5cm seam allowance, join the pieces. Zigzag the raw edges together.

16 Fold the seam allowance to the back and top stitch across the front of the shoulder, 1cm from the fold.

Sew different

There is no reason why aprons shouldn't be pretty as well as practical, as long as the fabrics are washable. A beautiful apron is great for parties when you need to serve food but still want to look fabulous! Make one to match your favourite party frock.

Book bag

I designed this bag to show off a special fabric. It leaves hardly any waste from half a metre so you can splash out on something lovely. For added style, this bag has boxed corners to make a flat base and has a stunning ribbon facing.

A medium-weight fabric works best. If you want to use a heavy-weight fabric, use a lighter one for the handles or they will be too thick to turn out. This isn't an ideal project for vintage fabrics as they would be too fragile to carry much weight. If you used a plain fabric you could decorate this style of bag with all sorts of trimmings and edgings.

You will need

50cm of fabric, at least 105cm wide
Sewing threads to match fabrics
Sewing machine
Scissors
Tape measure
Iron
Fabric marker
Pins
75cm of 3-cm wide ribbon
Hand-sewing needle

Cutting list

Two 37 x 46cm pieces of fabric
Four 46 x 6cm strips of fabric

Techniques

Folded fabric tubes, page 83
Sewing a seam, page 36
Turning a corner, page 49
Zigzagging allowances together, page 37
Pressing and steaming, page 23
Tacking stitch, page 27

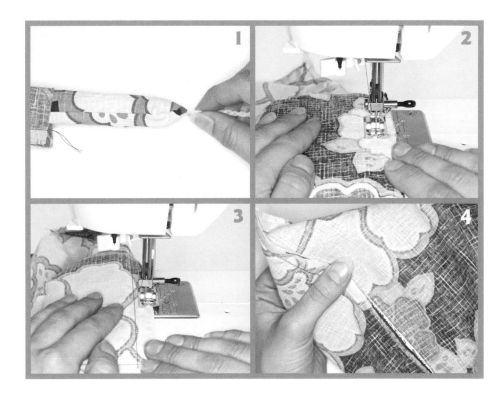

1 Join two pairs of 46 x 6cm strips at the short ends to make two strips, each one 90cm long. Make these into two flat tubes for the bag handles.

2 With the right sides together, sew the 37 x 46cm pieces together along one long side, across one short side (the bottom of the bag), and up the other long side, turning the corners neatly.

3 Zigzag the seam allowances together. Turn the bag the right way out and press the seams flat.

4 Turn the bag inside out. Put your hand inside and separate the front and back fabric to open up the corner and create a point. Make sure the seams match up and there are no creases, then press the corner flat.

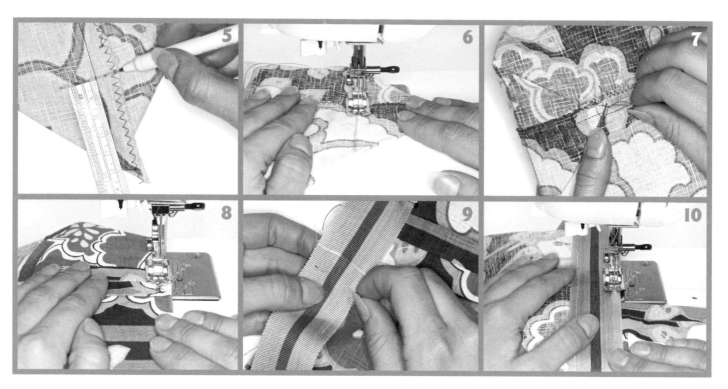

5 Measure 5cm from the point and mark a line across the folded corner. Make sure this line is at right angles to the seam or your corner will be wonky.

6 Sew across the corner. Repeat with the other corner. Turn the bag the right way out and press the new seams flat.

7 Sew the points of the box corners to the seam allowance along the bottom of the bag to stop them flapping about.

8 With the handle seam facing up, pin one end of a handle to the right side of the front of the bag, 8cm from a side seam and with the raw edge aligned with the top edge of the bag. Making sure the handle isn't twisted, pin the other end to the other side of the bag front, 8cm from the other side seam. Don't worry that the handle seems to be the wrong way up – it will work! Sew the handles on using zigzag stitch close to the raw edges. Go over the line of stitching two or three times. Repeat to attach the other handle to the back of the bag.

9 Fold under one end of the ribbon. Pin the ribbon to the right side of the bag, with the top edge just covering the raw edge of the bag. Tack the ribbon in place by hand, then remove the pins.

10 Turn the bag inside out and fold the ribbon to the inside; the handles will now lie the right way up. Adjust the position of the ribbon so that a little of the bag fabric shows above the ribbon all around. Making sure the bobbin thread matches the main fabric and the top thread matches the ribbon, sew around the top edge of the ribbon. Then sew around the bottom edge of the ribbon. Remove the tacking stitches. Turn the bag the right way out and press it again.

You will need

84 scraps of fabric to make 28 blossoms,
  each scrap at least 10cm square
Circle template about 10cm diameter
Vanishing fabric marker
Scissors
Pins
Embroidery thread
Large-eyed sharp needle
Hand-sewing needle
Sewing thread
20cm embroidery hoop
Narrow double-sided tape or fabric glue
1.2m of 2.5-cm wide ribbon
Fishing line

Falling blossom

This hanging decoration would look stunning in a window, casting shadows in the sun, or make a longer version to hang in a stairwell. It's also a great way to use up small scraps of fabrics. The decoration can be made up with as many sets of blossoms as you want; this one uses 28 sets, each made of three circles of fabric.

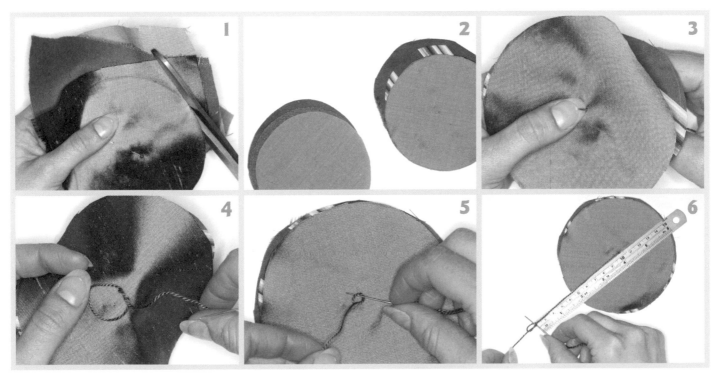

1 Cut as many circles as required. Each blossom needs about three circles, though you may want more if your fabrics are thin or less if they are thick. Cut about ten circles at the same time: cut rough circles or squares big enough for your circular template and pin them together in the middle. Place the template on the top fabric and draw around it with a vanishing marker. Cut around the circle through all layers.

2 Arrange the circles into sets of three and pin them together. The circles on the top will be the most visible, so make sure you vary the fabrics that are on top of each set.

3 Make each strand in the following way, varying the lengths as you wish. Cut a 1m length of embroidery thread and thread the needle. Make a big knot at the other end. The first set of circles you attach will be at the bottom of the strand. Push the needle through the centre of a set of circles from the underneath. Remove the pin.

4 Tie a loose knot right up against the top fabric circle.

5 Put the needle through the loop in the knot and hold it where you want the knot to sit. Pull on the free end of the thread to tighten the knot so it sits right on top of the fabric circles.

6 Measure 10cm along the thread and make another knot (you can space the blossoms out at different intervals). Make a loop at the 10cm point, put the needle through it and pull on the thread to tighten the knot. Thread on another set of circles, knot and repeat to complete the strand. Leave the remaining thread free at the top to attach the strand to the hoop. Make up the rest of the strands, laying them flat on a table to avoid tangling.

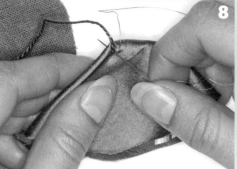

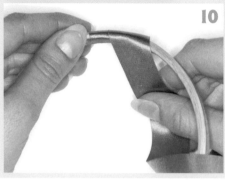

7 Thread the hand-sewing needle and knot the thread. From underneath, bring the needle and thread through the circles next to the knot. Fold each set of circles into quarters.

8 Make a couple of tiny stitches through the fabrics to hold the folded circles together and fasten off the thread.

9 Remove the inner ring of the embroidery hoop. Stick a length of tape or a thin line of fabric glue around the inside of the ring.

10 Starting on the sticky inside, wrap the ribbon around the hoop, making sure you don't leave any gaps. Make sure you finish on the inside of the hoop and stick the end of the ribbon down with a tiny spot of glue. Leave until completely dry.

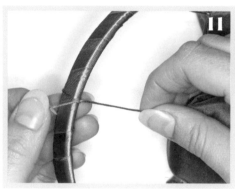

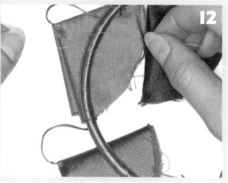

11 Tie the strands of blossom onto the hoop as desired, making sure that it will be fairly well-balanced.

12 Cut two lengths of fishing line, each about 40cm long, and tie them across the top of the hoop to form a cross. Hang the garland from the crossed fishing line.

Sew simple

This garland has one string each of seven, six, five and four blossoms and two strings of three blossoms. You could make the strings any length you want and change the distance between each blossom. You could also use different-sized circles in layers.

Pocket handbag

Handbags never have enough pockets for me, so this one has decorative outside pockets and internal pockets you can tweak to suit your needs. The bag is made from wool tweed and is perfect for winter.

You will need

Pattern pieces on page 295
Scissors
1m of medium-weight wool tweed
30cm of medium-weight iron-on interfacing
Pins
Iron
50cm of lining fabric
30 x 13cm of lining fabric with one long edge on the selvedge (for the internal pocket)
Sewing machine
Sewing threads
Hand-sewing needle
30cm zip

Techniques

Pattern markings, page 246
Iron-on interfacing, page 255
Sewing a seam, page 36
Turning a corner, page 49
Trimming seam allowances, page 38
Pressing and steaming, page 23
Darts, page 48
Tacking, page 27
Bias strip, page 68
Bias tubes, page 82
Lapped zip, page 86
Purse zip, page 91
Single hem, page 52
Slip stitch, page 29

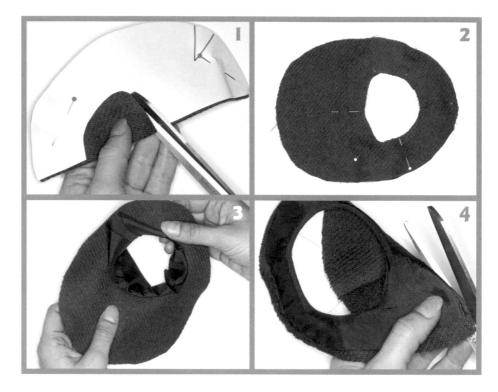

1 Using the pattern, cut out two main bag pieces on the straight grain of the fabric. Cut two pieces of interfacing and iron them onto the reverse of the fabric bag pieces. Cut two main bag pieces from the large piece of lining. Cut two outer pocket pieces from main fabric and two pocket pieces from the large piece of lining, placing the pattern piece on the fold of the fabric.

2 Pin the pocket lining and pocket fabric right sides together, pinning in a star shape around the hole.

3 Sew around the hole, using a 5mm seam allowance. With most machine feet, line up the edge of the foot with the raw edges of the fabrics to get this seam allowance. Sew slowly, pivoting the needle slightly when you need to make a turn. Trim the seam allowance by about half. Turn the lining through the hole and first finger press then press the lining flat with an iron. You will need to use steam and patience to make the turning neat.

4 Make the darts marked on the pattern through both layers. Trim away part of the dart to reduce the bulk; don't trim too close to the stitching.

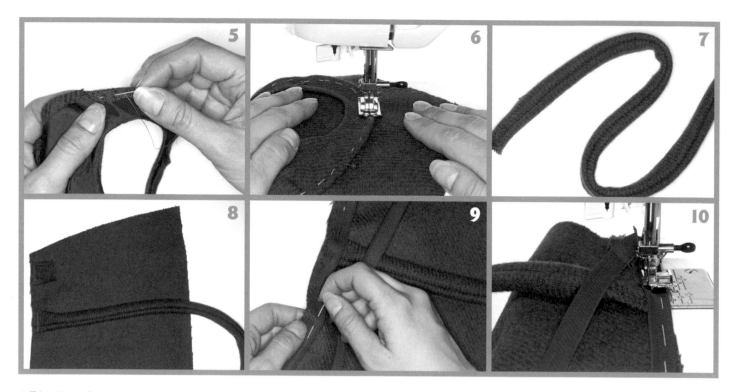

5 Trim 5mm from the seam allowance on the lining only. Turn under the main fabric seam allowance, tacking as you go, and press the edge.

6 Place the pocket on the front bag piece, using the pattern as a guide. Pin in place and sew all around the pocket, very close to the folded under edge. Repeat Steps 2–6 with the other pocket.

7 Cut two pieces of bias strip from the main fabric, each 62cm long by 7cm wide. Make these into two bias tubes for the handles.

8 Cut 2.5cm from each of the handle tubes to use as tabs. Tack one handle onto the bag front and one onto the bag back using the pattern markings as a guide and positioning the handles as shown. Tack the tabs at either end of the bag front 1cm in from the end, with raw edges matching, so the tabs hang down like the handles, as shown. Using a zigzag stitch, sew backwards and forwards near the raw edge to firmly attach the handles and tabs.

9 Open out the zip and, placing it face down, centre one end on the left tab and pin then tack it all along the length of the opening. The other end of the zip should be centred on the other tab.

10 Sew the zip in place along this side following Steps 3–5 of Lapped Zip (page 86), Use a zip foot and take it very carefully.

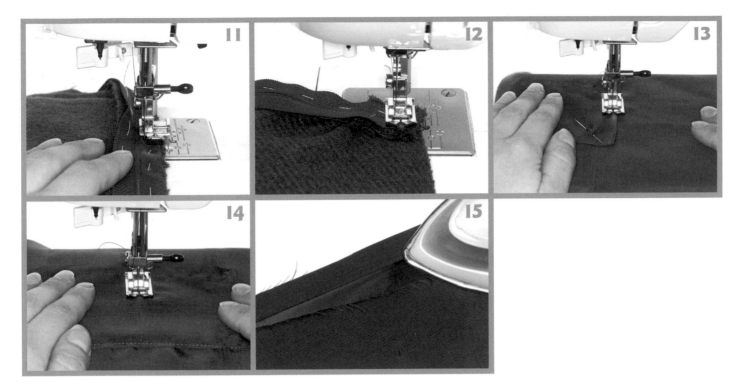

11 Repeat this with the other side of the bag, again matching the tab (attached to the main piece of bag) 1cm from the edge, as before. Place the other side of the zip centred on the tab and sew together as before. Open the zip halfway.

12 Pin all around the sides and bottom edge of the bag and start sewing at the zip end of the side seam. Hold the zip flat and sew right through it and the tab. Sew around the bag and then through the zip and tab at the other end, making sure you flatten the zip in the same direction. Make sure the zip is open part way before you sew the bag up. Turn the whole thing the right way out and press around the zip area and the other seams if you wish.

13 Fold under the selvedge edge of the internal pocket piece of lining fabric and machine a single hem. Fold under the remaining seam allowances and press. Right side up, sew the pocket onto one piece of the bag lining, placing it in the centre. Start sewing at the top edge of the pocket, 1cm down from the top. Set the machine to reverse and on zigzag stitch. Sew backwards to the top of the pocket piece then forwards again to where you started. Then change to straight stitch and sew all around, pivoting at the corners. Do the same two rows of zigzag stitch at the other top edge of the pocket.

14 Sew the pocket divisions at 8cm, 10cm and 4cm intervals in the same way. You can alter these divisions according to your technology or handbag contents.

15 Iron the lining to get any wrinkles out, then place the two lining pieces right sides together and pin. Sew down the sides and along the bottom, starting and ending the side seams 1.5cm down from the top. Turn the top seam allowances under and press.

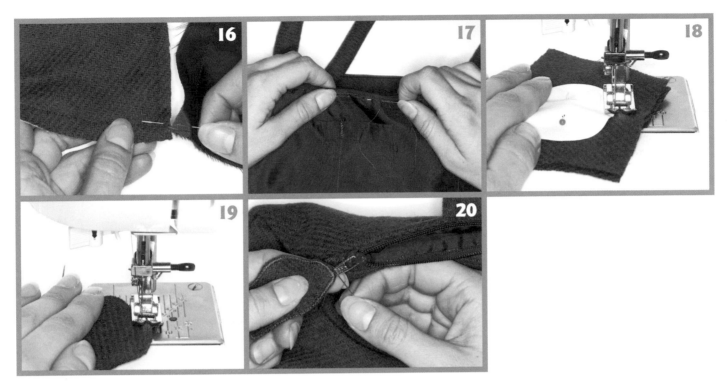

16 Turn the main bag inside out. Make two or three large stitches to join the bottom corners of the bag and lining together.

17 Turn the lining right side out, over the main bag. Match the side seams together and pin the folded top edge to the zip. You may need to try this a few times and fiddle it to get it to fit perfectly. Slip stitch the lining to the zip, making sure your stitches are firm and the knots secure as this seam will take some strain.

18 Make the zip pull. Cut two squares of wool a few centimetres bigger than the template. Pin the template to the fabric and sew all around through both layers of fabric.

19 Remove the template then use a small zigzag stitch to go back over your stitched line. Cut it out close to the stitching, then zigzag over the raw edge a third time.

20 Sew the tag onto the zip by holding the edge of the tag over the hole in the zip puller and sewing through and around it.

Mr Mouse

Felted stripy jumpers make great toys, for both children and adults. This little mouse puppet can be made to fit any size hand, just enlarge the templates appropriately.

You will need

Templates on page 296
Scissors
Pins
One felted wool jumper, preferably striped
Hand-sewing needle
Sewing thread to match jumper
Embroidery needle
Embroidery threads
Hessian or hemp yarn for whiskers
Beeswax

Techniques

Felting, page 179
Whipstitch, page 29

 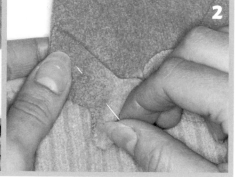

1 Cut out the templates. Pin the body template to the jumper with the straight edge of the template against the bottom of the jumper ribbing. Cut out one body, then re-pin the template, again with the straight edge against the ribbing, and cut another body. Cut out the other templated pieces, cutting two heads, two paws and two ears. Cut a narrow strip of felt for the tail.

2 Pin the paws to the right side of the front body piece, with the hands facing inwards and the ends aligned with the side edges, about 2cm down from the top edge.

 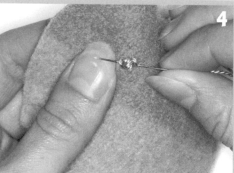 

3 Right sides together, place the back body piece on top of the front piece. Whipstitch along both sides, making sure you catch the paws in the stitching.

4 Embroider the face using the main photograph as a guide.

5 Make the whiskers. Run the hessian through the beeswax to stiffen it. Knot one end and thread the other into the embroidery needle. Stitch through from the back and trim the whisker to length. Make four whiskers. Using sewing thread, sew over the whisker knots on the back so they don't fall out.

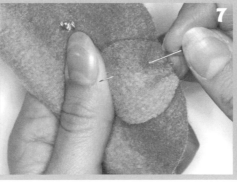

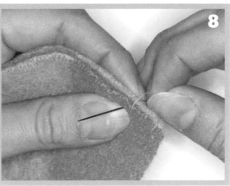

6 Shape the ears by pinching a small pleat in the straight edge. Tack the pleats in place.

7 Pin the ears to the face, with the pleated edge aligned with the side of the face, and tack in place.

8 Place the back head piece on top of the face, right sides together. Whipstitch the pieces together around the sides, leaving the bottom edge open.

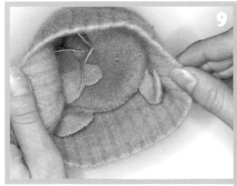

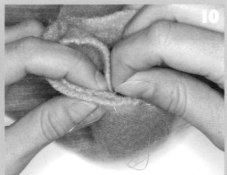

9 Turn the head right side out, but leave the body section inside out. Right sides together, place the head inside the body so that the raw edges line up.

10 Match the side seams of the head and body, then whipstitch all around the edge. Turn the mouse right side out.

11 Sew on the tail at the side seam or at the back of the body.

Decorative Techniques

Frills and ruffles

Ruffles are one of my design trademarks. I love using them on cushions, bags and scarves and to cover clothes with excessive frills. The basic techniques are really very simple, so experiment and enjoy!

Edge finishes

Frills and ruffles are made of strips of fabric, in whatever width you like. The strips can be cut on the straight grain, which will need finishing in some way, or on the bias, which won't. Experiment with different edge finishes as they will affect how the fabric folds and ruffles.

The simplest edge finish is to cut the strips with pinking shears (page 36).

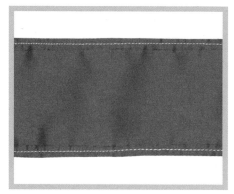

The edges can be finished with a narrow double hem (page 52). This gives a very crisp edge that won't gather up as much as the other finishes.

Sew different

There are other ways of finishing the edges of ruffles. You could try using a scallop-edge rotary cutter (see page 280) to get a wavy raw edge or try tearing the fabric (page 21) into strips and using the raw, fraying edges as a feature. Zigzag the edges in a thicker, contrast colour thread for a decorative edge.

You can finish the raw edges with zigzag stitch or machine overcasting (page 37).

Strips cut on the bias (page 68) won't fray and will ruffle and gather beautifully.

Hand-sewn ruffle

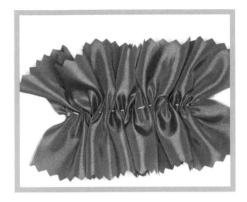

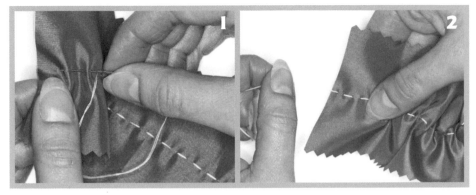

This simple ruffle is gathered along the middle and this technique is ideal if you have a long strip to ruffle up. For extremely long ruffles, start in the middle and sew in two directions (page 27).

1 Knot the end of the thread firmly. Work running stitch down the centre of the strip. Experiment with the size of the stitches to get the look you want. Small stitches work well on fine fabrics and will produce tight gathers. Thicker fabrics need larger stitches.

2 Leave the needle in and pull up the thread. Arrange the ruffles as loosely or tightly as you want. Use the threaded needle to fasten off the thread by making three tiny stitches close together (page 27).

Machine-sewn ruffle

This method works well with short to medium lengths of ruffle and produces very tight gathers. The gathers are made with large machine stitches that are pulled up. It is not suitable for thick fabrics as the threads can break.

1 Set the machine to the longest stitch length. Reverse to fix the thread and sew to the end. Leave long tails of thread.

2 Pull the bobbin thread to the front (page 34).

3 Gently pull up the bobbin thread, easing the gathers down the strip as you go.

4 Tie the two threads firmly together to fasten off.

Single-edge ruffle

This can be hand- or machine-sewn. It produces a curved ruffle that can be sewn down straight if required.

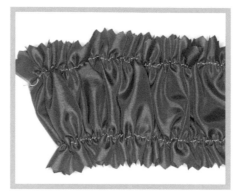

I Machine-sew (page 131) a line of stitches about 5mm from one edge of the strip. Gather up in the usual way.

Double-edge ruffle

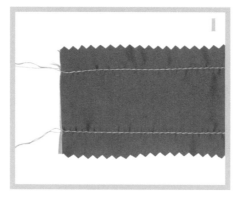

This is best made with strips cut on the straight grain, not cut on the bias. It works well with soft fabrics.

I Machine-sew (page 131) rows of stitching 5–10mm from both edges. Pull up both sets of stitching from the same end. You can adjust the amount of gathering on each side differently, so you get a curved ruffle.

Layered ruffle

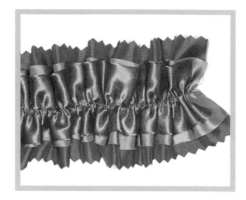

For a very decorative effect, try layering several fine fabrics together, ideally bias cut or pinked strips. Thicker fabrics will gather better with hand sewing.

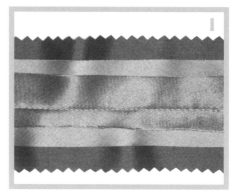

I Pin all the layers together then hand- or machine-sew down the middle and gather up (page 131).

Narrow knife pleat

Pleating the fabric strip as it goes into the machine is a very quick way of producing irregular but very effective ruffling. It works with thick fabrics as well as fine ones. I have used this technique in the Pleated Corsage project (page 204).

1 Set the machine to a medium to large stitch length. Start sewing, then pause and use a ruler or flat edge to push a tiny pleat of fabric under the foot.

2 Make another couple of stitches over the pleat then pause and push another pleat under. Go slowly and gently and you will be able to make a series of tiny pleats. If you miss a few pleats, then run the piece through the machine again and catch the gaps.

Pleats, folds and tucks

The possible variations among pleats, folds and tucks are almost endless. Fabrics will hold creases and pleats to different degrees; linen and cotton are the best for sharp pleats.

Hand pleats by machine

The simplest way to make a pleated trim for curtains or as an embellishment for a skirt is to hand-pleat straight into the sewing machine. The pleats are somewhat irregular, which is part of the charm, though with practice your pleats will become more even.

1 Start sewing along the edge of a piece of fabric as normal. Pause in the sewing with the needle down and take a pinch of fabric ahead of the presser foot.

2 Hold the pleat flat and continue to sew, slowly, over the pleat.

This late 19th-century Chinese skirt has panels of pleats running from the hips, which make it swing when worn. Groups of knife pleats radiate out, facing left and right from a central box pleat. Each pleat is edged with contrasting fabric to create flashes of colour with movement.

Knife pleats

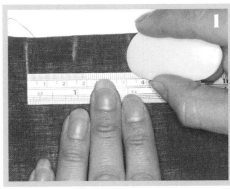

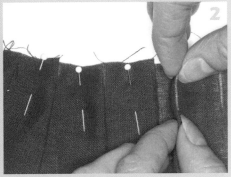

Knife pleats have sharp, straight folds and are much more regular than hand pleats.

1 Along the top edge of the fabric, mark the pleating points, in this sample, 2.5cm apart.

2 A pleat is made over three marks. Pinch the fabric on the first mark.

3 Lift up the pinched pleat and put a ruler against the second mark.

4 Fold the pleat over the ruler to meet the third mark.

5 Pin the pleat vertically. Continue making all the pleats in this way.

6 Sew across the top edge of the pleats to secure them, taking out each pin just in front of the presser foot.

Sew different

Sew lengths of ribbon onto the fabric, positioned to appear along the edges of the pleats to get an effect similar to the Chinese skirt, opposite.

Sewn-down knife pleat

This is a variation on the knife pleats (page 135), and is the way traditional pleated skirts are made.

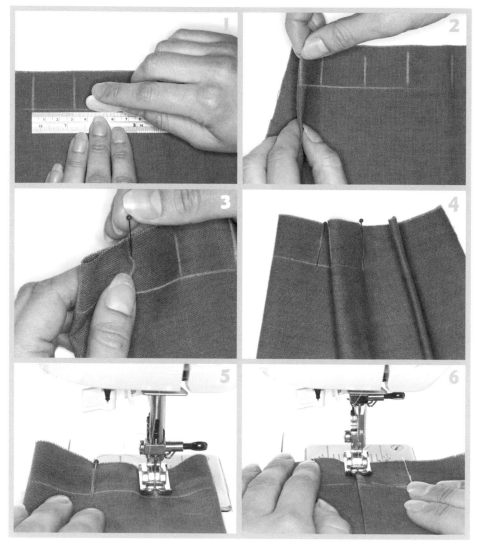

1 Mark the top edge of the fabric with a vertical line every 3cm. Mark a horizontal line 3cm down from the edge joining them all.

2 Fold the fabric at the second mark.

3 Pin the pleat, putting the pin through the first and third marks. Leave a space of one mark then repeat the pleat and pin.

4 Continue until all the pleats are pinned.

5 Using a medium stitch, sew along the pinned marks from the top edge as far as the horizontal line.

6 Press the pleats flat then top stitch (page 38) along the folds as far as the horizontal line to hold the pleats flat.

Box pleat

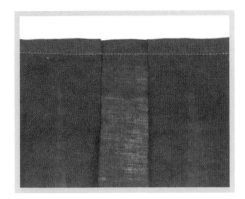

Box pleats are deep, flattened pleats of the type found on the back of some jackets. When making just one or two spaced pleats, use this method. When making several box pleats in a row, use the measuring technique from the Decorative Box Pleating Masterclass (page 140).

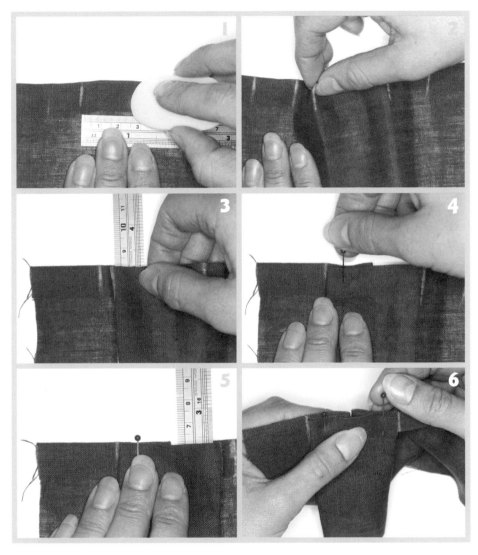

1 On the top edge of the fabric make six marks the following distances apart: mark one, then 2.5cm to mark two, then 2.5cm to mark three, then 5cm to mark four, then 2.5cm to mark five, then 2.5cm to mark six.

2 Counting from the left, pinch mark three.

3 Place a ruler to the left of mark two, and fold the pleat over the ruler, so that mark three meets mark one.

4 Pin the pleat vertically.

5 Then make the other side of the box pleat by pinching mark four, folding it over the ruler on mark five to meet mark six.

6 Pin the pleat vertically. Sew along the top edge to hold the pleat in place, or attach it to your garment or project as required.

Inverted box pleat

Inverted box pleats are exactly the same as box pleats but are worked the other way up.

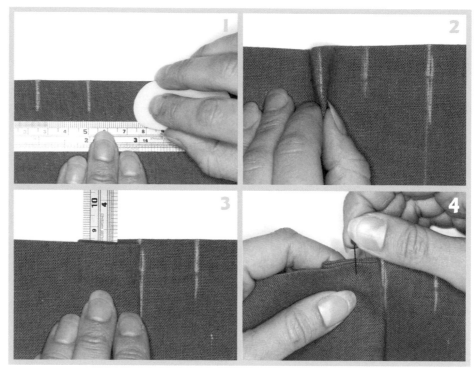

1 Make five marks, all 2.5cm apart. Make mark three, the centre mark, longer.

2 Counting from the left, pinch the fabric at mark one.

3 Place a ruler to the right of mark two and fold the pleat over the ruler so that mark one meets mark three.

4 Pin the pleat vertically.

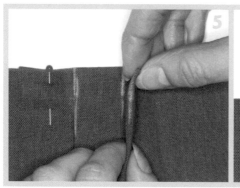

5 Pinch the fabric at mark five.

6 Place a ruler to the left of mark four and fold the pleat over the ruler so that mark five meets mark three.

7 Pin the pleat vertically. Sew across the top to hold the pleat in place.

Double inverted box pleat

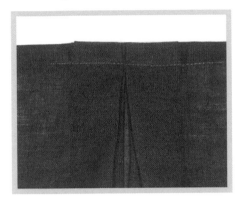

This is another variation on the box pleat and is wonderfully decorative on a skirt or the back of a jacket.

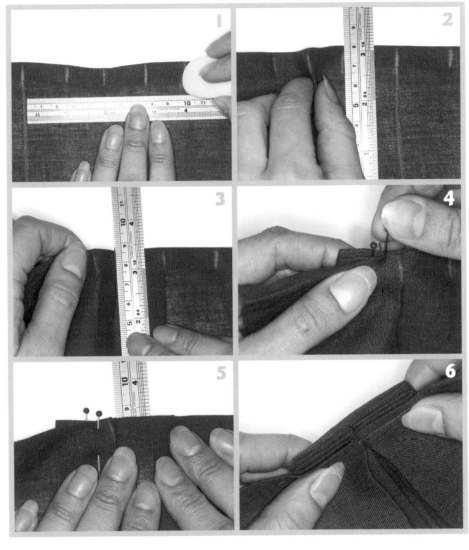

1 Make nine marks, all 2.5cm apart. Make mark five, the centre mark, longer.

2 Counting from the left, place a ruler to the right of mark four, pinch mark three and fold it to mark five. Pin the pleat vertically.

3 Place a ruler to the right of mark two, pinch mark one and fold it to mark five.

4 Pin vertically through all the layers.

5 Repeat the process on the other side.

6 Sew across the top to hold the pleat in place. This creates a double layer of folds and pleats.

Decorative box pleating masterclass

This decorative box pleated trim has formed the basis of some of my most popular designs and is based on 18th-century dress trimmings. I always enjoy experimenting with the possible variations and have included a number of them on the following pages.

The pleating takes up two-thirds of the length of the finished trim, so for 30cm of trim, cut 100cm of ribbon. This leaves a few centimetres at each end of the trim. The pleats you will make need to be the same width as the ribbon or fabric used, so each half-pleat is half the width of the ribbon. This sample is based on a 5-cm wide ribbon, so the half-pleats will be 2.5cm deep.

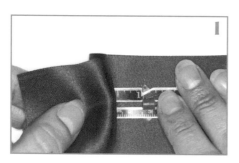

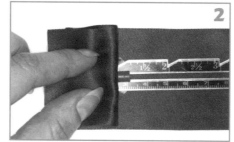

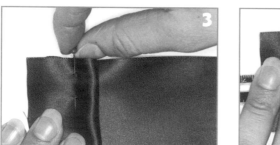

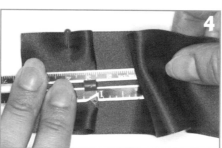

Sew simple

You will need a sewing gauge (page 281) or ruler. A standard ruler can be used instead of a gauge, but be aware that the measurements often start a little way along the ruler so you will need to measure to about 2cm rather than 2.5cm. Mark the correct point on your ruler with masking tape, or make a guide from a piece of cardboard with tape markings.

1 Start with the ribbon or fabric the wrong side up. Set the sewing gauge marker to half the width of your ribbon. Measure in from the end three times the width of the ribbon (in this sample, 7.5cm) and place the very end of the gauge on this point.

2 Keeping the sewing gauge in place, fold the ribbon back over the gauge so the fold meets the 2.5cm mark.

3 Holding the pleat in place, remove the sewing gauge and pin the pleat vertically. You have made your first half-pleat.

4 Place the gauge the other way up, with the 2.5cm marker on the fold.

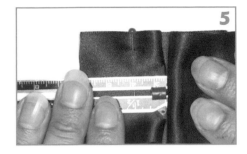

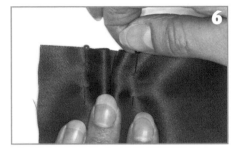

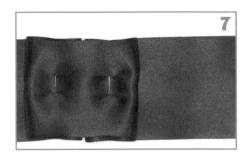

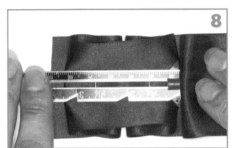

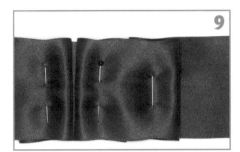

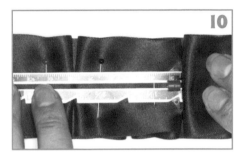

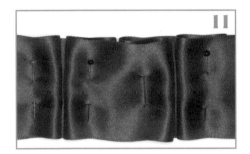

5 Fold the ribbon back over the gauge as in Step 2.

6 Pin the second pleat.

7 Turn the whole piece over.

8 Place the seam guide with the 2.5cm mark on the fold to the right, fold the ribbon over and pin, as before. Make sure the folds are touching.

9 Turn the whole piece over again.

10 Measure, fold and pin, as before.

11 Turn over and continue until the full length of the ribbon is pleated. Go back and straighten up any pleats that don't line up neatly with the one next to them. Slippery ribbons may need two pins in each pleat to stop them shifting about.

12 Sew the pleats in place. Using a sewing machine or hand sewing, sew along the centre of the pleated ribbon, keeping the line of stitching as straight as possible. Remove the pins as you go.

When all the pins are removed, you can press the whole trim if desired. You may prefer to leave the pleats unpressed for a softer effect. On the following pages, the soft box pleat is unpressed while the other samples are pressed.

The pleated ribbon sewn and unpressed.

The pleated ribbon sewn and pressed.

Soft box pleat

In this unpressed variation of standard box pleating, the tops of each pleat are hand-sewn together.

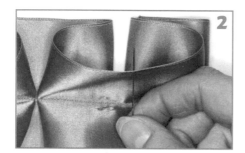

I Pick up the centre of one half of the pleat, and make a securing stitch through the edge of the ribbon.

2 Sew into the other pleat from the inside, as shown.

3 With the two edges held together, make two or three small stitches through all layers.

Point to point

This version is made with pressed pleats. Alternate which corners are folded in to get different patterns.

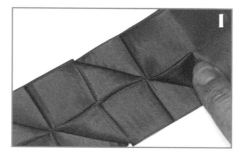

I Fold one corner of a pleat to the centre.

2 Press the fold.

3 Fold the opposite corner to the centre and press the fold.

4 From the back, put the needle through the middle and then through one corner.

5 Pick up the other corner and sew them together or sew them down into the centre of the pleat.

Squares

In this sample, all four corners are folded in and pressed. On the left of the strip they are sewn down; on the right they are pressed but not sewn.

Envelopes

In this sample, only three corners of each pleat are folded in. On the left of the strip they are pressed but not sewn; on the right, each of the three points has been sewn down.

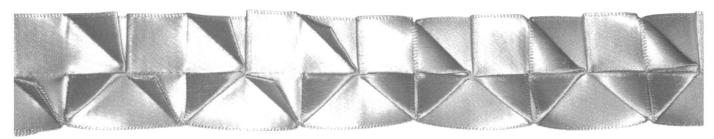

Diamonds

The pleats in this sample are folded in a different way to create diamond shapes in the ribbon.

1 From the bottom, lift up the centre edge of the pleat. Hold the underside of the pleat in place. Make sure the pleat is neat and the folds underneath match up.

2 Press the folded-up section of the pleat in place.

Saw-tooth diamonds

This is a variation on Diamonds (page 143) in which the diamonds create a zigzag along one edge of the pleated ribbon.

1 From the top, lift the centre edge of the pleat. Let the underside folds of the pleat come up.

2 Pull the top edge of the pleat over to the bottom edge, so that the underside folds form triangles.

3 Flatten then press the pleats.

Arrows

In this variation of folded box pleats the triangles created by folding the pleats are all facing in the same direction.

1 Hold the top right corner fold of one pleat.

2 Pull the corner over to meet the bottom right corner, allowing the underside folds of the pleat to make a triangle.

3 Fold the other half of the pleat so that it also forms a triangle.

4 Flatten the pleat so both triangles are equal. Press the triangles. On the next pleat, fold from the bottom to the top, so you get gaps on alternate sides of the ribbon.

Top stitched box pleat

This is a variation on the inverted box pleat (page 138), but it is made in a different way. The top part of the pleat is sewn down. As long as the stitching is neat, either side can be the right side.

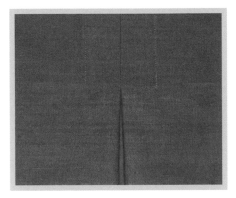
The pleat from one side.

The same pleat from the other side.

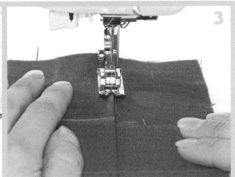

1 Fold the fabric in half and mark 6cm from the fold. At the marked point, sew a vertical line 6cm long.

2 Unfold the fabric and with the pleat uppermost, open out the pleat and press it.

3 From the top, sew a 6cm line along the fold. Repeat on the other side of the pleat.

Sew simple

This technique is commonly used on skirts, and is sometimes called a kick pleat. The same pleat could be used all around a skirt to create a formal ruffled effect at the knees, which would be very effective if the top stitching was in a contrast thread. You could also fill in the inside of the pleat with contrast fabric that would show when you walk. Use fusible webbing (page 188) to attach a small piece of contrast fabric before you sew up the pleat.

Pin tucks

These narrow tucks are somewhat wider than pins, but you can make them as small or as big as you want. Always make sure that you allow space between each tuck. In this sample the space is twice as wide as the tuck, though you could make them closer together.

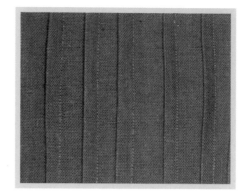

Press the tucks all to one side then the other to make them stand up.

This is the same size of pin tuck, but the tucks are spaced further apart.

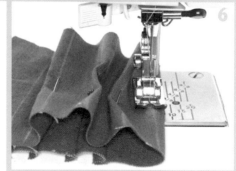

1 Mark pairs of lines 1cm apart all the way down the fabric, with a gap of 2cm between each pair.

2 To make the tuck, fold the fabric in the middle of a 1cm pair of lines; this will create a 5mm tuck. To match up the lines, insert a pin through one of the lines and out through the other.

3 Pin the tuck along the marked lines.

4 Pin through all the pairs of lines in the same way.

5 Sew along the marked lines, folding the excess fabric back out of the way.

6 Work from the right-hand end of the fabric, so the finished tucks are underneath as you are sewing the next pinned one.

Tuck and fold

This technique uses pin tucks to create pressed and sewn waves. Make a panel of pin tucks, each 2cm wide and 1.5cm apart. Press the tucks all to one side then press them to the other side to make them stand vertically.

1 Press the tucks along one edge of the pleated panel in one direction. Press the edge only, not the whole piece.

2 Sew across the edge, in the direction of the flattened tucks.

3 Press the tucks along the other edge in the other direction. Sew as before.

Trimmings

I find it all too easy to run riot in a shop full of ribbons and trims and buy lots of stuff just because I can't go home without it. I've also got a vast collection of vintage lace, beads, buttons, yarn and other such pretty things. I hope this section will inspire you to use some of your stash!

Attaching trimmings by machine

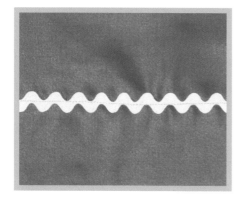

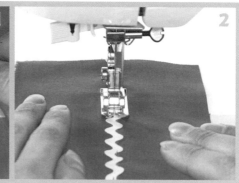

Ribbons and braid can easily be sewn on by machine. Ric-rac and other narrow trimmings can be sewn on straight down the middle.

1 Firstly, mark the position of the line of trimming on the fabric.

2 Pin the trimming in place and hand tack if necessary. Use a medium stitch length, position the needle in the centre of the trim and stitch slowly and carefully to keep the stitching straight.

Sew different

Use top stitch, machine embroidery thread or a narrow decorative stitch to make a feature of the sewing.

Narrow ribbon

Narrow ribbon, cords and many other lightweight trimmings can be stitched on decoratively using zigzag stitch. Experiment with a few scraps to establish whether you want the stitch to stay within the ribbon or to overlap the edges.

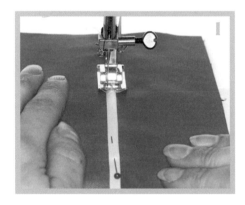

I Set the stitch to the required width and length. Start by turning the flywheel by hand to bring the needle down into the fabric and make sure you have the stitch position correct, then carefully sew down the centre, going slowly to keep the stitching straight.

Sew simple

If it is hard to sew the trimming on with pins in it, use a wash-out glue (page 18) to hold it in place temporarily.

Wide ribbon

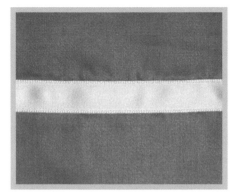

Wide ribbons must be sewn in the same direction along both edges to make them lie flat.

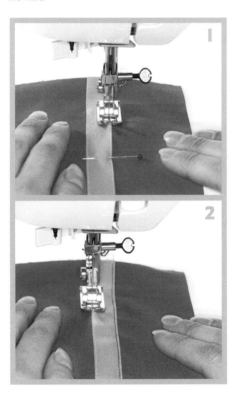

I Stitch very close to one edge with a small to medium stitch length.

2 Stitch along the other edge, starting from the same end as you did when you stitched the first line.

Upholstery braid

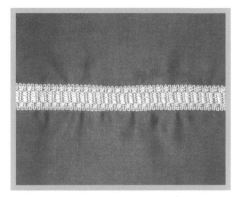

Upholstery braid is designed to be glued onto furniture, not sewn, so it is often too thick to pass under the presser foot. Any such chunky trimmings need to be stitched where the braid is thinnest, usually at the edge. Use a large stitch length or consider sewing on the trim by hand instead. Your machine may have a special braid foot with a channel on the underside to sew thick trimming.

I As this braid is fairly thin, it can be stitched near the edges using a large machine stitch. As with Wide Ribbon (left), sew the second side in the same direction.

Attaching lace by machine

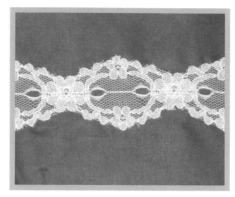

Lace trimming varies a lot, but generally it can be sewn on by machine. Vintage or handmade lace should always be sewn on by hand (right).

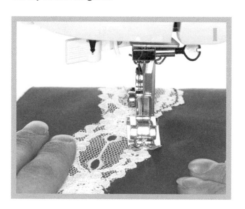

I Set the machine to a narrow zigzag stitch and guide the pinned-on lace under the presser foot. Keep the stitching fairly close to the edge of the lace. Pivot the needle (page 49), if required for sharper curves. Sew the other side in the same direction, as with Wide Ribbon (page 149).

Attaching trimmings by hand

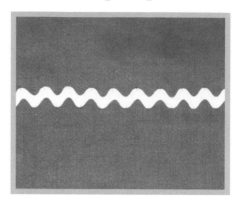

Some delicate trimmings are better sewn by hand, or you may prefer the finished effect of hand sewing rather than that of machine sewing.

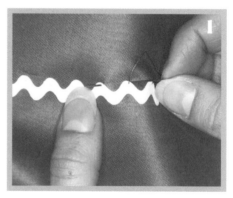

I Use slip stitch (page 29) and a thread that matches the trimming to catch the very edges of the trimming. Sew all along one edge then the along the other.

Gluing trimmings

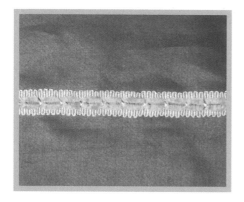

Glue can be useful for thick or chunky trimmings that won't sew well. Bear in mind that the glue might make the trimmed area stiffer.

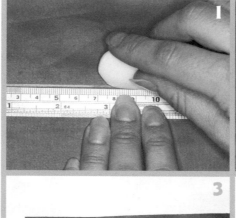

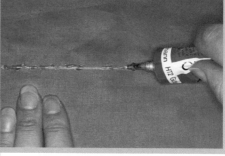

1 Mark the line of the trimming.

2 Run a small bead of glue along the marked line. Leave it to partially dry.

3 Press one end of the trimming onto the glue, making sure it is correctly positioned. Work along the trimming, pressing it into place bit by bit.

Attaching trimming with fusible webbing

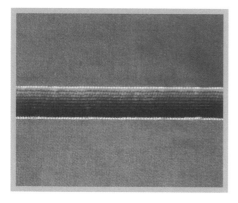

Fusible webbing is a great way of applying ribbon that can be pressed. Very thick trimmings will be hard to press, so this technique is not advised. Use hemming webbing (page 56) cut into long, narrow strips, a few millimetres narrower than the ribbon.

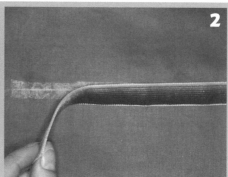

1 Mark line of the trimming. Place a strip of webbing on the line.

2 Position the trimming over the webbing carefully, without shifting the webbing off the marked line.

3 Carefully cover the ribbon with a pressing cloth and press, following the webbing manufacturer's instructions.

In-seam trim masterclass

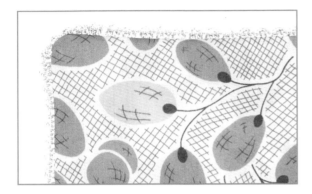

I absolutely love putting trimmings and decorations into seams. I've used this technique with ribbons for the Pinstripe Pincushion (page 214) and with braid on the Gingham Purse (page 218). It's also the same as putting in piping (page 79). Experiment with other types of trims and edgings that could be sewn into the seams of bags, clothes, cushions and almost anything else.

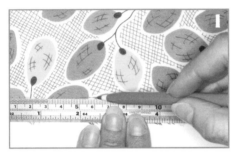
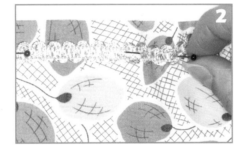
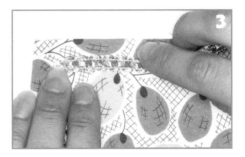
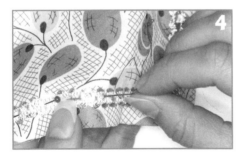
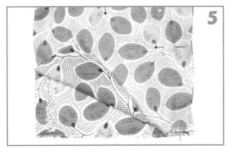

1 First mark the seam line on the right side of the fabric. This needs to be accurate.

2 Pin the trimming along the marked seam line. If there is one edge that you want to have showing, make sure that that edge is the one facing inwards; the edge that will be hidden faces the raw edge of the fabric.

3 To go around corners, make a neat fold.

4 Hand-tack the trimming in place along the centre of it, so you are sewing right on the seam line.

5 Place the other piece of fabric on top, right sides together and raw edges matching.

6 Pin the layers together.

7 Sew the seam with the line of tacking facing up. Follow the line of tacking very precisely. Remove the tacking, turn right side out and press.

Frog fastenings

I've never been quite sure why these are called frogs – they are much nicer than they sound. I have developed this easy technique that works well with narrow bias tubes. If you use cord, or anything else that is hard to pin, you will need to sew as you go along rather than pinning then sewing at the end.

Make lengths of narrow bias tube (page 82) for each fastening. This sample needs about 40cm of tube.

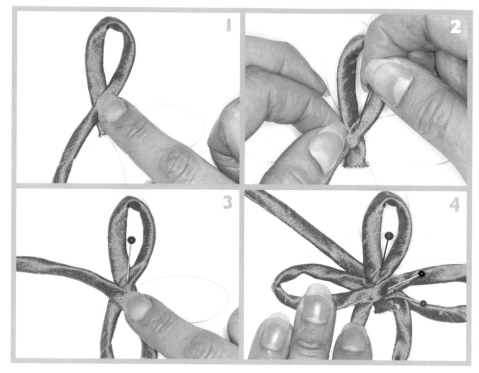

1 Draw a template of the required size and design on paper. Starting in the centre of the template, with a slight overlap, make the first loop.

2 Lift the tube off the template and pin through both layers.

3 Replace on the template and make the second (bottom) loop in a figure of eight. Then make the left loop, pinning as you go.

4 On the last loop, put the working end underneath the centre so it can be cut and sewn down invisibly.

5 On the back, tuck the starting end under the working end and slip stitch (page 29) it in place.

6 Go around the frog, sewing all the layers together on the back. Remove the pins as you go.

7 Cut off the long working end, leaving a very short tail.

8 Tuck under the tail end and sew down.

9 Sew the frog to a garment edge with half of one loop projecting over the edge. Use slip stitch around the outside edges to sew the frog in place.

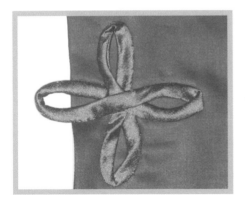

The frog fastening sewn on at the edge.

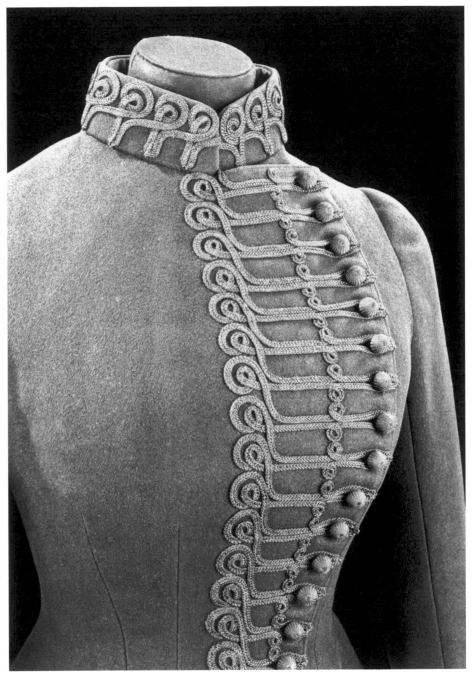

This riding jacket from 1885–1886 has a very fashionable braid decoration inspired by highly-decorated military uniforms. This version is based on a design known as 'crow's foot'.

Single beads

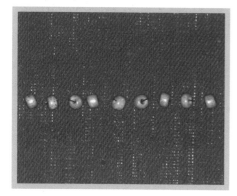
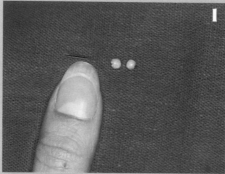
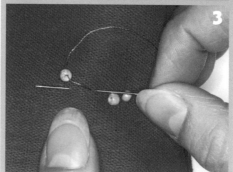
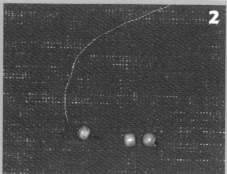

Beads can easily be sewn onto clothes, bags and other projects. Use beading thread and a beading needle. You could also wax the thread (page 27).

This technique works well for single beads or a few, randomly-spaced beads.

1 Fasten the thread on the back of the fabric. Bring the needle up through the fabric in the correct bead position.

2 Thread the bead on to the needle.

3 Make a tiny backstitch to secure the bead and come up through the fabric in the right position for the next bead.

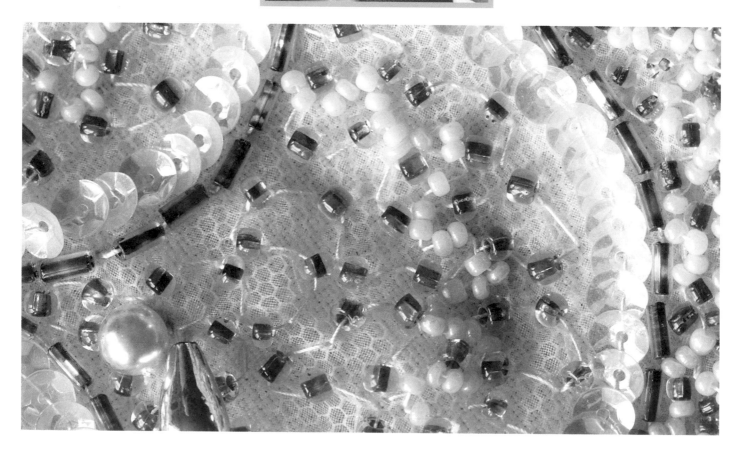

Line of beads

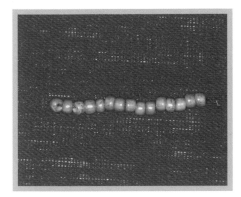

Where a close line of beads is required, try this technique.

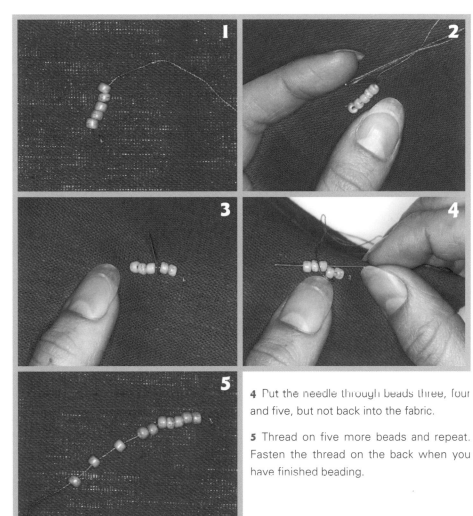

4 Put the needle through beads three, four and five, but not back into the fabric.

5 Thread on five more beads and repeat. Fasten the thread on the back when you have finished beading.

1 Fasten the thread on the back of the fabric. Bring the needle up through the fabric in the correct bead position and thread on five beads.

2 Pass the needle to the back of the fabric at the end of the row of beads.

3 Bring the needle up between beads two and three.

Sew different

Don't try and sew large or heavy beads onto delicate fabrics as they will pull the fabric out of shape. If you want a heavily-beaded motif, try sewing the beads onto a small piece of thicker fabric and then cutting it out and sewing it onto the garment.

Single sequin

This technique works well for single sequins. It is more hard-wearing and less likely to catch on things than the beaded technique (opposite).

1 Fasten the thread on the back of the fabric. Bring the needle up and thread on a single sequin.

2 Take the needle down on one side of the sequin and bring it out on the other side, making sure you are very close to the edge.

3 Bring the needle back down through the centre hole of the sequin. You can leave it like this, or follow the next two steps to make a star-shaped stitch.

4 Bring the needle out at the side of the sequin, making sure it is exactly between the first two stitches, then take it back through the centre hole. Do the same again on the opposite side.

5 Take the needle through the centre hole for the final time and fasten the thread on the back.

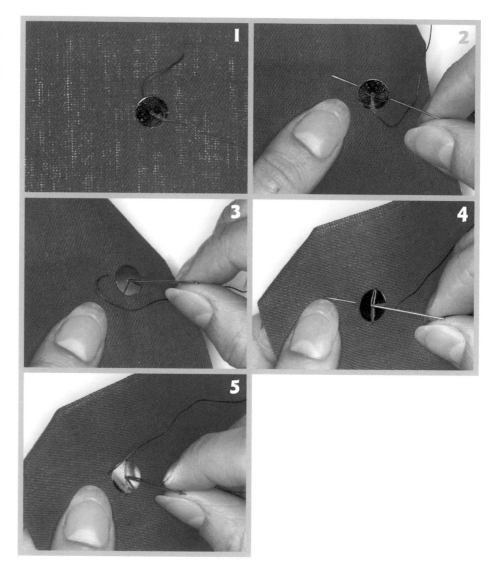

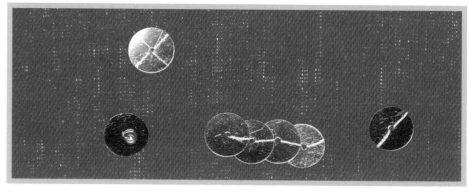

Top, star-stitch sequin; bottom left to right, beaded sequin, line of sequins, straight-stitch sequin.

Single sequin with bead

A small bead can be used to attach a single sequin.

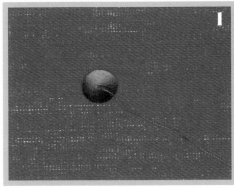 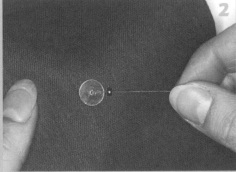 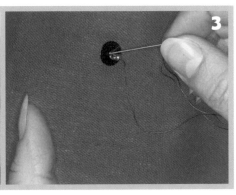

1 Fasten the thread on the back. Bring the needle up and thread on the sequin.

2 Thread on a bead.

3 Take the needle back through the sequin but NOT the bead. Fasten the thread on the back.

Line of sequins

A row of sequins is very easy to sew on.

1 Follow Steps 1–2 of the Single Sequin technique (opposite).

2 As the needle comes out right at the edge of the first sequin, thread on the second sequin. Take the needle down through the hole in the first sequin and come out on the other side of the second sequin. Repeat to sew on the whole line of sequins.

Sew different

In this sample I have used flat sequins. Cup sequins are curved and have facets to reflect more light. They are best sewn on with a bead. You can also buy sequins joined together in a braid. These are best sewn on down the centre by machine.

Tassels

Tassels can be made with all sorts of yarns, including embroidery thread and knitting yarn. Cut a card template slightly longer than the desired finished tassel length. This sample is 8cm long. When you wind the yarn, keep count of how many wraps you make, so you can make subsequent tassels the same size.

1 Wrap the yarn around the length of the card the required number of times. The more wraps, the fuller the tassel will be.

2 Cut a 20cm length of the same yarn, or a stronger one if it breaks easily. Slip the tie under the loops. If this is difficult, thread the yarn on to a tapestry needle first. Tie the yarn in a double knot. Hold the first knot with your finger while you do the second knot.

3 Cut the other end of the wrapped loops using small, sharp scissors.

4 Cut another length of yarn about 30cm long (again a stronger yarn if needed), to tie the neck. Wrap the yarn around the tassel then tie a double knot, as before.

5 Wrap the long ends of the tie yarn around the neck. Make as many wraps as you wish, but leave enough yarn at each end to finish. A contrasting yarn is very effective for this step. Tie the two ends of the yarn in a double knot, as before.

6 Thread both ends of the neck-binding yarn into a tapestry needle and push the needle through the binding into the middle of the loose yarn ends (the tassel skirt). Pull the ends of yarn through and remove the tapestry needle.

7 Hold the tassel in your fist to keep the skirt compressed, and trim the ends of it with medium-sized, sharp scissors.

Pom-poms

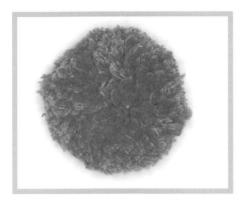

I love pom-poms and often make huge ones from entire balls of knitting yarn. If you are making lots of pom-poms, it's worth buying a pom-pom maker. These plastic gadgets make the whole process easier and faster and come in different sizes. Check the instructions in case your pom-pom maker is different to mine.

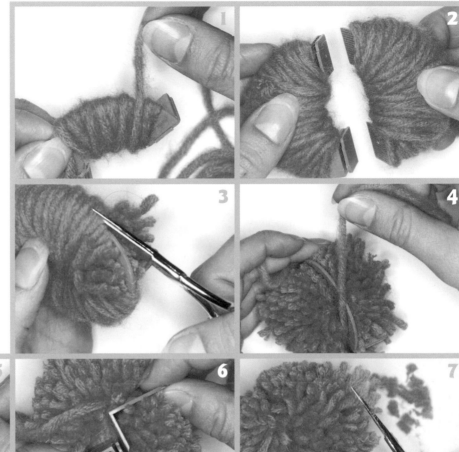

1 Wrap yarn around each half of the pom-pom maker until the semi-circle is full.

2 Clip the two halves of the maker together.

3 Using small, sharp scissors, cut around the edge. Try cutting the top layers first then work down through the thicknesses. While you are cutting, hold the centre firmly to stop the short lengths of yarn falling out.

4 When all the threads are cut, wrap a length of strong yarn around the middle, on the flat side of the maker.

5 Knot the yarn firmly around the middle.

6 Unclip the two halves of the maker.

7 Trim stray threads to a consistent length. One drawback of a pom-pom maker is that one side has more stray long threads than the other, but a trim will neaten it up.

8 If you are working in the traditional way, cut two circles of card the diameter of the finished pom-pom. Cut large inner circles. Cut the yarn into lengths and wrap it through the hole until the circle is covered and the hole is full. You will need a tapestry needle to get the yarn through the centre once it starts to fill up. Tie and trim as above.

Faggoting seams

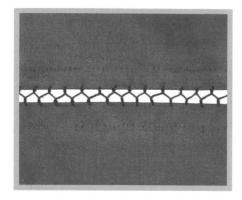

Faggoted seams are really pretty and look like tiny corset lacings. Use this technique to join two finished edges that don't take much strain, like shoulder seams. If the machine tacking leaves marks, use silk thread or tack by hand.

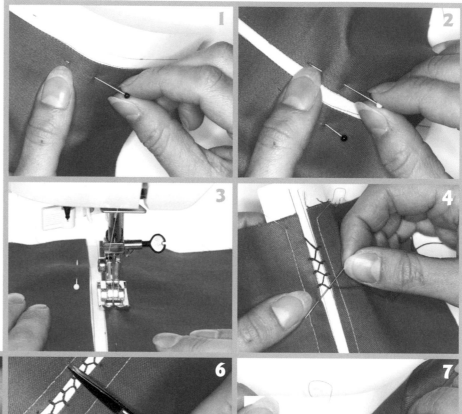

1 Draw two lines 5mm apart on paper. Press under the seam allowances of the two pieces of fabric. Pin one folded edge to the paper against one line.

2 Pin the folded edge of the other piece of fabric to the other line.

3 Machine tack both pieces in place, about 5mm from the fold. Remove the pins.

4 Start the thread by coming through the folded edge. Make the first stitch by going diagonally across the opposite fold, about 5mm down from the starting point.

5 Turn the whole piece around and make the next stitch by going under the end of the previous stitch, diagonally across the gap and making a tiny stitch in the opposite edge. Continue to the end of the seam, keeping the stitches even and well spaced. You could use a vanishing fabric marker to mark the distances between stitches.

6 To remove the paper, snip the machine tacking stitches.

7 Carefully pull off the paper, making sure you don't strain the decorative stitching, and remove the tacking threads.

Frayed edge

A decorative, frayed edge can be very attractive on a suitable fabric, such as linen. For this effect, you need to sew along the straight grain of the fabric, so use something with a very obvious grain. Mark a line along the grain using a vanishing fabric marker.

1 Machine-sew along the marked line using a very small stitch and matching thread (here, a contrast thread has been used for clarity). This stitching marks the end of the fraying and stops the edge from unravelling further. Use the tip of a needle to pull out a few threads on the raw edge of the fabric.

2 Unpick a few threads at a time, working several loose at the end before you start pulling them out along the whole length.

3 Pull the threads out a couple at a time. Don't try to pull them all at once or the short threads will tangle. Remove the threads up to the stitching line. Leave the stitching in place to prevent further unravelling.

Scalloped edge masterclass

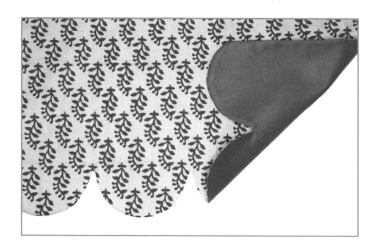

Scalloped edges on garments and curtains are very attractive. They are fiddly, but not difficult to make. Use a medium-weight fabric and be very accurate with the machine sewing for the scallops to look neat and professional. Make a paper template of the required size by drawing around suitably sized pots or jars. Leave a small gap between each semi-circle.

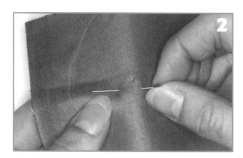

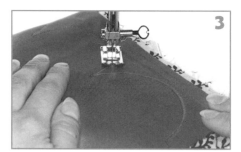

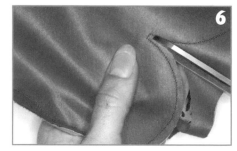

1 Draw around your template on the wrong side of one of the fabrics, drawing the scallops close to the edge of the fabric.

2 Place the two fabrics right sides together, with the drawn outline facing up. Pin the layers together, pinning through the scallops.

3 Using small machine stitches, sew along the marked line. Go very slowly to make sure the curves are accurate. Pivot the fabric around the needle (page 49) if required to go around the curves.

4 Pivot at the inner corners. Turn the flywheel by hand to sew accurately around these tight spots.

5 Cut out the scallops, cutting about 5mm from the stitching.

6 Cutting carefully, cut a slit down into the narrow gaps.

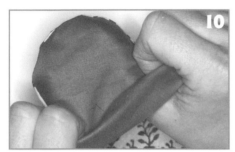

7 Cut notches into the curved edges, but do not cut into the stitching (page 45).

8 Make very tiny clips into the corners of the small gaps (page 44).

9 Turn the piece right side out.

10 Push out the scallops from the inside and finger press (page 24) the edges so that the lining doesn't show on the right side.

11 Press the finished piece.

Sew different

You can also make a decorative edging with reverse scallops (left). Leave wide gaps between each semi-circle and clip the corners very carefully. Finger press and then press the square ends very neatly.

Fabric manipulation

Fabric manipulation is all about exploration and experimentation. I love to push the boundaries with these techniques to discover what new things can be created. I've included a range of techniques in this section, from machine-felting recycled knitwear to various gathering, puckering and shaping techniques, both traditional and modern.

Straight row gathering

This is very simple gathering. I have worked this on gingham so that you can clearly see how the stitches create neat folds, almost like pleats. To make this with plain fabric, mark dots 1–2cm apart on the fabric. This technique is used in the Gathered Scarf project (page 220).

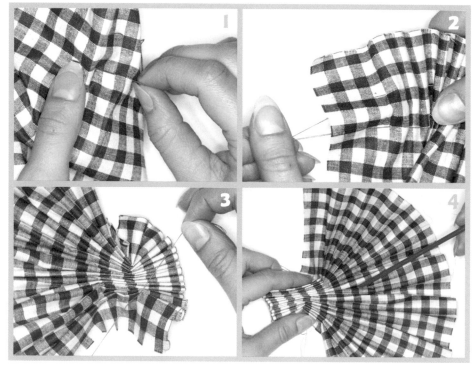

The edge is almost ruff-like. Narrow strips can be pleated like this to make tiny ruffles.

1 Knot the thread firmly. Make two rows of evenly-spaced running stitches, making the rows about 2cm apart.

2 Pull up both sets of threads, pulling them one at a time if the fabric is thick. Ease the gathers down the threads – don't pull hard.

3 Trim the excess threads, leaving a tail of about 20cm on each. Knot the threads together or re-thread them into needles and sew in the ends to secure them.

4 Stroke the pleats into shape with a knitting needle. Steam (don't press!) the pleats to help hold the shape (page 24).

Random gathers

In this variation of gathering, the running stitches cover the whole fabric and are not regularly spaced, to give uneven, undulating gathered fabric.

Random gathers worked on shot silk.

1 Secure a thread at the starting edge.

2 Sew a line of uneven running stitches; some big stitches, some small ones, some that are large on the front and small on the back, and some vice versa.

3 Make another row of running stitches about 1cm away from the first line, spacing the stitches differently.

4 Continue to sew rows across the fabric.

5 Gently pull up all the threads.

6 Ease the gathers down towards the knots.

7 Trim the long threads to about 20cm.

8 Knot or sew in the ends of the threads.

Suffolk puff masterclass

These gathered circles, called yo-yos in the USA, were traditionally used for patchwork. They were made from scraps of fabric and sewn together edge-to-edge. I like to use them in appliqué for their sculptural, decorative effect when sewn flat and overlapped, as on the Silk Cuff (page 206).

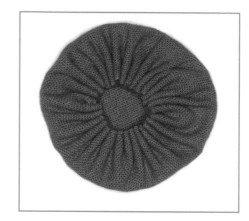

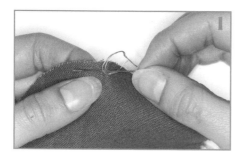

1 Cut a circle of fabric, slightly more than twice the desired finished diameter of the puff. Secure a doubled thread (page 26) in the seam allowance on the wrong side of the fabric.

2 Take the needle through to the right side.

3 Fold the edge over the securing stitches.

4 Work a medium-sized running stitch around the circle, folding over the edge as you go. Keep the stitches evenly spaced and not too small.

5 Take the needle to the outside on the last stitch, taking it through the hole made by the first stitch.

Sew different

Thick fabrics don't gather up well enough to make small, neat Suffolk puffs, but they will work for large ones. With very thin fabrics, the centres gather up to nothing, rather than leaving a nice hole in the middle.

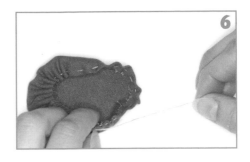

6 Leave the needle attached and pull up the threads, easing up the gathers neatly around the circle.

7 With the gathers pulled up, take the needle through to the inside edge, taking it through the same hole.

8 Secure the thread with a couple of small stitches on the inside.

9 While holding the middle of the puff, pull on the edges to even out the pleats.

Shirring

Shirring is traditionally used to make fake smocking on babies' dresses but I like to use it to make sculptural, puckered fabrics. For this technique, shirring elastic is wound, by hand, onto the bobbin. Make sure you wind it in the right direction. Wind it with slight tension, but don't over-stretch it.

This technique only works on fine fabrics that pucker easily and is very effective on viscose or silk velvet.

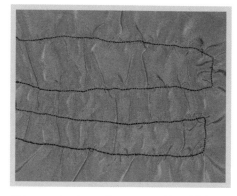

This sample shows the wrong side with just stitching running in just one direction.

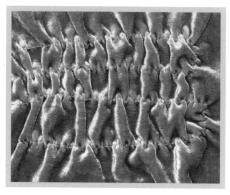

The right side with stitching in just one direction. The rows of stitching can be made much closer together for a more traditional shirred effect.

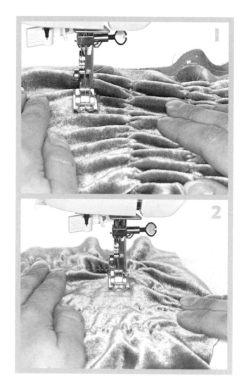

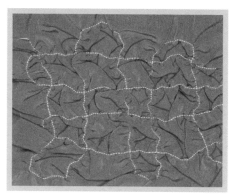

This is the effect on the back with lines of stitching running in both directions.

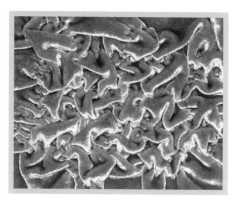

The fully gathered fabric from the front.

1 With the fabric face up, fasten the thread by making two very short stitches (page 34). Using a large, straight stitch, start sewing in a straight line across the fabric. At the end of the row either fasten off, or turn, sew along a couple of centimetres and then turn back to do the next row.

2 To make the very puckered effect, sew lines in both directions across the fabric.

This dress from 1878–1880, is heavily inspired by 18th-century styles. The central panel of the bodice is made from fine silk, shirred or gathered to create a soft, decorative texture.

Stitch and slash masterclass

Stitch and slash is a very satisfying technique. Several layers of fabric are sewn together in close rows, then the upper layers are cut to reveal the layers underneath. More layers can be added, and the sewing can be closer together than in this sample. After cutting, the slashes can be manipulated, pressed and sewn by hand or machine. The stitching is made on the bias (pages 16–17) so the edges don't fray too much. The foundation layer needs to be quite sturdy and it works best if the layers contrast in colour.

Special gadgets for slashing are available. They are similar to rotary cutters, but have an extended piece along the bottom to stop you cutting the foundation layer. They are available in different widths, depending on how close your rows of stitches are.

Sew different

Quilters use this technique to create unique fabrics called faux-chenille, by layering lots of loose-weave cotton fabrics together, sewing very close rows then cutting. Washing and tumble-drying the fabric helps to fluff up and fray the raw edges to create an effect similar to chenille pile.

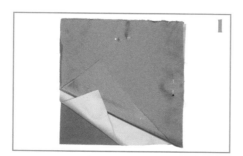

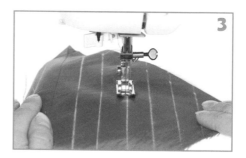

1 Pin at least three layers of fabric together, making sure that they are all on the same grain alignment.

2 Mark diagonal lines along the bias grain of the top fabric.

3 Sew the lines with a medium stitch. Start with the middle line then sew one row on either side of the centre and then work outwards. Turn the work each time so you sew in the opposite direction on each line.

4 Insert scissors between the bottom and middle layers and cut through them, making sure you don't cut the foundation layer.

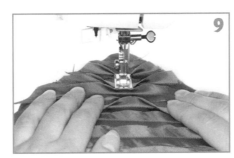

5 Cut along the centre of the channel between the rows of stitching.

6 To use a slash cutting tool, make a snip in the top two layers with the scissors. This makes it easier to start the slashing tool.

7 Slice along the centre of the channel with the tool.

8 The finished piece can then be machine washed and dried, and the edges scrubbed with a stiff brush to fluff them up if required.

9 To make folded-back layers, sew across the slashes. Fold each layer over as you come to it, or pin them all before you sew.

Layers folded back and sewn across.

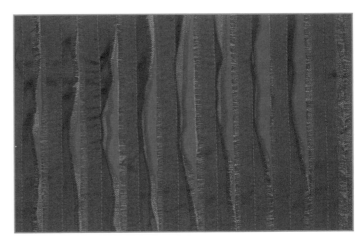

In this sample the fabric is deliberately cut on the straight grain so that it frays a lot and the lines of stitching are widely spaced.

Direct smocking

Direct smocking is a fun and easy way to manipulate checked or spotted fabrics. It is traditionally worked on gingham, which shows the puckering and folding to best advantage.

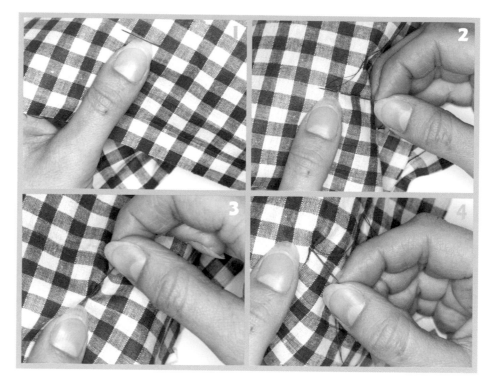

1 Bring the needle out on a corner of a square in the gingham pattern.

2 Make the first stitch by picking up a couple of threads at the corner to the right of where you started.

3 Pull the thread taut to bring these two corners together.

4 Put the needle back in at the same point and then bring it up diagonally, one square to the left.

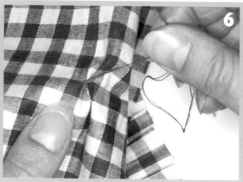

5 Repeat the stitch in Step 2 by picking up the corner to the right of the thread, then coming back to the same place.

6 Pull up the second stitch.

7 Put the needle in at the same point and take it down diagonally, one square to the left. Continue in this way.

One row of smocking complete.

In this sample, the row of smocking has been worked starting on a different square, so the little triangles formed are white rather than dark blue.

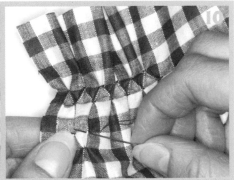

8 Start the second row of smocking two squares down and one square across from where you started on the first row.

9 Start by making the first stitch downwards and to the right.

10 Continue working across the row in the same way as for the first row.

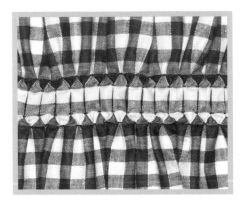

Two finished rows of smocking.

Sew different

Explore old sewing books for different patterns for direct smocking or 'counter-change' as it is sometimes called. Look for old aprons and children's garments made using this technique for ideas. Or just experiment and see what you come up with.

American smocking masterclass

American or 'lattice' smocking is worked with similar stitches to direct smocking, but on the back of the fabric. The stitches don't show on the front and a heavily textured pattern slowly appears. I have developed my own way of marking the fabric. It is traditionally done with rows of dots, but I find the numbered grid easier to keep track of. The co-ordinates are given with the across numbers first, then the down numbers, so 3:2 is 3 across and 2 down. The stitches are alternately pulled up or left slack.

Experiment with the size of the grids to suit your fabric and the effect you want. In this sample, the grid lines are about 2cm apart.

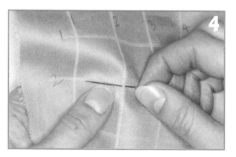

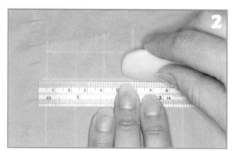

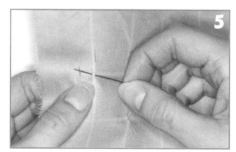

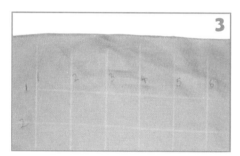

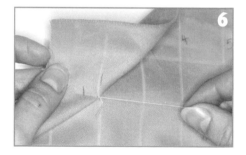

1 Mark the horizontal lines.

2 Mark vertical lines to make squares.

3 Number each line as shown.

4 Fasten the thread at 2:2.

5 Stitch diagonally to 1:1 and pick up a few threads at the cross point.

6 Pull up the stitch.

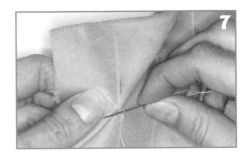

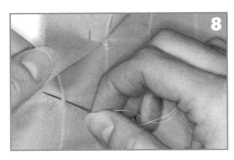

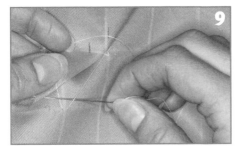

7 Knot the thread to hold the stitch. Put the needle through the stitch with the working thread on the left. Pull up to fasten.

8 From this point, take a stitch to 1:3. DO NOT pull up this stitch.

9 Fasten the thread as in Step 7. Continue the row all the way down, stitching down to 2:4, pulling up, then down to 1:5 and not pulling up.

10 To start the second row, begin on 2:3, then stitch diagonally up to 3:2 and pull up. Continue downwards to 3:4 and don't pull up, then to 2:5 and pull up, and so on.

This diagram shows how the stitches are made to produce this smocking pattern. Turn to page 294 for more diagrams showing different patterns.

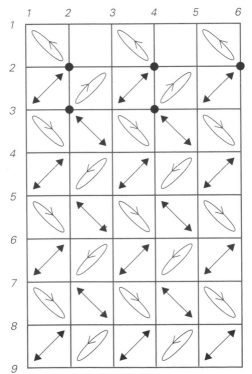

Stitch pulled up.

Stitch not pulled up.

Starting point for row of smocking.

The finished smocking will pucker up to produce a lattice design.

The wrong side, showing four rows of smocking stitches.

Felting

Felting (or more technically, 'fulling') pre-knitted wool in the washing machine is very easy. The combination of hot water, agitation and soap makes the wool fibres fluff up, grab each other and mat together, creating a thicker, fluffier version of the woollen fabric that went into the machine. Felting knitwear produces a medium-weight fabric that doesn't fray. Different knits come out as different thicknesses – the only way to find out how thick is to try.

Both the Customised T-shirt (page 276) and the Pebble Cushion (page 278) use small pieces of felted wool, while Mr Mouse (page 124) uses about half a jumper. I have a vast collection of felted jumpers, originally bought in charity shops, but if you only need a small around, then it might be easier to knit squares of pure wool yarn and felt them. Whichever you do, only use fibres that are hand-wash only. Some wool is treated to stop it shrinking in the wash and it won't felt. The jumper or yarn needs to be mostly wool, or another animal fibre like alpaca, angora or cashmere. A little synthetic yarn won't hurt. There is no way to predict how the wool will come out once it's felted, so every time is an exciting experiment.

Wash the jumper or knitting on a hot wash, ideally in an old pillowcase tied with string, in a load with towels or jeans. The felting will be improved if there is more in the machine and it is more ecological to wash a full load. Be aware that dyes will run from the knitwear spectacularly, so either wash similar colours or put in a dye catching cloth (page 20).

Once the wash has finished, hang up the pieces immediately, as the spin cycle can leave creases in the wool that are hard to get out. There is no need to tumble-dry felted wool. If it hasn't felted as much as you want, put it through another wash.

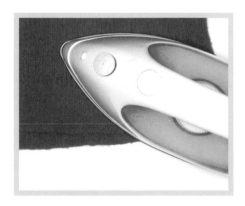

When dry, press with a very hot iron and lots of steam to get any remaining creases out.

Hand knit before felting.

Hand knit after felting.

Cut along the side seams and around the sleeves. Cut along the sleeve seams and press the pieces of felt flat.

Machine knit before felting.

Machine knit after felting.

Quilting, appliqué and patchwork

These techniques have masses of potential for creating interesting, imaginative, decorative and practical projects. A traditional bed quilt is only one thing you can make with quilting techniques. The quilted projects in this book include the Trapunto Cushion (page 225), the Patchwork Needlebook (page 211) and the Quilted Placemats (page 216).

Quilting basics

A quilt is, very simply, two or more layers stitched together.

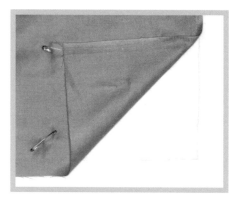

Cotton wadding.

Usually a quilt would have a layer of thick wadding between two layers of fabric, the top fabric (which will be the right side of the quilt) and the backing fabric. Lots of different sorts of quilt wadding are available including cotton and polyester. There is more about wadding on page 292. I prefer cotton wadding over polyester.

Polyester is much cheaper, but has a habit of what is called 'bearding', where fibres start to come through the surface of the quilt after sewing. Bearding doesn't really show much on a white quilt, but on a dark fabric it shows badly.

Cotton wadding is generally thinner, but can be layered to make a thicker quilt. It will shrink slightly when you wash it. To preshrink it, immerse it in hot water and leave it

Polyester wadding.

until the water is cool. Air-dry it and press lightly. Cotton wadding is naturally a creamy colour with some black flecks in it. Bear this in mind if you are using a thin or pale fabric.

To hold the quilt together and to stop the wadding wrinkling or tearing, the quilting lines must be fairly close together. For cotton the minimum distance is around 5cm, while for polyester it is more like 10cm. Each type of wadding will be different, so check the manufacturer's information.

Cut the lining fabric and wadding a few centimetres bigger than the top fabric to allow for shrinkage while quilting.

Washing and pre-washing

Many quilters prefer not to pre-wash quilt fabrics and wadding and enjoy the vintage-effect puckering that occurs after the first wash. If you don't want this shrinkage effect, pre-wash or shrink all materials.

Quilting equipment

Special thread for hand quilting has a higher twist than normal sewing thread, making it more suitable for long lines of running stitch. To avoid getting the thread tangled, always use it in the direction it comes off the spool; use the already cut end in the needle and knot the freshly-cut end. Quilting is always worked with a single thread.

Quilting needles, called betweens, are short and fine to make it easy to work the close running stitch (page 28).

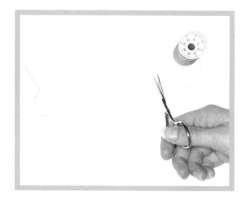

Quilting designs

If you wish to use a decorative quilting design, draw this onto the top fabric before putting the layers together to make the quilt sandwich. Wash-out fabric markers are usually the best thing to use, as the marks will last throughout the quilting process.

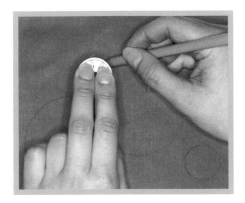

Joining wadding

If the wadding is too narrow for the project, the pieces will need hand-sewing together. Butt the edges up and sew them together.

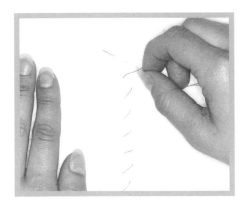

Making the quilt sandwich

You will need a large table, clean floor or bare mattress covered in boards to lay out the quilt fabrics fully.

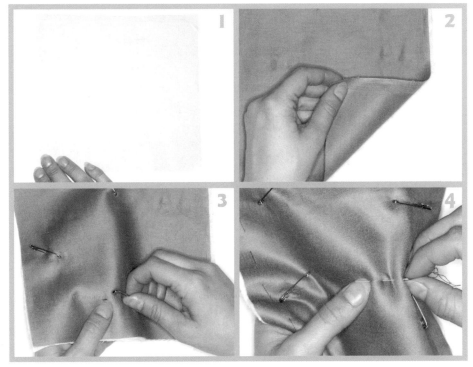

1 First place the lining right side down, ensuring that it is square and free of creases and wrinkles. For large pieces, a helper is very useful at this stage! Use masking tape to keep the lining in place.

2 Place the wadding on top of the lining and then the quilt top fabric, face-up.

3 Pin the layers together with long, straight pins or safety pins.

4 Using long threads, tack the layers together, starting by tacking around the outside edges. Then tack in a cross through the centre and finally across the rest of the quilt in lines about 15cm apart.

Sew simple

Use safety pins instead of normal straight pins on large pieces of quilting as the former don't fall out or snag.

Hand quilting masterclass

Quilting can seem rather complicated for the non-expert but you don't have to have a quilting frame to do basic hand quilting. Even a large quilt can be quilted using the method shown.

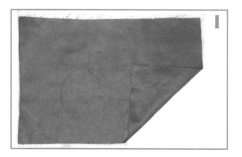

1 Make a quilt sandwich of the three layers (page 181).

2 Pin in several places then tack the layers together (page 181).

3 Start the quilting using a thread about 40cm long. When starting the thread at the edge of the work, fasten the thread in the edge that will be covered by the binding.

4 To start a thread in the middle of a piece of work, make a small knot and insert the needle into the top layer of fabric some distance from where you want to start sewing. Pass the needle through the wadding layer to come out where the stitching is to start. Pull sharply on the thread to pull the knot through the fabric so it sticks in the wadding layer. Alternatively, you could try using an extra-long thread (page 26).

5 Quilting stitch is basically a small running stitch that looks the same on the back as the on the front. The stitches are worked in an up and down motion, so the needle goes horizontally through the layers.

6 Make several stitches at the same time by keeping the quilt sandwich in the left hand and manipulating the fabric to pass the needle through. It does take practice to get neat, even quilting stitches. Finish the thread at the edge of the quilt if you can.

7 Otherwise work a tiny securing stitch (page 27) over the last quilting stitch.

Sew simple

Always make all the layers slightly bigger than the required finished size of the quilt. The process of quilting will shift the fabrics around slightly and the quilt will shrink a little.

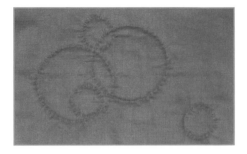

8 Then push the needle out at a distance and pull the thread taut.

9 Make a small knot in the thread. Cut it after the knot, then pull it through in the same way as you did to start in Step 4.

When quilting is complete, trim the edges neatly and use a binding technique (pages 68–78) to bind the edges.

Sew different

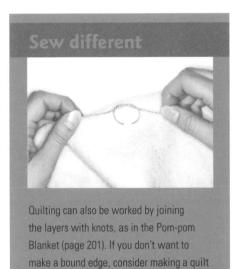

Quilting can also be worked by joining the layers with knots, as in the Pom-pom Blanket (page 201). If you don't want to make a bound edge, consider making a quilt in the same way as the Quilted Placemats (page 216), where the sandwich is made inside out, turned and then quilted. This works well for small quilts.

Machine quilting

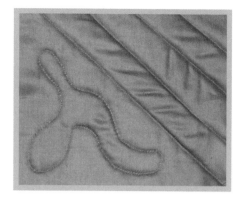

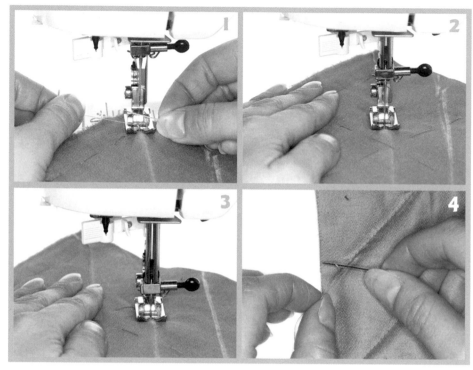

Quilting by machine is undoubtedly quicker than hand quilting, though the finished effect is somewhat different. Close-quilting by machine will produce a flatter and more solid quilt than a similar one quilted by hand. Getting a large quilt under the machine can be difficult. Roll or fold the part of the quilt not being sewn and hold the roll with bicycle clips or clamps to keep it in check. Machine quilting is done in the same way as normal sewing, by holding the fabric and moving it around under the presser foot.

You can buy a special machine foot for quilting called a walking or even-feed foot. This helps to stop the layers moving about as you sew, but you can use a normal foot. I find a clear foot makes it easy to see what is going on.

Always practice on a quilt sandwich made from offcuts. You may need to adjust the top thread tension (page 35) to get the stitches to sit correctly on the thickness of the quilt.

Quilter's masking tape is narrow, low-tack tape that can be stuck on the quilt surface. You can use this tape to mark the required quilting lines rather than drawing them on if you prefer.

1 Turn the flywheel and put the needle up and down a couple of times. Pull on the thread to bring the bobbin thread to the surface. Hold both the threads when you start sewing to avoid tangles. Start the sewing using the reduced stitch length method (page 34).

2 Start quilting along lines in the centre, then lines halfway through each half of the quilt, to anchor the layers together. Quilt from the centre outwards when working on very large pieces.

3 Use a quilting guide (page 281) to keep the distance between the rows, or mark the lines on the fabric.

4 End the sewing in the same way as you started, by reducing the stitch length. Pull up the bobbin thread and cut off each thread as you go.

Sew different

It is also possible to quilt in random patterns by using the free-machine technique, similar to machine embroidery (page 194). Use a large needle, set the stitch length to 0 and hold the work in an embroidery hoop: you can buy enormous hoops for this purpose.

Trapunto masterclass

Trapunto quilting uses stuffing to create small areas of padding on an otherwise flat fabric. The fabric is backed with something firm, like calico, and outline shapes are sewn through the two layers. The backing layer is cut open and stuffed. Use merino wool tops if the piece is non-washable and polyester wadding if you want to wash it (page 293). Trapunto works best on plain fabric with a sheen. Remember to use hollow, outlined shapes that can contain the stuffing.

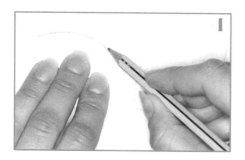

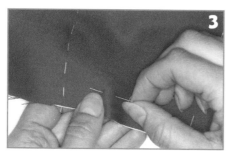

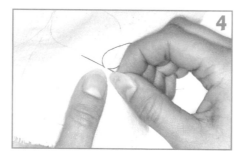

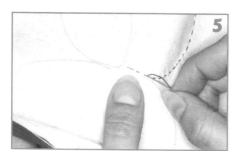

1 Draw the design onto the backing fabric.

2 Place the front fabric face down with the backing fabric on top, design uppermost.

3 Pin then tack the piece around the edges and in a cross through the centre to stop the layers moving around.

4 Start the sewing by anchoring the thread through just the backing fabric (page 27), just outside the stitching line.

5 Sew around the outline with a small running stitch, taking care to keep the stitches even on the underside, which is of course the finished right side. Remove the tacking stitches.

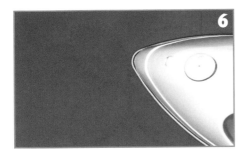
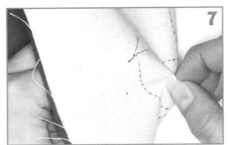
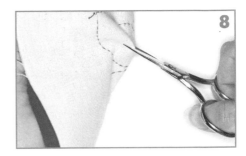

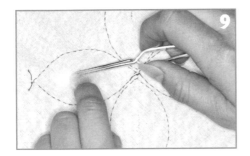
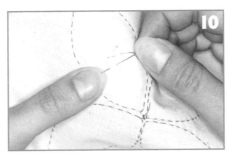

6 Press the front of the fabric before you start stuffing, as this is the last chance to do so. It will also help the stitches to sink into the fabric more.

7 When the whole design is sewn, separate the front and back layers by pinching the fabrics between your forefinger and thumb.

8 Holding the backing fabric only, make a tiny snip in the fabric and cut carefully to enlarge it slightly.

9 Stuff wadding into the space, a small amount at a time. Use tweezers or a knitting needle to poke it into place. Stuff the edges of the shape first then fill the centre. Do not over-stuff as this will cause the fabric to pucker around the stitching.

10 Sew up the slit by sewing across it, taking the needle from the inside to the outside on every stitch.

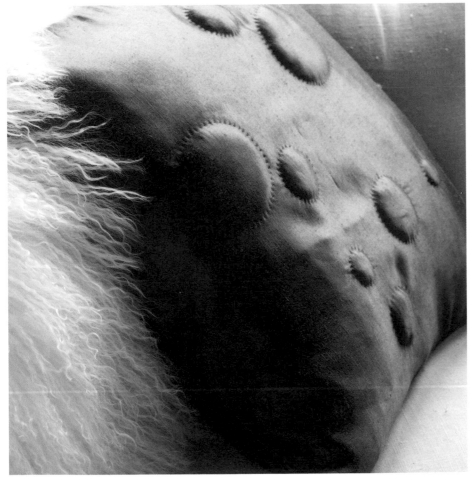

Fusible webbing appliqué

Using iron-on fusible webbing is a quick and easy way to do appliqué. Fusible webbing is paper with a layer of fabric glue attached to it that is activated by the application of heat. The paper is removed in the final stage when the appliqué is heat-bonded to the fabric. This technique also makes it easy to do complicated shapes that would otherwise be very tricky to cut out of fabric.

Fusible webbing for appliqué is available in a small package or by the metre for larger projects. The finished appliqué is usually washable, but check the manufacturer's instructions. Use a Teflon pressing cloth (page 284) or baking parchment when ironing the fusible webbing onto fabric.

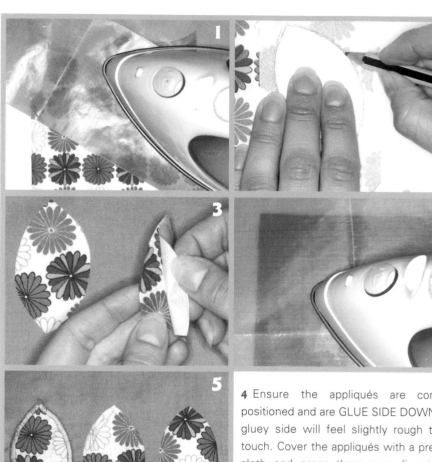

4 Ensure the appliqués are correctly positioned and are GLUE SIDE DOWN. The gluey side will feel slightly rough to the touch. Cover the appliqués with a pressing cloth and press them according to the manufacturer's instructions.

5 The appliqués can be sewn if required. From the left, they are shown with satin stitch (page 33), with straight stitch sewn 5mm in from the edge and with no stitching.

1 Cut enough fusible webbing for the motifs you wish to cut out. Iron the webbing onto the WRONG SIDE of the fabric, following the manufacturer's instructions and using a pressing cloth.

2 Draw the designs directly onto the fusible webbing paper using a pencil. Cut them out with sharp paper scissors.

3 Arrange the motifs on the fabric and when you are happy with the arrangement, peel off the paper backing. If it is hard to remove, crumple the edges of the appliqué slightly, which will release the paper.

Hand-sewn appliqué

There are many different ways of making appliqué, this is just one of the easier methods for simple shapes in fabrics that fray. The interfacing helps shape the appliqué and makes it easier to turn the seam allowances under.

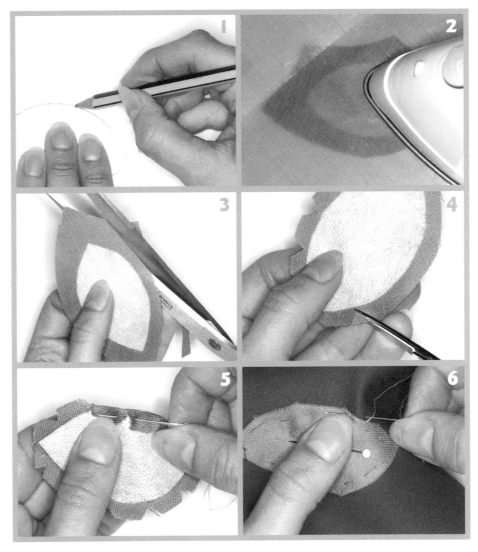

Sew different

Embroidery stitches can be used to attach the appliqué, particularly blanket stitch (page 198).

1 Draw the desired appliqué shape onto lightweight iron-on interfacing and cut it out.

2 Press the interfacing shape onto the WRONG SIDE of the appliqué fabric, using a Teflon pressing cloth or baking parchment.

3 Cut out the shape with a 5mm seam allowance all around.

4 Notch (page 45) or clip (page 44) the seam allowance if the edge is curved.

5 Turn the seam allowance over to the back and tack it down.

6 Position the appliqué shape, pin it on and slip stitch (page 29) all around it, making sure to catch any stray threads or corners. Remove the tacking stitches.

Machine-sewn appliqué

This appliqué variation uses interfaced fabric sewn down by machine. The interfacing stabilises the fabric so it doesn't stretch or fray while you work.

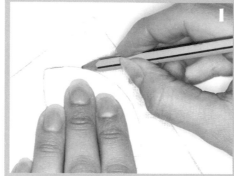

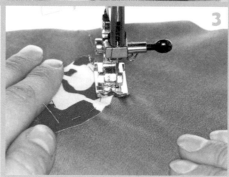

1 Apply interfacing to the WRONG SIDE of the appliqué fabric and draw the shape. For a neat edge, interface more fabric than you need and then cut out the shape so the interfacing goes right to the edge.

2 Cut out the shape. Position the appliqué and tack it in place.

3 Sew around the edge using a medium zigzag stitch, satin stitch or machine blanket stitch (page 33). You may find it easier to use stabiliser under the fabric (page 194).

3-D appliqué

Appliqué has many possibilities. I like to experiment with 3-D shapes as well as flat ones. I used this technique in the Silk Cuff (page 206) by applying the Suffolk puffs to the fabric with slip stitching. The shape used in this sample is just one of many possibilities. This technique can be used for brooches by adding more petals and sewing a button in the middle.

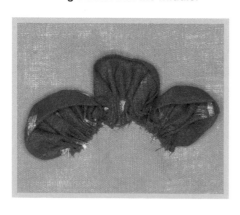

1 Cut circles of a soft fabric. Fold the circle in half, fasten the thread and sew a small running stitch (page 28) along the raw edge.

2 Pull up the thread and arrange the gathers as required, then fasten off the thread.

3 Slip stitch (page 29) the appliqué to the base fabric. Overlap the shapes if you don't want the raw edges to show.

Using unusual materials

For decorative work, all sorts of materials can be sewn to make interesting, textural appliqué. I love working with felt and leather, particularly in appliqué because they don't fray and are easy to sew. Other materials, such as plastic, can be very effective but rather hard to sew down unless you pierce holes first. Plastic bags, leaves and paper (particularly handmade paper) can all be sewn by machine or by hand, but throw away the needles afterwards as they will be blunt. Found objects like washers and broken jewellery can all be sewn down by hand for interesting textural effects.

LEATHER

Fine leather or suede can be sewn with a normal, fine, sharp sewing needle. For thicker leather, use a special leather needle (page 282).

1 Fasten the thread on the back then bring the needle up into the edge of the appliqué. Do not sew too close to the edge as leather can tear.

2 Use slip stitch (page 29) or an embroidery stitch (pages 196–199) to attach the appliqué to the background fabric.

FELT

Because felt doesn't fray, there is no need to use interfacing. It can be cut and sewn directly onto the background fabric by hand or machine. Blanket stitch is a very effective way of attaching felt.

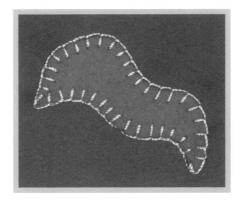

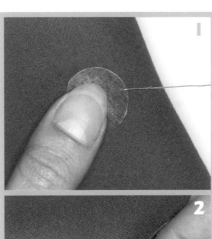

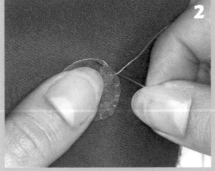

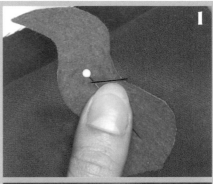

1 Fasten the thread on the back then bring the needle up by the edge of the appliqué.

2 Make the blanket stitch (page 198).

3 On the last stitch, stitch the loop down to make the leg neat.

Reverse appliqué masterclass

Reverse appliqué simply means back-to-front appliqué, where the applied fabric is on the back of the main fabric and the main fabric is partially cut away. It has great potential for decorative effects. The raw-edge version is very effective in felt or other fabrics that do not fray. More layers of fabric can be added and cut away to different degrees.

machine-sewn reverse appliqué

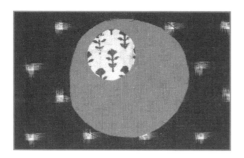

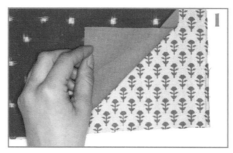

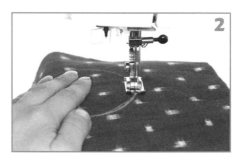

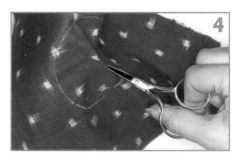

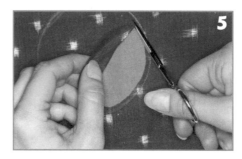

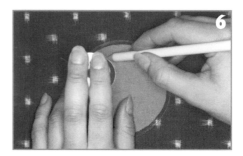

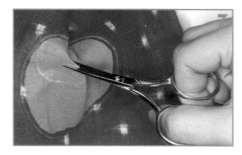

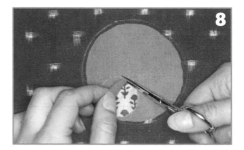

1 Layer three fabrics together, all face up.

2 Draw the required design on the top fabric. Sew the design through all layers using a small to medium stitch length. Fasten the threads neatly on the back.

3 Pinch and separate the layers within the sewn area, making sure you are holding only the top layer.

4 Cut a small snip in the top layer.

5 With small scissors and taking great care, cut away most of the top layer of fabric within the sewn area. Cut to about 5mm from the stitching.

6 Draw the second design on the middle layer. You can machine around this as in Step 3 if you wish, but I haven't on this sample.

7 Separate the layers and make a snip in the middle fabric within the marked area.

8 Cut away the middle fabric as required.

Hand-sewn reverse appliqué

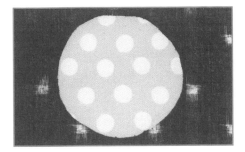

In this version, the raw edge of the cut out is turned under and sewn by hand. More layers can be included and the layers cut and sewn in turn.

1 Layer two pieces of fabric, with them both right side up.

2 Tack the layers together.

3 Draw the design on the top fabric.

4 Pinch and separate the layers within the marked area, making sure you are holding only the top layer.

5 Cut a small snip in the top layer.

6 With small scissors and great care, cut away most of the top layer of fabric within the marked area. Cut to about 3mm from the marked line.

7 Fasten the thread on the back, then sew the edge with tiny slip stitches (page 29), folding the seam allowance under as you go.

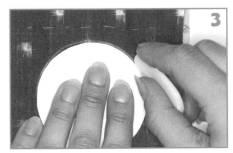

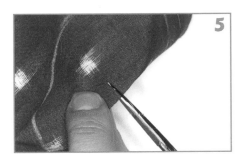

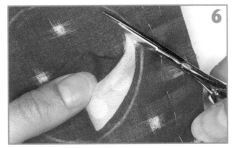

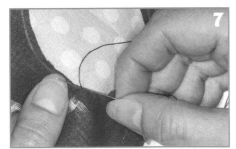

Sew different

This technique is very effective if you use lots of layers of fine fabrics and alternate which areas you cut away and sew down. You can also use decorative stitches to sew down the raw edges.

Free machine embroidery

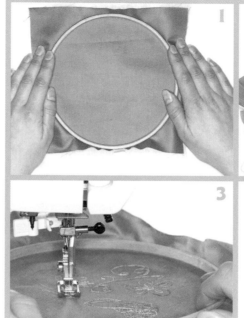

Free machine embroidery enables you to create your own designs on fabric using an ordinary sewing machine. The design is created freehand, although you can draw guidelines onto the fabric first. To support the fabric, you will need to use a stabiliser behind it. Tear-off stabiliser is designed for machine embroidery. If you are using a fine fabric, try a wash-out stabiliser that will disappear completely.

The easiest way to learn free machine embroidery is with the fabric in a hoop. You hold on to the hoop and move it, and the fabric, around under the needle. Without the hoop it can be hard to move the fabric sufficiently, unless the fabric is very firm.

You will need to drop the feed dogs (page 13) on the machine. Check the manual to find out how to do this. Most new machines have a switch, but some older machines may have a metal plate that you fit over the feed dogs.

Use an embroidery or darning foot and use machine embroidery thread in the top of the machine. A co-ordinating sewing thread will be fine in the bobbin.

1 Place the stabiliser underneath the fabric and put it all in an embroidery hoop.

2 Position the hoop under the presser foot. If the hoop won't go under the presser foot, then remove the foot, put the hoop in place, then replace the presser foot.

3 Set the stitch length and width to 0; moving the fabric under the needle creates the stitches. The further you move it, the bigger the stitches will be. Put the presser foot down. Start with the machine running slowly and move the hoop around to create lines and swirls. Follow a drawn design if you prefer. You will be able to speed up as you get more practice.

Patchwork masterclass

Like quilting, patchwork can seem rather difficult; there are endless variations and versions and many specialists doing intricate and complicated things. This masterclass shows a simple way of exploring machine-sewn patchwork, where small sections are made then joined together. This technique is used on the Patchwork Needlebook (page 211).

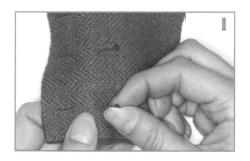

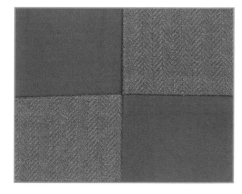

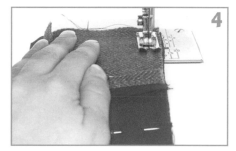

1 Work out the design and cut out scraps of fabric to test the layout. Cut out the pieces with 1cm seam allowances. Place the first two pieces right sides together, matching the raw edges.

2 Sew the two pieces together using 1cm seam allowances.

3 Debate rages in the patchworking community about whether it is better to press seam allowances open or to one side. It will depend on what you are using the patchwork for. If you want to quilt the finished patchwork, then press the seam allowances to one side, as this will be stronger, and allows you to machine quilt along the sewn patchwork lines. If you are making something else from the patchwork, like the Patchwork Needlebook (page 211), a scarf or a cushion cover, I recommend pressing the seam allowances open so the finished fabric is as flat as possible.

4 The easiest way to create a large piece is to make strips by joining one piece to the next and so on in a long row, then join the rows together along the long edges.

Sew different

Try the inset corner technique (page 51) to include an L-shaped piece in your patchwork design.

Sew simple

If the fabrics you are joining are bulky and the seams are lumpy, follow the instructions for intersecting seams (page 43) to achieve a flatter result.

Embroidery

Simple embroidery stitches are useful for all sorts of projects, from customising clothes to embellishing appliqué. I prefer to keep it simple by using pretty fabric, good-quality thread and patterns created from groups and lines of stitches.

    The key to good embroidery is getting the stitches even. If you are learning, use a fabric on which you can see the woven threads – medium to heavy linen is ideal. Then all you have to do is make each stitch cover the same number of threads as the previous one. I've used wool tweed for these samples because it contrasts well with the shiny perlé thread, but even-weave linen might be easier to start with.

    Use an embroidery needle, as they have blunter tips and larger eyes than normal sewing needles. Some people like to work with the fabric stretched in an embroidery hoop. I don't find this works for me on small areas of embroidery, but experiment and find out if it is easier for you.

Chain stitch

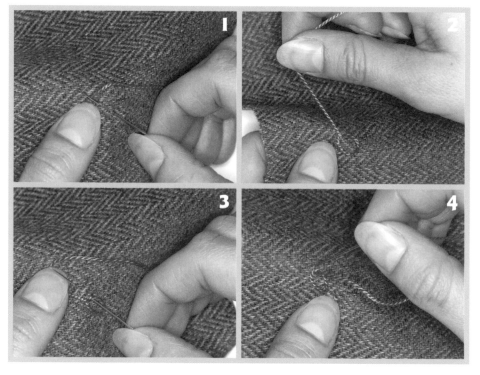

Chain stitch is a very effective stitch for lines and circles.

1 Bring the thread through to the front, make a loop with the thread and hold it with your left thumb. Insert the needle close to where it came out and come out again a small distance away. Make sure the looped thread is under the tip of the needle.

2 Pull the thread up gently.

3 Repeat, putting the needle into the edge of the loop to stretch the leg.

4 To finish, stitch over the top of the last loop of chain stitch.

Ladder stitch

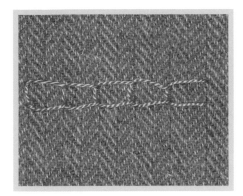

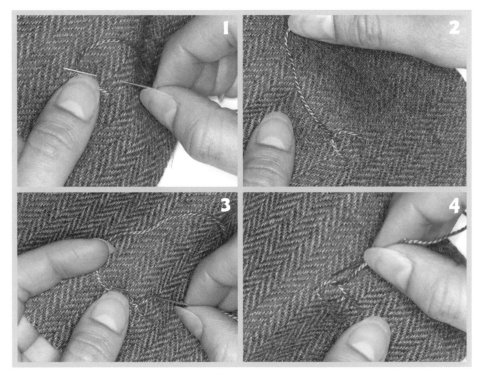

Ladder stitch is made in the same way as chain stitch, just wider.

1 Bring the thread through to the front, make a loop and hold it with your left thumb. Insert the needle a small distance to the right of where it came out and come out again a small distance up and diagonally to the left.

2 Pull the thread up gently.

3 Repeat, putting the needle into the edge of the loop to stretch the leg.

4 To finish, stitch over both corners of the top of the last loop.

Seed stitch

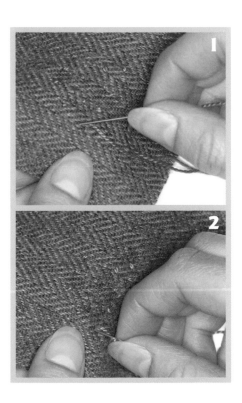

Seed stitches are randomly-placed short stitches. They are used as a filling stitch to cover a small area in a decorative pattern. The key is to make the stitches fairly even and not pull them up too tight.

1 Bring the needle to the front then make a small stitch in any direction.

2 The needle should come out where you want the next stitch to be.

Blanket stitch

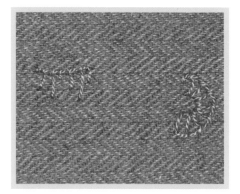

Blanket stitch can be worked in the round or with legs of different lengths, as well as for an edging (page 30). At the end of a row, catch down the last loop in the same way as Step 4 of chain stitch (page 196).

1 Bring the needle out of the fabric and make a loop and hold it with your left thumb. Put the needle in diagonally below where the thread came out, and back out again in line with where it came out.

2 Pull up the stitch and continue in this way.

French knot

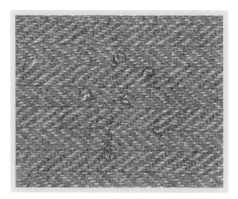

French knots are pretty stitches that are great for filling, like seed stitch (page 197), and can also be worked in lines. They are fiddly to make and take practice. Use a thick thread and whatever you do, don't pull too hard! French knots are quite delicate, so don't use them on something that will get a lot of wear.

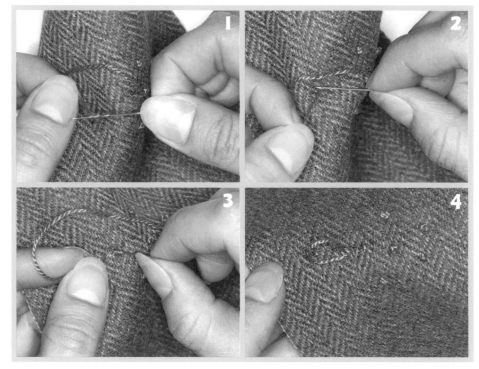

1 Hold the thread taut and twist the point of the needle around it three times.

2 Keeping the thread taut, pull the needle back slightly so the wraps slide down.

3 Insert the needle back into the fabric right next to where it came out.

4 Gently pull the needle through until the wrapped threads are held on the surface.

Couching

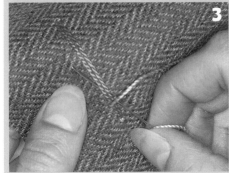

Couching uses two threads: the first is laid on the surface of the fabric, while a contrasting one is used to stitch it down. This is very useful for thick or metallic threads that won't easily stitch through the fabric. You can couch a single thread or, as here, a double thread.

1 For neat ends, bring the thread to be couched up on the right side of the fabric and then down again at the end of the line. If using a thick thread, poke a hole between the fabric threads to make space for it.

2 Bring the couching thread up at one side of the flat thread and make a stitch straight over the top of it.

3 Bring the needle out diagonally under the flat threads ready to make another stitch.

Cross stitch

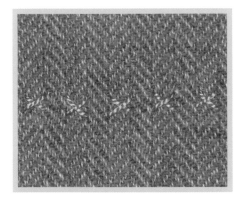

These cute stitches are very easy, but you really need a fabric with obvious threads to make sure you get them even, or draw lines to follow.

1 Bring the needle out at top left.

2 Stitch to bottom right, then bring the needle out at bottom left.

3 Finally, stitch to the top right corner.

Pom-pom blanket

I love the cosy feel of wool blankets, but they can be too scratchy against the skin. I solved this problem by backing a blanket with cotton fabric and using a small amount of special fabric to make the edge binding. All these pom-poms will take a while to make, but they aren't difficult.

You will need

Wool blanket – this one fits a double bed
Scissors
Tape measure
A piece of fabric for the backing, the same size as the blanket. I used two second-hand curtains joined together. A sheet or cut-up duvet cover would also work.
Safety pins
½m of patterned fabric for the binding
Iron
Pins
Sewing machine
Sewing thread to match patterned fabric
Two balls of DK or Aran multi-coloured knitting yarn for the pom-poms
Pom-pom maker or cardboard circles
Embroidery thread
Large-eyed, sharp-pointed embroidery needle

Techniques

Single-fold binding, page 75
Tearing, page 21
Mitred corner, page 78
Sewing a seam, page 36
Pom-poms, page 161

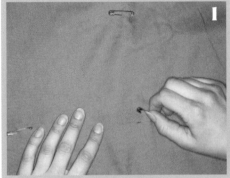

1 If the blanket has an edging, cut it off. Cut a piece of backing fabric the same size as the blanket. Lay the blanket flat face down on the floor. Lay the backing fabric face up on top of it. Starting at the centre, safety pin the backing fabric to the blanket, being careful to keep the fabric smooth and flat.

2 Make the binding strips. Work out the amount you need by adding up the length and width of the blanket and doubling it. This will give you the length of strip you need to make an edging all the way around. You will have to add seam allowances and some extra for turning the corners to this length. Cut the patterned fabric into 6cm strips across the width. Depending on the fabric, you may be able to tear it. Join all the strips together to make a continuous strip long enough to go around the blanket, and leave plenty to overlap at the ends: don't trim it to length until you have bound the whole blanket. Press a 1cm fold on one long side of the binding strip.

3 Attach the binding to the blanket, stitching through the patterned fabric and blanket and so holding them together around the edges. Remove any safety pins that are in the way and mitre the corners neatly.

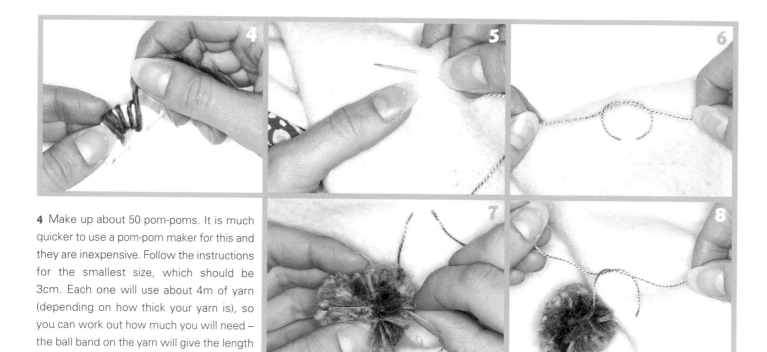

4 Make up about 50 pom-poms. It is much quicker to use a pom-pom maker for this and they are inexpensive. Follow the instructions for the smallest size, which should be 3cm. Each one will use about 4m of yarn (depending on how thick your yarn is), so you can work out how much you will need – the ball band on the yarn will give the length in the ball.

5 From the blanket side, make large single quilting stitches about 15–20cm apart to join the blanket and backing fabric together. Using the embroidery thread and sharp needle, go through all the layers and make a stitch about 5mm long.

6 Tie the ends of thread in a firm double knot and trim the tails to about 1cm long. Remove the safety pins as you make the quilting stitches.

7 Attach a pom-pom to some of the quilting stitches, spacing them regularly over the blanket. Make the stitch as before, leaving a long tail, and thread the needle through the yarn tied around the middle of the pom-pom.

8 Push the pom-pom down to the surface of the blanket then remove the needle and firmly tie the ends of the embroidery thread together to hold the pom-pom in place. Trim the ends to about 1cm long.

Sew different

You could make this project with a patterned blanket, fleece throw or large piece of fabric. If you use bought fabric, like wool or fleece, you will need to join two lengths together to make a piece wide enough for a double bed.

Pleated corsage

I love making corsages, they look fabulous and are a great way of using small pieces of precious fabric. You could attach the corsage to a headband or hair clip instead of sewing on a safety pin.

You will need

60cm strip of 4-cm wide bias strip (or two shorter pieces joined)
Sewing machine
Sewing thread to match fabric
Hand-sewing needle
Two 4cm circles of felt
2.5cm button
Small safety pin
Scissors

Techniques

Bias strip, page 68
Sewing a seam, page 36
Narrow knife pleat, page 133
Single or double thread, page 26
Hand-sewn ruffle, page 131
Slip stitch, page 29

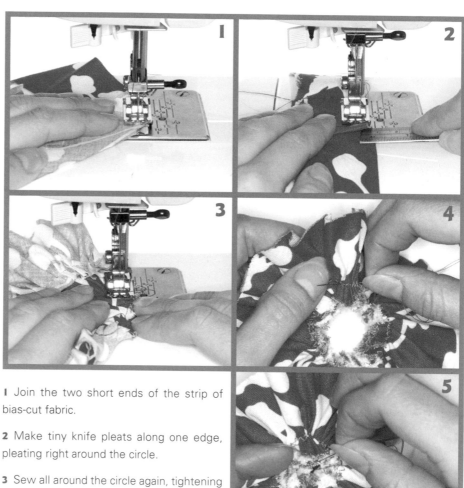

1 Join the two short ends of the strip of bias-cut fabric.

2 Make tiny knife pleats along one edge, pleating right around the circle.

3 Sew all around the circle again, tightening up the pleats as you go along, squashing them closer together.

4 With a double thread, work big running stitches along the pleated edge and gather the circle up even tighter so the centre hole almost disappears. Knot the thread firmly.

5 Sew the ruffled fabric to one of the felt discs, stitching over the edge of the fabric and down through the central hole.

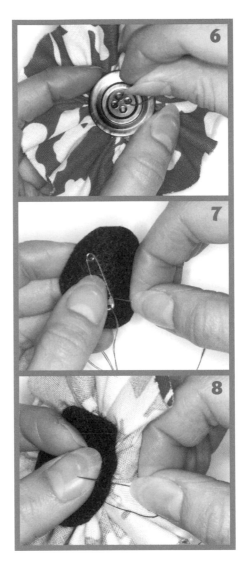

6 Place the button over the hole and, using double thread, sew it onto the felt disc.

7 Sew the safety pin onto the other felt disc, about two-thirds of the way up. Make sure the safety pin is the right way around so you can open it!

8 Place the disc with the safety pin against the back of the corsage, and slip stitch the two discs together around the edges.

Silk cuff

Peacock blue and scarlet is one of my favourite colour combinations, reminiscent of jungle birds. You could make this cuff in something more subtle, but bear in mind that the puffs look best in a plain fabric. A small print pattern would be good for the contrast centres.

You will need

Main fabric – I used silk dupion, which is just the right stiffness for this project. If you want to use a fabric that is very thin and floppy, back one of the main cuff pieces with interfacing or an alternative. Make sure this is the underside when you sew the cuff up.

Fusible webbing

Pencil

Compasses

Scissors

Scraps of contrasting fabric

Iron

Ironing board

Hand-sewing needle

Sewing thread to match main fabric

Sewing machine

Two small buttons

Techniques

Suffolk puff, page 168

Sewing a seam, page 36

Turning a corner, page 49

Outward corners and points, page 50

Iron-on interfacing, page 255

Pressing and steaming, page 23

Top stitch, page 38

Machine buttonhole, page 92

Button with a thread shank, page 98

Slip stitch, page 29

Cutting list

Two 22 x 10cm pieces of main fabric for the cuff

One 16cm diameter, one 13cm diameter, one 11cm diameter and two 9cm diameter circles of main fabric

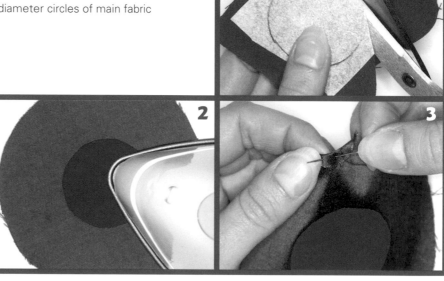

1 For the contrast insides, draw one 7.5cm diameter, one 6cm diameter, one 5.5cm diameter and two 4cm diameter circles onto the paper side of the fusible webbing. Make sure you leave a 1cm gap between circles. Write the size of each in the middle of the circle so you don't get them confused. Cut out the circles roughly, leaving at least 1cm around each. Following the manufacturer's instructions, iron the fusible webbing onto the reverse side of the contrast fabric and cut out the circles neatly.

2 On an ironing board, lay out the main fabric circles with the wrong side facing up. Peel the backing paper off the 7.5cm contrast circle and lay it in the centre of the 16cm main fabric circle. Iron it in position. Repeat with the other circles, matching the 13cm main fabric circle with the 6cm contrast circle, the 11cm main fabric circle with the 5.5cm contrast circle and the two 4cm contrast circles with the 9cm main fabric circles.

3 Make the circles into Suffolk puffs.

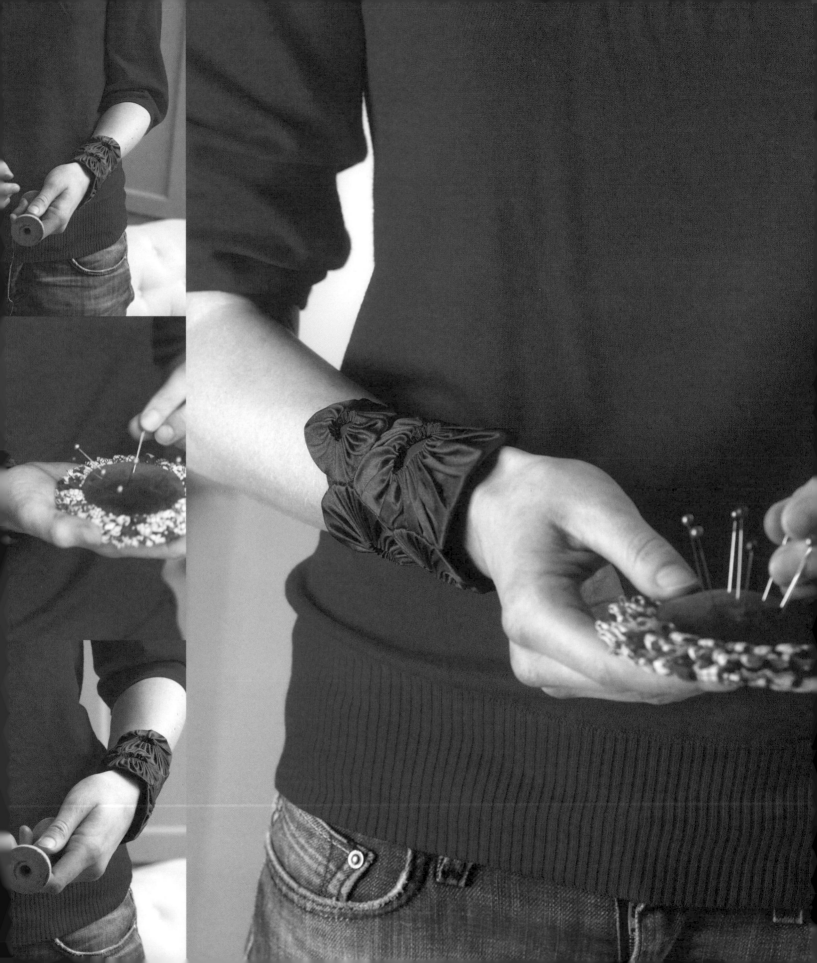

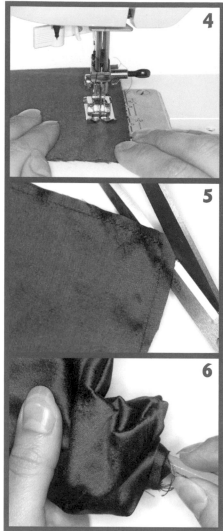

4 With the right sides together, sew the two rectangles of main fabric together around the edges, using interfacing if required. Use a 1cm seam allowance and leave a 4cm gap in one long side.

5 Trim the seam allowances to 5mm and clip the corners.

6 Turn the cuff the right way out through the gap in the side. Use a knitting needle to push out the corners.

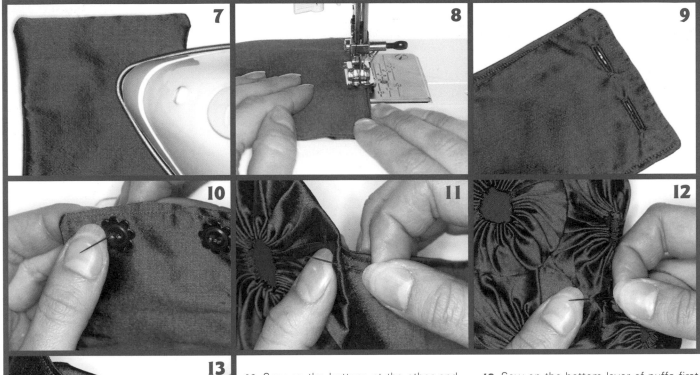

7 Press the cuff flat, making sure the seam allowances of the opening are turned to the inside.

8 Top stitch all around the cuff, 5mm from the edge. If you have used interfacing, make sure the interfaced piece is the underside of the cuff.

9 At one short end make two buttonholes suitable for your buttons, about 1cm in from the end.

10 Sew on the buttons at the other end, adjusting their placement so the cuff fits comfortably around your wrist.

11 Arrange the Suffolk puffs in a pleasing design on the cuff, leaving space around the buttons and buttonholes. The puffs can overlap the edges of the cuff and each other. Pin the puffs in position. Using a tiny slip stitch and matching thread, sew the puffs to the cuff. Catch only the top layer of cuff fabric, so the stitches don't show on the underside. Fasten off the threads with a tiny knot somewhere unobtrusive.

12 Sew on the bottom layer of puffs first, then any that overlap them. Slip stitch the puffs to themselves, catching the fabric of the bottom layer of puffs only.

13 Where a puff overlaps an edge, slip stitch along the edge of the cuff catching the back of the puff to hold it in place.

Patchwork needlebook

Use simple patchwork and quilting techniques to make the most of tiny scraps of favourite fabrics and create a needlebook to store your needles stylishly and safely.

You will need

Scraps of patterned fabric
Thin quilt wadding, such as organic cotton
Print fabric
Pins
Sewing machine
Sewing threads
Iron
Scissors
Hand-sewing needle
1m of bias binding
Felt, either purchased or made from
    recycled knitwear

Cutting list

Scraps of fabric at least 15cm in one
    direction, in three designs
15 x 23cm of print fabric
15 x 23cm of thin quilt wadding
Two or three pieces of felt for the inside
    pages, measuring approximately
    11 x 19cm, 10.5 x 18.5cm and
    10 x 18cm.
    Cut the edges with pinking shears or
    a scalloped rotary cutter

Techniques

Patchwork, page 195
Pinked, page 36
Pressing and steaming, page 23
Machine quilting, page 184
Continuous bias strip, page 70
Making bias binding, page 72
Single-fold binding, page 75
Mitred corner, page 78
Slip stitch, page 29

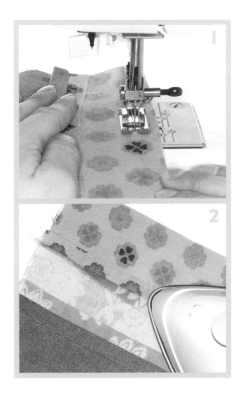

1 Make a patchwork for the needlebook cover. Using a 1cm seam allowance, join the scraps along their long sides in whatever arrangement you prefer, with the largest piece in the middle. The finished patchwork fabric needs to measure 15 x 23cm.

2 Press the seam allowances open.

3 Make the quilt sandwich: place the patchwork piece face down, place the quilt wadding on top and the inside fabric face up. Pin together.

4 Quilt the fabric in straight lines 3cm apart along the width of the piece.

5 Trim the edges to make a piece measuring 14 x 22cm.

6 Sew one edge of the bias binding to the quilted side of the needlebook. Mitre the corners neatly.

7 Fold the binding over the edge of the quilt sandwich and slip stitch the other edge, just catching the lining fabric.

8 Lay the felt 'pages' centrally in place on the inside of the needlebook and pin in place. Sew down the centre of the needlebook to sew the pages in position. Make sure the bobbin thread matches the middle fabric on the outside of the book, and the top thread matches the colour of the innermost felt page.

Pinstripe pincushion

What could be more appropriate for pins than pinstripe? This fabric is called pinstripe because the lines are the width of pins. It is perfect for showing off glass-headed pins and is suitably non-girlie for those who don't go in for pretty-pretty sewing kit.

I used scraps of wool suiting – an old suit will yield enough fabric for loads of pincushions: you could scale the design up and make a cushion with the rest. The ribbon for the edging needs to be a lightweight floppy one, not modern stiff polyester satin. I used a roll of vintage silk ribbon, but you can buy new silk ribbon and other fine ribbons at specialist shops (see page 302).

You will need

Pinstriped fabric
Pins
Sewing machine
Sewing thread
Iron
7m of 1-cm wide silk ribbon
Scissors
Wool or other stuffing
Hand-sewing needle

Cutting list

16cm x 13cm piece of pinstriped fabric
    for the front
Two 10cm x 13cm pieces of pinstriped
    fabric for the back, with the stripes
    running in opposite directions

Techniques

Right sides together, page 247
Sewing a seam, page 36
Pressing and steaming, page 23
In-seam trim, page 153
Turning a corner, page 49
Slip stitch, page 29

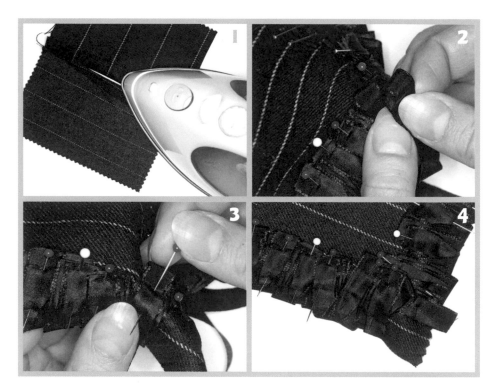

1 Right sides together, pin the two back pieces along the long edges. Using a 1cm seam allowance, sew 4cm in from each edge, leaving a gap of 5cm in the middle of the seam. Press the seam allowance open.

2 Cut the ribbon into 1m lengths to make it easier to work with. Holding the ribbon against the edge of the front piece of fabric with your thumb, make three or four loops of ribbon, each slightly different lengths, on top of each other.

3 Pin the loops to the fabric, with the pin heads towards the centre of the fabric.

4 Pin each set of loops in place before you move on to the next. Leave 1cm on each edge free at the corners.

5 Lay the be-ribboned panel face up. Place the back panel on top of it, face down with the opened seam allowance facing up. Pin the two pieces together around the edges. Using a 1cm seam allowance, sew around the edges, turning the corners and being careful of the pins holding the ribbons in place. Remove the pins holding the two fabric pieces together.

6 Carefully put your fingers through the gap in the back of the pincushion and remove the ribbon pins. Turn the whole pincushion right side out, watching out for any stray pins. Turn the corners out with a knitting needle or pencil.

7 Stuff the pincushion firmly with wool or other stuffing, making sure the corners are well-stuffed.

8 Slip stitch the opening closed.

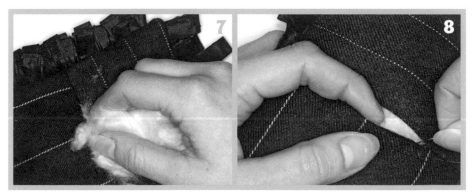

You will need

For four placemats:

½m of patchwork cotton for main fabric
½m of patchwork cotton for backing fabric
Lightweight washable wadding, such as
    organic cotton quilt wadding
Scissors
Tape measure
Sewing machine
Sewing thread
Hand-sewing needle
Knitting needle
Quilting thread

Cutting list

Pre-wash all fabrics including wadding
    (unless marked as non-shrink)
Four 25 x 35cm pieces of main fabric
Four 25 x 35cm pieces of backing fabric
Four 25 x 35cm pieces of wadding

Techniques

Sewing a seam, page 36
Turning a corner, page 49
Pressing and steaming, page 23
Slip stitch, page 29
Hand quilting, page 182

Sew different

If you are using a fairly large-scale print,
as here, a different area of the design will
be on each mat. Quilting these different
areas of pattern will make each mat unique.

Quilted placemats

I couldn't resist this lovely summery fabric with its retro print. These placemats should probably be saved for best, because they will need hand-washing unless you choose to quilt them by machine rather than by hand.

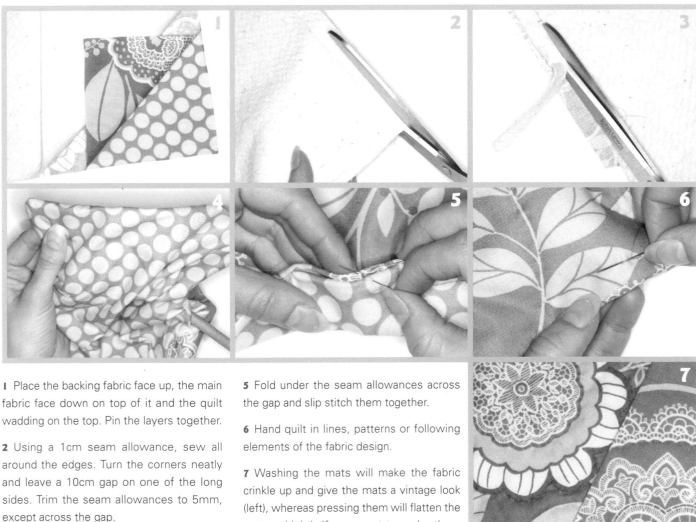

1 Place the backing fabric face up, the main fabric face down on top of it and the quilt wadding on the top. Pin the layers together.

2 Using a 1cm seam allowance, sew all around the edges. Turn the corners neatly and leave a 10cm gap on one of the long sides. Trim the seam allowances to 5mm, except across the gap.

3 Trim the wadding away from the gap but leave the fabrics.

4 Turn the mat the right way around and poke out the corners with a knitting needle. Press the mat lightly.

5 Fold under the seam allowances across the gap and slip stitch them together.

6 Hand quilt in lines, patterns or following elements of the fabric design.

7 Washing the mats will make the fabric crinkle up and give the mats a vintage look (left), whereas pressing them will flatten the pattern (right). If you want to make them even more quilt-like, don't pre-wash the fabrics before making the mats and when you do wash them, they will come out all crinkly and soft.

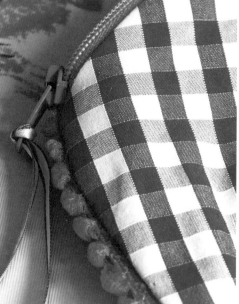

You will need

Pattern on page 296

Two pieces of fabric 25 x 20cm

Scissors

Vanishing fabric marker

Pins

Tacking thread

Hand-sewing needle

½m of trim

12cm zip

Sewing machine

Sewing thread to match fabric

Scrap of narrow ribbon

Techniques

Sewing on the bias, page 250

Tacking stitch, page 27

In-seam trim, page 153

Purse zip, page 91

Bias seams, page 47

Zigzagging allowances together, page 37

Gingham purse

Purses are a great way to use up scraps of fabric. This purse is made from the sleeves of a shirt I recycled and teamed with vintage trimming.

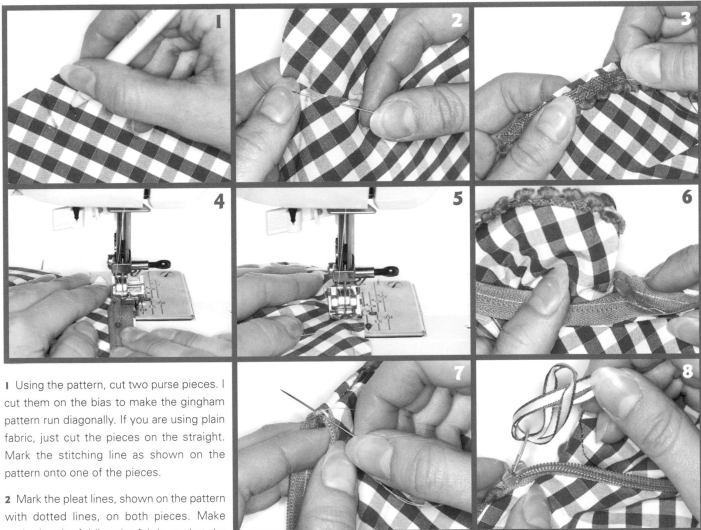

1 Using the pattern, cut two purse pieces. I cut them on the bias to make the gingham pattern run diagonally. If you are using plain fabric, just cut the pieces on the straight. Mark the stitching line as shown on the pattern onto one of the pieces.

2 Mark the pleat lines, shown on the pattern with dotted lines, on both pieces. Make each pleat by folding the fabric so that the marks meet and tack the pleats in place.

3 On the piece with the stitching line marked, pin then tack the middle of the trim to the stitching line. If the trim has one fancy edge, make sure that this points inwards.

4 Sew in the zip. Open the zip halfway.

5 Pin the purse pieces right sides together and sew all around them and over the ends of the zip, making sure they are folded in half.

6 Remove the tacking thread and turn the purse the right way out. You could zigzag the raw edges if your fabric frays a lot.

7 Tidy up the ends of the zip with a few stitches if required. Press the purse.

8 Add a zip pull made from a small loop of narrow ribbon.

Gathered scarf

I love pleats and gathers with a passion and came up with this design after making miles of pleats for an 18th-century-style jacket. This is a pretty simple and very effective use of small gathers.

You will need

Front fabric
Back fabric
Scissors
Sewing machine
Sewing thread to match fabric
Hand-sewing needles
Tape measure
Ruler
Vanishing fabric marker

Cutting list

2m x 30cm of front fabric
2m x 30cm of back fabric
You can join smaller pieces of either of the fabrics together to get a 2-m long piece. I used a silk dupion for the top fabric and a printed chiffon for the backing. One of the fabrics should be reasonably stiff and the other soft, or both medium-weight. Do not use something transparent for this project as the seams will show through.

Techniques

Sewing a seam, page 36
Turning a corner, page 49
Outward corners and points, page 50
Trimming seam allowances, page 38
Slip stitch, page 29
Single or double thread, page 26
Starting and stopping, page 27
Straight row gathering, page 166

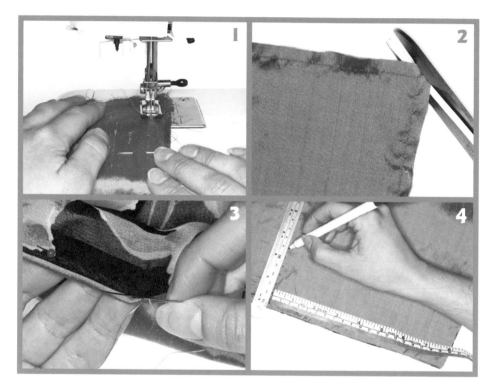

1 With the right sides together, pin the pieces and sew around the edges. Turn the corners neatly and leave a 15cm gap at the middle of one long seam.

2 Trim all the seam allowances and clip the corners.

3 Turn the scarf right side out, press the seams flat and turn under the seam allowances across the gap. Slip stitch the opening closed.

4 With a vanishing marker pen, mark a row of dots 1cm apart right across each end of the scarf, 20cm from the end and starting right by the edge. Mark another row 2cm above the first row.

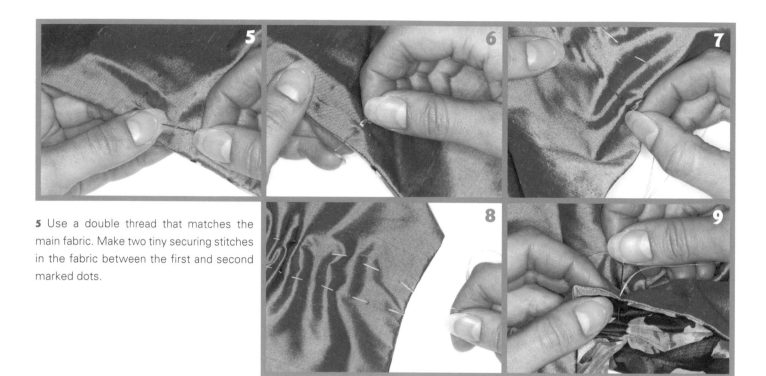

5 Use a double thread that matches the main fabric. Make two tiny securing stitches in the fabric between the first and second marked dots.

6 Take the needle between the two layers of fabric and come out at the first dot.

7 Use a large running stitch to go in and out of all the dots, ending on the front side of the scarf close to the edge. Do not pull up the stitches or cut the needle off the thread. Repeat on the second row of dots with another needle and thread.

8 Pull up both sets of threads to gather up the fabric.

9 Take the first needle back though the fabric a couple of millimetres away from where it came out and pull the gathers tight. Make three small securing stitches buried in the valley of the gathers. Repeat with the other needle and thread. Repeat Steps 5–9 at the other end of the scarf.

Sew different

You could try using different gathering techniques to create the ends of this scarf. Random Gathers (page 167) would be very effective. You could also try using Direct Smocking (page 174) by marking dots to follow and sewing through both layers.

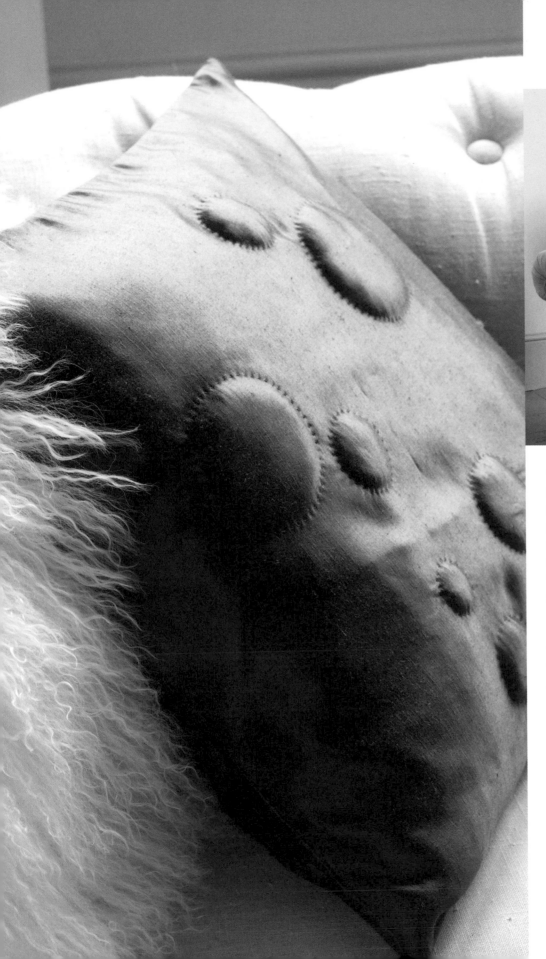

You will need

Main fabric

Backing fabric

Pencil

Cotton reels, bottles and jars

Hand-sewing needle

Tacking thread

Sewing thread

Iron

Small, sharp scissors

Wool or kapok stuffing

Tweezers

40cm square cushion pad

40cm zip

Sewing machine

Trapunto cushion

Trapunto quilting is one of my favourite techniques. I love the bumpy, raised surface you get, which is wonderfully tactile. This technique works best on fabrics with a bit of sheen.

Cutting list

43cm square of plain cotton sheeting or other similar backing fabric. If the main fabric is pale, make sure the backing fabric doesn't have a pattern or colour that shows through.

43cm square of fabric for the front. Medium-weight satin or silk works well for this. I used organic hemp silk.

Two 43 x 23cm pieces of matching or contrasting fabric for the back.

Techniques

Tacking stitch, page 27
Trapunto, page 186
Pressing and steaming, page 23
Back zip cushion, page 240

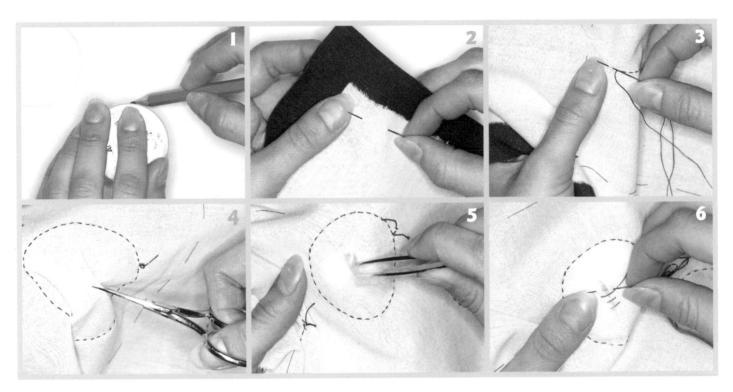

1 Using the pencil, draw circles in a design on the backing fabric, drawing around cotton reels, bottles and jars to get a variety of sizes of circle. Don't draw tiny circles because they are hard to stuff.

2 Lay the front fabric face down with the backing fabric on top of it, facing up. Pin and tack the pieces together around the edges and in a cross through the middle to stop the layers shifting.

3 Using a thread that matches the front fabric, start the trapunto stitching. Start and end your thread in the backing layer only, just outside the circle. When you have sewn all of the design, remove the cross tacking threads and iron the whole piece from the front. This is the last chance you will have to iron it all, so make sure you do it perfectly.

4 Using the scissors, make a snip incision into the backing fabric inside a circle.

5 Stuff the circle lightly with the wool or kapok. You will find tweezers useful here.

6 Sew up the slit. Use either the technique that is shown in Step 10 of the trapunto masterclass, or just oversew the edges together. Make up the cushion backing with the zip and sew the front and back panels together. Remove the tacking stitches around the edges.

Using the Techniques

Curtains

Good curtains can do amazing things for a room. The colour and the softness will make a bare room warm and comfortable and they will change the look, the feel, the light and the temperature. There are some really stunning contemporary curtain fabrics around and making curtains really isn't difficult, so there is no need for ready-made basics.

If you have large windows then curtains can get very expensive, so look out for sale fabrics or consider taking apart old curtains and patching them back together to get the right size and shape. Vintage fabrics can also be used but as they will be more fragile, line them to protect them from the sun. Long-term exposure to sunlight damages fibres and will fade the colours. Bear this in mind if you want to use very special fabrics. Dressmaking fabrics can be used, but they are usually narrower so will need more piecing together. Try to avoid anything that might stretch or your curtains will develop an unattractive sag.

Measuring for curtains

The most important part of curtain-making is measuring correctly. If you don't have enough fabric the curtain will never work. First, put up the curtain pole or track so you know where to measure from. You need to work out the length and the width. In order to get a nicely gathered, full curtain you will need several widths of fabric. The number of widths will depend on the type of curtain tape you are using but it is usually two or three times the width of the window. Most curtain fabric is 150cm wide so you will need to join lengths to make it wide enough.

1 Starting with the length, measure from the top of the pole or track to where you want the hem to fall. For floor-length curtains, take 1cm from the measurement. This is the finished length.

2 Then work out the width. Measure the full length of the pole and divide by two if you are making a pair of curtains.

3 Multiply the length of the pole by the fullness required (usually two or three times the width).

4 Add seam and hem allowances of about 5cm to join the panels if required and 5cm to each side.

5 Divide this by the width of the curtain fabric (usually 150cm) and round up to the nearest half or quarter. This is the number of lengths you will need to piece together to make one curtain.

6 Then work out the length required. Take the finished length and add hem and heading allowances as required for the type of curtain (usually about 10cm for the top and 20cm for the hem). This is the panel length.

7 Multiply the panel length by the number of panels required for each curtain. This is the amount of fabric you need to buy. Add a little extra for safety's sake. If you want to match patterns, you will need to allow more (see opposite).

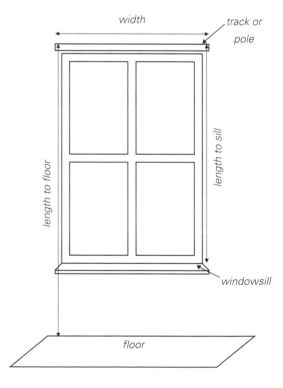

width

track or pole

length to sill

length to floor

windowsill

floor

Pattern matching

Before you buy the fabric, find out what the pattern repeat is. This is the distance between the start and end of each repeating motif of the design. If the pattern repeat is 20cm, then allow 20cm extra for each panel length.

If the pattern is very bold and you need to ensure that you position the same motif at the same level on several curtains, allow extra for that, too. Pattern matching is important for very obvious, bold motifs. If the pattern is small or very busy, then you don't need to worry. However, always make sure you join the panels the right way up!

To cut the panels with patterns matching, decide on the placement of the motif relative to the curtain pole and cut the first panel. Place the remaining fabric beside it and adjust to match the pattern and cut the second panel. Repeat and keep track of which bits match to what, and keep them the right way up. Some fabrics will show the pattern repeat marked on the selvedge (pages 16–17), which makes it very easy to match. Most printed or patterned fabrics will have an arrow in the selvedge to show which direction is the top. Make sure you keep this correct!

Sew simple

Floor length curtains look very elegant if there is lots of space around the window. The hem should be 1cm off the floor. Curtains that bunch up attractively on the floor are called puddle curtains. It's best to only try this with very soft, drapey fabrics. Sill-length curtains should just skim the windowsill. Make sure you measure very accurately for these, and test the almost-finished curtains before you hem them.

Curtain weights

Curtains can be weighted down with small lead buttons sewn into the hems. This helps to keep them hanging straight and keep the pleats in place. It also stops them flapping about too much in the breeze.

The buttons can be sewn straight on to the hems, but they might clatter on the wall or damage paintwork, so it is best to make small bags to contain them, and sew the bags to the outside of the hem allowance, under the lining if required. Cut two squares of fabric the diameter of the button plus 1.5cm seam allowances. Sew up three sides, then turn. Insert the button and either machine- or hand-sew the opening closed. Sew the bag onto the hem using small stitches through the corners.

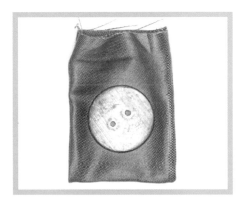

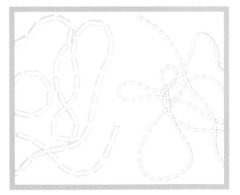

Tape weight (above) is like lead-shot in a fabric tube and should be fed through the curtain hem. Lightweight is best for sheer curtains, while heavier stuff will tame weighty curtains. Remove weights before you wash curtains.

Tapes

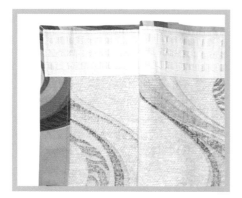

For standard tapes, measure the width of the finished curtain and allow 10cm extra of tape.

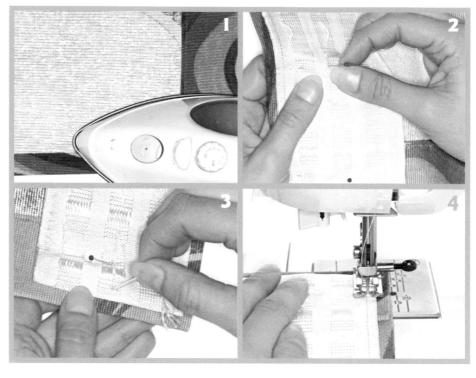

1 Make the side hems then turn over 2cm or more at the top edge, as required. Press the fold.

2 Position the tape so that it covers the raw top edge. Some tapes have a coloured line to show which is the top. Turn under about 5cm on one end and pin the tape in place across the curtain, making sure the tape is straight across the whole curtain.

3 At the other end, make sure the pull-up cords are pulled through to the front and turn under the end, as before.

4 Set up the machine with the bobbin thread matching the curtains and the top thread either the same or white.

Start by sewing from the bottom edge up across one folded end, pivot at the corner (page 49) and continue along the top of the tape and down the other folded end. Be sure not to catch the pull-up cords in the sewing. Go back to where you started sewing and sew along the bottom of the tape. Start and finish the sewing by pulling threads through to the back and knotting them (page 34).

Sew simple

When you have pulled up the cords to pleat up the curtains, don't cut off the cords. When you clean curtains, the pleats will need to be let out so the curtain is flat. Twist the cords around one another so that they form a neatly coiled rope. Either loop up the rope and use a safety pin to pin it to the side seam, or feed the rope through the cords at the back of the pleated heading.

Decorative pleating tapes

There are lots of different types of tape, some simple and plain, and some really fancy. Standard tape is available in various widths and creates neat pencil pleats when pulled up fully, and gently rippled gathers if not pulled so tight. With pencil pleats you will need at least two times the width, or one-and-a-half to two times the width for a gently gathered look.

Decorative tapes need a bit of practice – you will need to allow extra tape to ensure that the pleats are placed centrally and not too close to the edges of the curtain. Usually they come with instructions or you can find information on the manufacturer's website. The choice of tapes will depend on the curtain fabric. A fancy tape, like smocking tape, would be lost on a busy patterned fabric and very deep headings need to be balanced by long curtains. Most of the decorative tapes need two-and-a-half to three times width, so they are very fabric-hungry. The type of heading you use will also depend on the type of curtain rail or pole you have. Check in the shop or on the manufacturer's website.

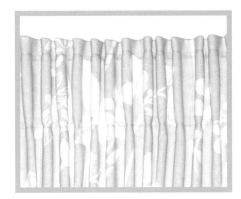

Pencil pleats using 8cm standard tape fully pulled up.

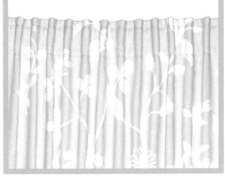

Gentle gathers using 4cm standard tape lightly pulled up.

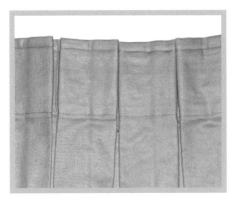

Box pleat tape.

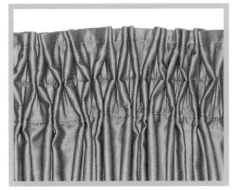

Smocking tape.

Tulip pleat tape, also used in Quick Curtains (page 262).

Making basic unlined curtains

Basic unlined curtains are fine for rooms where keeping out light isn't essential. Follow the steps for Quick Curtains (page 262).

A separate cotton lining can be added to these basic curtains or to ready-made ones if they have pull-up pleating tapes at the top (see opposite). Adding linings to other types of curtains can be more complicated.

Sew different

For very quick unlined curtains, you can finish the side hems with single hem (page 52) if the edge is a selvedge or double hem (page 52) if it is not. You could even use fusible webbing (page 56) if the curtain isn't going to be washed.

When you have to join panels to get sufficient width, use French seams (page 40) or mock-French seams (page 41) for a very hard wearing finish.

Lining fabrics are usually white or cream, but coloured cottons are available and look fantastic from the outside. Beware of the colour showing through light curtains during the day – it may cast a strange light if you close the curtains against the sun.

Making lined curtains

Linings give you more privacy, let in less light and help keep out the cold. Linings also protect the curtain fabric from mould caused by condensation and from fading caused by sunlight.

This is the easiest way to make lined curtains with cotton, blackout or thermal lining. Work out the fabric needed (page 228), but make the side hem allowance 10cm. Join panels if required.

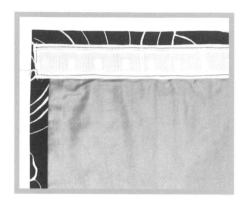

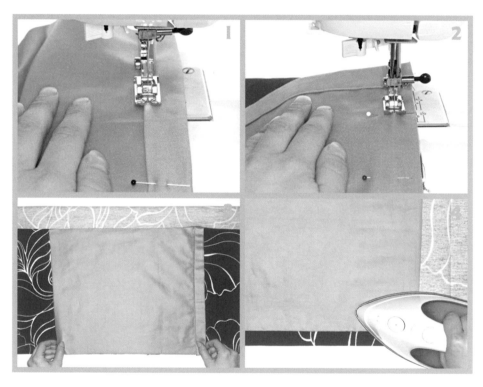

1 Cut the lining 20cm narrower than the finished curtain width and 8–10cm shorter. Make a double hem along the bottom edge (page 52).

2 Place the curtain fabric face up and place the lining with the hem side up along the right-hand side edge, 10cm down from the top. Pin and sew the seam (page 36) with a 1.5cm seam allowance. Start sewing at the top and finish the seam just before you reach the lining hem.

3 Pull the free lining edge over to the left edge of the curtain and again position the top of the lining 10cm down from the top edge. Sew the seam as before.

4 Turn the whole curtain the right way around and flatten it out. The narrower lining fabric will draw the curtain fabric edges around to the back of the curtain. Press the seams flat (page 23).

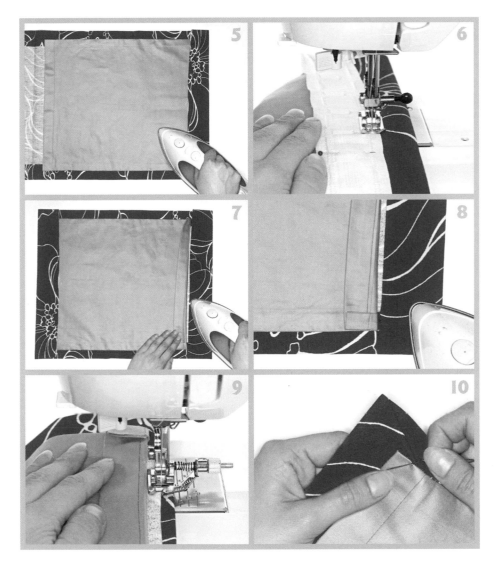

Removable linings for curtains with heading tape

Removable linings are preferable where you definitely have a damp or condensation problem, as they can be easily removed and machine-washed without having to have the whole curtain dry-cleaned. Remember to pre-wash the lining first though, or it will shrink when you machine-wash it.

1 Measure the curtain. You will need the length from the middle of the header tape to the top of the curtain hem, plus 10cm for the hem and 5cm for the heading. Work out how many widths you need, and add seam allowances for hems and joining (5cm at each side should do). Add about 5% to the total to allow for shrinkage. Machine-wash and iron the lining. Re-measure it and cut it into panels as required.

2 Follow the basic curtain making instructions for Quick Curtains (page 262), but use a single or a double hem (page 52) rather than a blind hem. Use narrow heading tape at the top.

3 Draw up the lining to the same width as the curtain and attach the lining to the hooks on the curtain tape, or a second set of hooks, depending on the type of hook used. Hang the lined curtain and allow it to settle for 24 hours, then pin the side seams of the curtain and lining together in a few places.

4 Take the curtains down and sew a few stitches to hold the lining and curtain together every 30cm or so down the length. Do the same along the hem so that doesn't flap about. Traditionally, bar tacks (page 32) were used to hold the lining and curtain hems together, so you can use those if you prefer, or try lock stitch (page 31).

5 Turn over the top hem so it just covers the raw edge of the lining fabric. Press the fold.

6 Sew on the curtain tape (page 230).

7 Hang the curtain and finalise the length. Mark this with pins. Make the bottom hem by folding over 2cm and pressing, then fold on the pinned line to make the full hem.

8 Turn under the corners of the hem so they will be hidden by the lining.

9 Fold the lining hem out of the way and make a hem on the curtain, using blind hemming (page 66) or another hemming technique (pages 52–67) as required.

10 Fold the lining back over the curtain hem and sew a couple of stitches at either side to hold the edge of the lining to the curtain.

Blackout and thermal linings

Specially treated linings are heavy and thick and won't drape well if sewn direct to pleating tape. These are best made as sewn-in linings (page 232). If you want, you can add a separate cotton lining for protection, added insulation and to give a nicer finish. Check the cleaning instructions for special linings as they might be different to the main curtain fabric.

Making sheer curtains

Plain cotton muslin, voile or patterned transparent fabrics can all be used to make sheer curtains. These thin fabrics don't work well with fancy decorative heading tapes so it is best to use standard narrow tape. For very sheer fabrics, you can buy a semi-transparent tape that will show less. Otherwise, allow extra fabric to make a deep double hem at the top, which will stop the tape showing through. Sheer curtains usually need two to three times width of fabric to window size.

Dyeing fabrics

Plain cotton muslin is cheap, readily available and can make great sheer curtains. Other plain cottons can also be dyed using purchased washing machine fabric dye. Make sure you weigh the fabric and get the right amount of dye, then follow the manufacturer's instructions carefully. Pre-wash the fabric before you dye it. You will need to dye all the fabric in one batch to make sure the colour matches – this won't work if you have huge curtains and more fabric than will fit in the washing machine.

Casings

Casings are a good way to hang curtains over a curtain pole. The technique is usually used for sheer fabrics and net curtains that won't be opened or for boats and caravans. Fabric two times the width of the window is probably enough.

Single casing

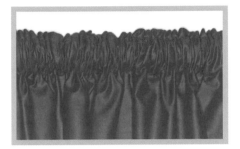

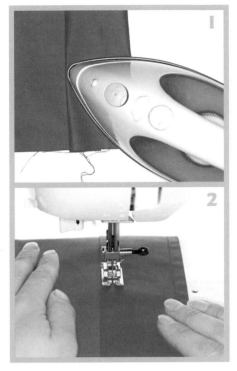

The size of the casing will depend on the curtain pole. Measure around the pole and add 1–2cm of ease, depending on the thickness of the fabric. This is the casing allowance. Add another 1cm for the hem allowance. Finish the side hems as desired.

1 At the top of the curtain, fold over the 1cm hem allowance to the back and then fold over the casing allowance.

2 Sew along the hem about 5–10mm from the edge and then top stitch (page 38) the same distance from the top fold. Hem the curtain as required (pages 52–67).

Double casing

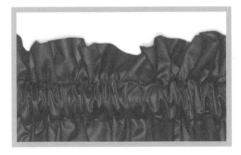

This version is much the same, but has a self-fabric frill above the rod. Work out the casing allowance as above, add a 1cm hem allowance and then add twice the required frill height. In this sample the casing allowance is 6cm and the finished frill is 4cm, so the frill allowance is 8cm, giving a total of 15cm. Finish the side hems as desired.

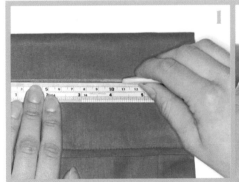

1 Fold over the hem allowance and then the casing allowance and half the frill allowance. Sew the hem, as above. Mark the frill line on the fabric.

2 Top stitch along the marked frill line.

3 Press the top edge of the frill. Hem the curtain as required (pages 52–67).

Tab-top curtains

Curtains with sewn loops are easy to make and don't require extra fullness of fabric as they hang flat. This makes them very economical in fabric. The number of tabs will depend on the weight of the fabric and the width of the tabs. Make a test tab and check the desired length and width, and make sure they will run smoothly along the curtain pole. Don't forget to allow for the seam allowances when you test the fit!

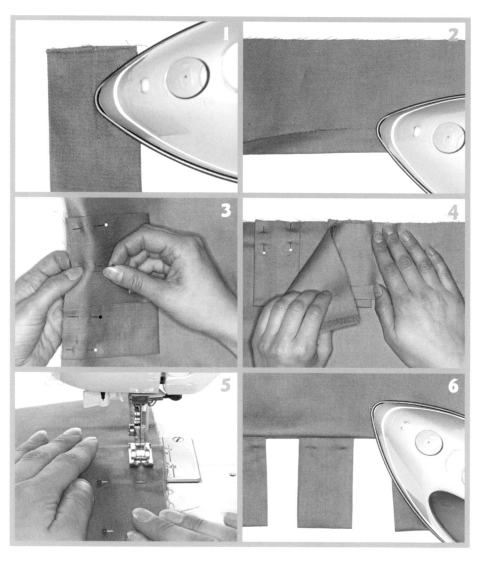

1 Finish the side hems as desired. Make the folded fabric tabs from the same or a contrasting fabric (page 83). To make lots of tabs, make a long tube and cut it into lengths. Press (page 23) the tabs in half widthwise, matching the raw ends.

2 Cut a facing for the top of the curtain. This is a strip of fabric the width of the curtain and 10cm deep. Press under one long edge.

3 Pin the tabs on to the front of the curtain, raw edges matching, making sure that they are spaced evenly and that there is a tab at each end.

4 Place the facing on top of the tabs, right side down and raw edges together, with the hem allowance facing up.

5 Sew along the top edge (page 36), catching in the tabs and using a 1.5cm seam allowance. Remove the pins.

6 Fold the facing to the back and press the top seam flat.

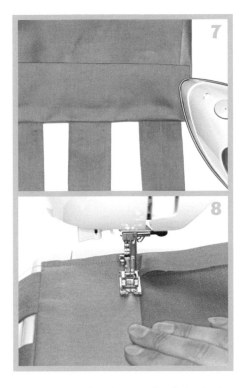

7 Fold under the short ends of the facing and press them.

8 From the back, sew down one short end of the facing, pivot at the corner (page 49) and sew along the bottom edge of the and up the other end, pivoting as before. Start and finish threads by pulling the threads through and knotting on the back (page 34).

Sew different

You could try making the tabs for tab top curtains from lengths of decorative ribbon, or from patterned fabric. You could also embellish the tabs with buttons or bows. As tab top curtains hang quite flat, you could decorate or embellish the hems with ribbon, applique, embroidery or even a border.

A note on curtain cleaning

Curtains usually need dry-cleaning, but there are ways of making curtains machine washable, either in your domestic machine or at the launderette if they are very big. Machine washing isn't normally advised because it can cause a fabric to shrink, but if you pre-wash the fabric then it will be ready-shrunk and shouldn't shrink any more, so you can make machine-washable curtains. They can be dried on the washing line and ironed. This isn't applicable to all fabrics, of course, and some weaves and finishes can be ruined by machine washing. So basically, if you want machine-washable curtains, use a fabric that will hold up to washing and test it first. Make sure you undo the cords in the heading tape (page 230) before you wash so the curtain is flat. Pre-wash (page 20) the lining fabric as well, unless you have separate linings.

Other household linen

Most household linen, such as sheets, duvet covers and pillowcases, is very easy to sew. Use a similar article you already have as a pattern and add seam allowances and extra for fastenings.

Making your own linen gives you the freedom to choose fabrics and mix and match to your heart's content. You can also add embroidery and other embellishments.

Extra-wide fabric called sheeting is available, which is wide enough to make king-size sheets and duvet covers. It is most commonly available in poly-cotton in quite a few colours. You may also find 100% cotton sheeting and organic cotton sheeting is now available, too. You can also buy white sheeting and dye it whatever colour you want (page 234).

I've used patchwork cotton to make up a stripy pillowcase for the project on page 268. Other cotton dressmaking fabrics would also work well, but bear in mind that they won't be wide enough for double sheets and duvet covers without putting a seam in the middle, which might be uncomfortable. Always pre-shrink the fabrics (page 20).

Tablecloths and napkins are also easy to make and are good canvases for embellishments and decorations, as long as they are washable. Napkins are just squares of fabric with narrow double hems (page 52) sewn on the machine, and tablecloths are much the same on a bigger scale. You could make a tablecloth and napkins to co-ordinate with the Quilted Placemats (page 216), or a set of coasters using the same technique.

Cushions

I love making cushions. They only need a small amount of fabric and are great canvases for decorative techniques or for showing off a small piece of special fabric. There are a few basic techniques that you can apply to all sorts of cushions.

Envelope back

This is my preferred method as it is quick, simple and above all, easy to get the cushion in and out.

Work out the fabric pieces:

For the front: measure the cushion pad and add 1.5cm seam allowances on all edges. So a 40 x 40cm finished cushion would need a 43 x 43cm piece of fabric for the front.

For the back (two pieces the same): the same height and half the width of the front, plus 10cm extra width on each. So the two back pieces for a 40cm cushion should each be 43cm x (half of 43cm + 10cm) 31.5cm. Round the figure up or down if necessary.

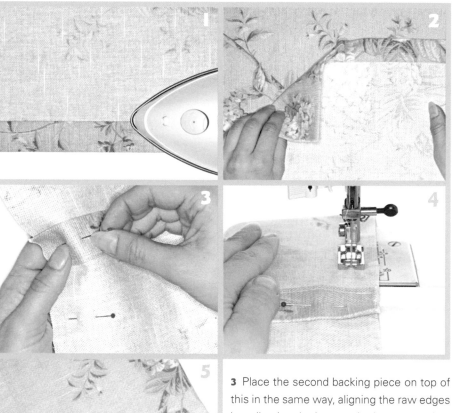

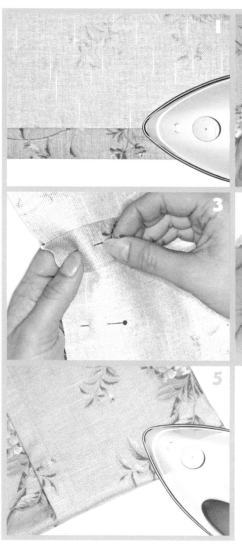

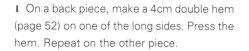

1 On a back piece, make a 4cm double hem (page 52) on one of the long sides. Press the hem. Repeat on the other piece.

2 Lay the cushion top face up. Place one back piece on top of it, right sides together and raw edges aligned. Pin in place.

3 Place the second backing piece on top of this in the same way, aligning the raw edges but allowing the hemmed edges to overlap. Pin in place.

4 Sew (page 36) around the whole cushion cover, using a 1.5cm seam allowance. Turn the corners neatly (page 49).

5 Remove the pins, turn out and press the edges (page 23). If required, finish the seams before turning out, using overcasting or zigzag stitch (page 37).

Box-edge cushion

This is a more fancy cushion with sides. It is suitable for chairs and can be filled with a foam square or a cushion pad. The cushion is made from front and back sections and a strip around the edge. One side of the strip has a zip inserted.

Work out the fabric pieces:

For the front and back: the size of the cushion, plus 1.5cm seam allowances on all sides. So, for a 30cm cushion, the front and back pieces will both be 33 x 33cm.

For the sides: The long strip needs to be the length of three sides of the finished cushion, plus two 1.5cm seam allowances. So, for a 30cm cushion this would be 30cm + 30cm + 30cm + (two 1.5cm seam allowances) 3cm = 93cm.

The height of the sides depends on the thickness of the cushion pad you are using. This sample has a finished height of 5cm. So the width of the strip needs to be the finished height plus two 1.5cm seam allowances, in this case 8cm.

The side with the zip needs to be made from two strips, each the finished length of the cushion plus 1.5cm seam allowances, so in this case it would be 30cm plus 3cm seam allowances. The width of the strips should be half the width of the long side strip, plus two extra seam allowances for where the zip is to be inserted. In this case the two strips are 33cm x (4cm + two 1.5cm seam allowances) 7cm.

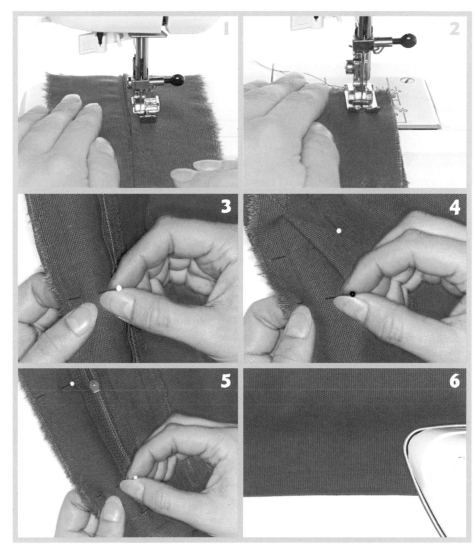

1 Insert the zip between the two appropriate side pieces following the inset zip instructions (page 88).

2 Join the zip panel to both ends of the long side strip, using 1.5cm seam allowances. Start and end the seams 1.5cm from the long edges.

3 Place the cushion back piece face up. With the strip inside out, and starting with the zip side, pin it to the cushion base. Continue working along the side seams, pinning them in place.

4 When you reach the corners, clip the seam allowance of the strip so it will turn the corner. Sew around the edges using a 1.5cm seam allowance and turning the corners (page 49).

5 Undo the zip halfway and pin the cushion front piece to the strip in the same way as the back piece, clipping the corners when you come to them. Sew as before.

6 Remove the pins, turn the cushion cover out and poke out the corners. Press (page 23) all the edges for a crisp finish.

Side zip cushion

A very simple cushion cover is just two squares of fabric with a zip set into one of the side seams.

Work out the fabric pieces:

For the front and back: the size of the cushion plus 1.5cm seam allowances on all sides. So for a 30cm cushion, the front and back pieces will both be 33 x 33cm.

Use a zip about 5cm shorter than the finished cushion size.

1 Insert an inset zip between the front and back panels (page 88).

2 Open the zip. Fold the cushion panels right sides together and sew (page 36) around the three remaining sides, using 1.5cm seam allowances and pivoting at the corners (page 49).

3 Remove the pins, turn out and press the edges (page 23). If required, finish the seams before turning out, using overcasting or zigzag stitch (page 37).

Back zip cushion

For a neater finish, the zip can be inserted into the back cover of the cushion.

Work out the fabric pieces:

For the front: the size of the cushion plus 1.5cm seam allowances on all sides. So, for a 30cm cushion, front will be 33 x 33cm.

For the back: two pieces the same height as the front and half the width, plus 1.5cm seam allowances on each piece. So the two back pieces will each be 33 x (half of 33cm + 1.5cm) 18cm.

Use a zip about 5cm shorter than the finished cushion size.

1 Insert an inset zip (page 88) between the two back pieces or use the lapped zip technique as shown here (page 86). For the lapped zip, allow 2cm seam allowances on the back pieces.

2 Lay the cushion front face up, place the back zip piece face down on top of it. Open the zip halfway and pin the pieces together around the edges.

3 Sew (page 36) around the edges, using a 1.5cm seam allowance and turning the corners neatly (page 49).

4 Remove the pins, turn out and press the edges (page 23). If required, finish the seams before turning out, using overcasting or zigzag stitch (page 37).

Oxford cushion

This type of cushion works best with a zip inset centrally in the back. Make a Back Zip Cushion (left), but make it 4–5cm bigger all around than the cushion pad. Choose a zip about 5cm shorter than the finished cushion size.

1 Make up the cushion cover as described for Back Zip Cushion, but don't zigzag the raw edges. Instead, trim the seam allowances to about 5mm.

2 Turn the cover out, push out the corners and press flat. On the front, mark a stitching line the desired distance from the edge: if the cover was 4cm bigger all around than the pad, the line will be 4cm from the edge.

3 Use a top stitch thread to sew neatly all around the marked line (page 38). Start and finish the sewing by reducing the stitch length (page 34).

Button cushion

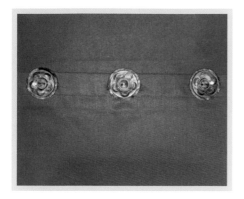

This can be an attractive fastening, especially if you use lovely buttons.

Work out the fabric pieces:

For the front: the size of the cushion plus 1.5cm seam allowances on all sides. So for a 30cm cushion, the front will be 33 x 33cm.

For the back: two pieces the same height as the front and half the width plus 6cm for the overlap and button placement. So the two back pieces would each be 33cm x (half of 33cm + 6cm) 22.5cm.

1 On each long edge of the back pieces, fold under 1.5cm then 3cm to make a double hem (page 52). Sew in place.

2 Work out the placement of the buttonholes in one hem and make them by hand (page 93) or by machine (page 92).

3 Place the cushion front face up, place the buttonholed piece face down on top of it, and the second back piece on top of that, also face down. The raw edges should align all around and the buttonhole area should overlap. Pin in place.

4 Sew (page 36) around the edges, using a 1.5cm seam allowance and turning the corners neatly (page 49).

5 Remove the pins, turn out and press the edges (page 23). If required, finish the seams before turning out, using overcasting or zigzag stitch (page 37).

6 Turn the cushion cover reverse side up. Use a pencil to mark through the centre of the buttonholes. Sew the buttons on in the marked positions (page 98).

Ribbon tie cushion

To fasten a cushion with ribbons or fabric tape, work out fabric pieces and follow the instructions for a Button Cushion (left), but sew lengths of ribbon to the hem allowance.

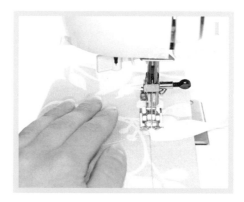

1 Fold under the raw end of the ribbon and pin in place. Sew a square across the folded end of the ribbon, making sure you don't catch the trailing ribbon.

2 Tie the ribbons together and pin the trailing ribbons down by the knots while you pin and sew the cushion together.

3 Place the cushion front face up, place the tied back piece face down on top of it. Make up the cover as for a Button Cushion.

Dressmaking

Making clothes is one of the most rewarding aspects of sewing, but it is fraught with danger. Bodies are complicated shapes to fit – all those in and out curves, moving parts and endless variations of length and girth!

Dressmaking takes practice. I've been making my own clothes for nearly 20 years and still make total disasters now and again. Tedious though it may seem, it is worth doing the preparation properly before you start. These are my most important ground rules for successful dressmaking.

• Know your real body measurements – not your shop dress size, but what you really are in centimetres or inches. Get a friend to measure you properly over the fullest part of your bust, around your real waist (narrowest bit if you have one, or around your belly button if you don't) and around your hips – the biggest bit of your bottom. These are the measurements you will need to buy patterns. There are lots more measurements you will need to make adjustments to the pattern (pages 248–249).

• Make sure the style suits you before you buy the pattern. Try things on in shops and make notes of what looks good in the mirror, or even take digital photos. Remember that the illustrations in the pattern books are of models, not real people. The outfit will not look the same on you as it does on her, unless you are built like a model. Don't waste time, effort and money on making clothes that you will never wear. Working out what fits properly and what really suits you isn't always easy. The style we love most may suit our body shape least. If you are unsure, look at one of the TV programme tie-in books about the right clothes for your body shape and try out some of their tips for your type of shape. See what works and ask for opinions from someone you trust. Alternatively you could try a personal shopper in a reputable shop and see what

they suggest. Another tip is to keep an eye out for women of your body shape who look fabulous and see what shape and style of garments they wear.

• Work out the measurements of garments in your own wardrobe that fit you well. Take measurements of the sleeve length, the back length, trouser leg-width and across the back of the shoulders. Use these as a basis for choosing or adapting patterns. If your favourite purchased trousers have a high waist and wide legs, then look for patterns with a similar shape.

• Start dressmaking with semi-fitted, loose shapes, like smock tops, tunics, loose dresses, elasticated trousers and A-line skirts. Pyjamas are a good thing to practise on – if they don't look perfect you can still wear them.

• Make a toile (or muslin as it is called in the USA) – always advised, rarely done. A toile is simply a version of the pattern made up quickly in cheap fabric to check the fit. You can leave out collars, zips and pockets, just make up the basic pieces and pin them together. One sleeve is usually enough to see how it fits. Cut off or turn under the seam allowances on necklines and hems to check the length. You might also find out at this stage that the style looks awful on you. I use old bed sheets to make toiles – they are very cheap from the charity shop – and the soft fabric will hang more like real fabric than cheap calico will. Make sure you transfer markings like bust and waist line so you can check that they end up in the right place. So does it really suit you? Is the length right, including in the body and sleeves?

• An alternative is to do a tissue-fit, where you pin or tape together the pattern pieces and hold them up to your body to assess where you might need adjustments. This is good for checking necklines, lengths and very basic fit, but not for detailed fitting, unless you know your body very well.

• Get a friend to help with these stages, ideally one who already knows how to sew! Or try a dressmaking evening class where you can get help with measuring and fitting.

• For your first few garments, use a fabric that has a clear right and wrong side (like a cotton print), so you don't end up getting the pattern pieces hopelessly mixed up and the wrong way around. It may seem like a good idea to use a fabric that is the same both sides so that it won't matter if you mix the right and left side pieces up – but beware, this is a good way to end up with two left sleeves! Also, stick with easy fabrics like cotton rather than trying slippery synthetics or anything needing special handling or advanced seam finishes.

Understanding commercial patterns

Patterns can look complicated and scary, but read through the notes below and you can approach them with confidence.

Pattern book information

The pattern book will give you a certain amount of information about each pattern, but for more detail you will need to look at the envelope. Most pattern books have a code of triangles and squares next to the pattern that are designed to show you what body shape suits these patterns best. Look up the key to these codes in the back of the book. Usually a triangle pointing down is a top-heavy or busty shape, while a triangle pointing up is a bottom-heavy or large-hip shape. A rectangle is no-waist shape and two triangles with the points together is an hourglass shape.

Easy, average, advanced

Not all pattern books show the skill level of the patterns, so it's something you may have to check on the pattern itself. Start with the very easy ones and work your way up. Advanced patterns really are advanced; don't try them until you are confident with all the techniques required.

As a basic rule, patterns with a small number of pieces are much easier than those with collars, panels, gores and ruffles.

Choosing patterns

Browse the pattern books of several companies and see whether they have any similar patterns. Make a shortlist of all the different patterns you are interested in. Ask to see all the envelopes so you can compare them and have a read through some of the instructions if you aren't sure. If the shop staff are helpful and knowledgeable, then make use of them. I recommend choosing patterns in a small shop where you can get more help, and going there when it's not too busy so you can take your time. Don't feel under pressure to buy the fabric in the same shop. Take your pattern away and read the instructions thoroughly before you choose the right fabric.

You could also make a shortlist then have a look on the Internet and see what other people made of the pattern, using review sites where you can also post your own report after making the garment. Alternatively you could do all your research online and browse all the styles, then read the reviews and order online. This works very well when you know which pattern company you prefer and are confident that you understand their definition of easy or average patterns.

Sizes

US and European standard sizes are all different to the UK sizing system, but most patterns will include UK size information as well. Having said that, you should use the dress size as a guide only and buy patterns based on your actual body measurements. The pattern envelope will include the body sizes for which it is designed. You should buy tops based on your bust measurement and trousers based on your hips. Skirts that fit at the waist then flare over the hip should be bought by waist measurement, but ones that fit on the hips should be based on hip measurement. Dresses that fit all over are tricky – it depends on the style and which part is going to be easiest to adjust to fit. You can always ask for advice in the shop.

Multi-size patterns

Most patterns include more than one size in the envelope. You need to buy the pattern according to your measurements, not your usual clothes size. Multi-size patterns allow you to adjust the pattern to fit better, using the different sizes. Your measurements may show that according to their scale you are a size 12 in the bust, but a size 10 in the waist. By using a multi-size pattern that includes a size 10 and a size 12, you can re-draw the cutting lines around the waist area, blending them in from 12 down to 10 and back out again for the hip if required. Make sure you do this on all the seams on all the relevant pattern pieces (page 248).

On the pattern envelope

There will be additional information on the envelope that the pattern pieces and instructions come in.

MISSES

This is an old term used more commonly when patterns were available in a wider range of sizes. 'Misses' basically refers to a pattern cut for a medium-sized woman, rather than 'Women's', which was for a fuller-figured woman, or 'Junior', which was for a smaller woman, and 'Teen', which is self-explanatory. 'Petite' and 'Junior Petite' also existed for short women. These categories tend not to be used anymore, but can be useful for buying vintage patterns. Newer terms – such as petite, tall and plus-size – are used today, but are not available for all patterns.

FABRICS

A list of suitable fabrics is included in the pattern information and you should pay attention to this. The fabrics listed may not be things you know by name, but you should be able to get an idea of what weight the fabric should be. If it suggests corduroy and wool then you should go for a sturdy fabric and don't try and make it from soft-drape synthetic. The pattern won't hold the right shape in a different weight of fabric. Likewise, a pattern for linen or soft silk will be a disaster in a stiff fabric – it will stick out rather than drape and be too thick for gathers and pleats. Ask for advice in the fabric shop if you are mystified. There is more about fabric drape and weight in Fabric (pages 16–17).

NOTIONS

This is the American term for haberdashery; other things you will need apart from fabric to complete the pattern.

VIEW A, VIEW B

This is just the name given to each variation of the pattern on the envelope. Some patterns have several garments in one envelope, which is a very affordable way to start sewing. Having said that, it can be a false economy if there is only one piece that you will actually wear. Where the different views include variations such as sleeve style or skirt length, you can often mix and match the pattern pieces to make up the style you want, as long as the basic bodice pieces are the same.

FABRIC REQUIREMENTS

This is the amount of fabric required to make one item as shown on the envelope. Patterns often have measurements in yards in English (as patterns are mainly produced for the US market) and in metres in French or Spanish. In Britain, fabric is sold by the metre, so you will need to use the French/Spanish information to find out how much fabric you need. This can be confusing, so work out which column you need in the English side, then cross-reference this to the metric columns.

WITH/WITHOUT NAP

Nap means a furry pile, like velvet or corduroy – a fabric that has a right and a wrong direction. You will need more fabric to make sure the pile or nap all lies in the same direction, usually downwards. The nap fabric requirements should also be used when you want to match patterns, prints, stripes or diagonals.

Pattern instructions

In the instructions that come with the pattern pieces you will find these elements.

DRAWINGS

The first thing you will see is a set of drawings of the garment, showing each view from the front and back and any variations of hem, sleeve, etc. Sometimes the drawings show the variations on the same garment, so you might see a long sleeve on the left and a short sleeve on the right.

Next are drawings of each of the pattern pieces showing the numbers they are all given and sometimes the grain lines (page 245). Follow the list for the view you are making to select which pieces you need.

Read through the general directions. These explain the notations used in this pattern and any special instructions, as well as general sewing information that you will need throughout the making.

When the pattern includes lining and interfacing, the diagrams can get confusing. If the pattern is complicated, then on all the diagrams try colouring in the right side, interfacing and lining in coloured pencils so that you can see at a glance which way around things are.

Stick the directions sheet to the wall by your sewing table so you don't have to go hunting for it and can check the instructions while you cut or sew.

FABRIC LAYOUTS

The pattern instructions will include suggested formats for placing the pattern pieces on the fabrics for each different garment style and for at least two widths of fabric. I strongly advise following them to make sure you get the right number of pattern pieces the correct way around. You may find that you can place the pieces closer together and be more economical with your fabric, but make sure you still follow all the grain lines (page 245) and get the pieces the right way up.

When making patterns with a nap fabric, you need to allow extra fabric so you can cut all the pieces with the pile running the same direction, or your garment will look very odd. Follow the nap layout for furry or single-direction fabrics and for directional prints. For these fabrics you usually have to cut the fabric in a single layer, or cut the fabric into two pieces and lay them on top of each other so the nap or pattern goes in the same direction on both pieces. If you simply fold the fabric in half, the nap on the top layer of fabric can face in a different direction to that on the bottom layer.

Most nap fabrics look best with the pile facing down. The 'with nap' amounts also apply to stripes, checks and plaids, where you will need extra fabric to match the lines (page 250).

If for some reason you can't follow the layouts (maybe you are using fabric of a different width) and are cutting the fabric in a single layer, make sure you cut out a left and a right of each pattern piece. The easiest way to do this is to draw around the pattern piece, then flip it over and draw around it again. Make sure you always flip it over or you will get two left or two right sides.

If you use two separate pieces of fabric laid on top of each other, make sure you have the right sides together.

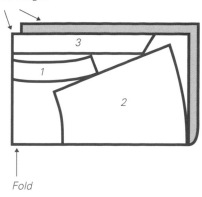

Selvedges

3

1

2

Fold

Fabric layout with the pattern pieces laid out on two layers of fabric. The darker colour represents the right side, folded under so that the right sides are together.

Selvedge

Selvedge

1

2

3

3

Fabric layout with the pattern pieces laid out on one layer of fabric. The dark-coloured pattern pieces have been traced then flipped over to produce right and left pieces.

GRAIN LINES

The grain of the fabric is explained on pages 16–17. It is vital that you match the grain markings on the pattern to the fabric grain to make sure your garment hangs properly. There are lots of ways to make it easier to match your grain.

You can mark the grain on the fabric with quilters' masking tape, so you can see through the pattern tissue.

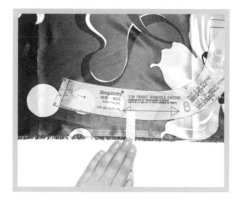

If the grain is hard to identify on the fabric, you can use the selvedge (pages 16–17) as your guide. Use a ruler or metre stick to measure from the selvedge to the grain line on the pattern. Make sure the measurement is the same at both ends of the grain line. For bias-cut clothes, the pattern pieces will have the grain line marked diagonally across the pattern piece, so it is easy to place the pattern correctly as long as you know where the straight grain is!

TALL AND SHORT FITTING ALTERATION LINES

Most patterns will have a very basic way of adjusting length in the pattern. In trousers there is usually a line around the knee that allows you to shorten or lengthen the pattern without disrupting the cut of the trousers. If you just shorten or lengthen the legs at the hem, the tapering of the trousers will be spoiled.

There will be a line in the waist-to-hip area that allows adjustment if you are long or short in the body. If you are long in the body, you will find that trousers try to cut you in half when you sit down, and if you are short in the body, you will find the crotch seam hangs rather low. Adjusting on this line will help you get a better fit.

The same applies to the body and the sleeves in dress or top patterns. Read the pattern directions and look for the pattern measurements for these key areas – this is often printed on the tissue itself rather than the instructions.

For the upper body, look for the neck to waist measurement and compare this with your own. Trouser patterns may have the crotch depth, but its more likely you will have to base the working out on a combination of inside leg, outside leg and trying a toile to see if it fits. Correct trouser fitting is the most difficult aspect of dressmaking, but it's well worth the effort.

There is more about altering patterns on page 248.

PATTERN MARKINGS

Pattern markings help you to construct the pattern. Always copy them onto the wrong side of your fabric before you take the tissue away from the cut pieces. With notches, you can either cut around them, making little points on the edge of your fabric pattern piece, or cut little Vs into the edge of the fabric, or mark them with chalk.

Circles are harder as you will have to draw them in with chalk because they aren't on the edges of the pattern. With the pattern and fabric flat, place a pin through the circle and into the fabric. Lift the tissue and then mark where the pin goes into the fabric. Keeping the pin in place, lift up both pieces of fabric and mark where the pin comes out on the other fabric pattern piece.

This pinning technique is also good for marking darts or any other markings you may need. Draw in the legs of the darts by joining the dots and notches. See page 48 for sewing darts.

Squares are also sometimes used on patterns as additional marking notations. Check the pattern instructions.

Dressmaker's carbon paper can also be used to transfer markings. There is more information about it on page 281.

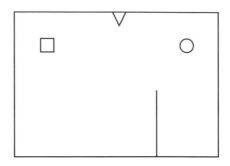

A sample pattern piece showing a notch, circle, square and grain line.

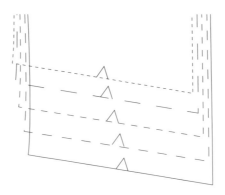

Notches shown on a multi-size pattern piece. Each size is delineated by a different style of dashed line.

WAIST AND BUST LINES

Many patterns will show a line on the tissue where the bust line (nipple to nipple) should be, and the waistline, whether or not these lines are seams. This is to help you check the fit when making a toile or a tissue-fit, or when measuring the pattern to see what adjustments you might need.

CENTRE BACK AND CENTRE FRONT

These lines are marked on the pattern whether or not they are also seams. They are useful in working out the construction and fitting of the garment.

CUT ONE, CUT TWO

This is the number of individual pieces of each pattern piece that you will need to cut in fabric. If you follow the layouts and have the fabric folded right sides together, you can usually cut two pieces out at the same time. The pattern will also say if you need to cut some pieces from lining and interfacing.

PLACE ON FOLD

This symbol is used where the edge of the pattern piece (always a straight line) should be placed on a folded edge of the fabric. The fabric layouts (page 244) will show you how to do this. It is often used for the front of skirts or dresses so you don't have a seam down the front. You usually only need to cut one piece, though for collars etc. you may need two. It will say on the pattern pieces how many of them you need to cut out.

EASE

Ease is the difference in size between your body measurements and the actual clothes. You need to be able to breathe, eat, lift up your arms and bend your legs, so you need the clothes to be a bit bigger than you actually are. Loose-fitting clothes have more ease. If you measure a pattern piece to see if it will fit, make sure you check how much ease it has built in – the pattern needs to be bigger than your body! Patterns vary in the amount of ease, with coats and jackets having more than fitted evening dresses. There is often plenty of ease in the bust, with less in the waist.

RIGHT SIDES TOGETHER

This is a classic sewing term that often causes confusion. Many fabrics have an obvious right side, or front, such as the printed side or the diagonal-weave side of denim. However, others, like plain linen or cotton, don't have an obvious right side.

The right side is the front of the fabric. When sewing pieces together, you usually need to place the right sides of both pieces of fabric facing each other, so when the seam is sewn and the piece turned the right way out, the seam in on the inside. French seams (page 40) and flat-fell seams (page 42) are the exception to this rule, as they are made in a different way.

In crafts it doesn't really matter which side you use as the right side, but in dressmaking it is really important. When both sides look the same, mark each pattern piece with a chalk X to show which is the wrong side. Make all your markings on this side and when you sew pieces right sides together, make sure the unmarked (right) sides are facing each other. If you don't do this you can run the risk of making up the pattern pieces inside out and ending up with two left legs!

Types of pattern

There are various kinds of patterns commercially available.

DESIGN YOUR OWN

These patterns make it easy to mix-and-match style variations, such as necklines and sleeves, on the same basic pattern. They are good for beginners, as long as you know the basic pattern will suit you.

PERFECT OR PERSONALISED FIT

These patterns are ideal for more fitted styles, such as jackets, trousers or jeans. They are usually very well illustrated with excellent directions for how to make all sorts of alterations to fit you perfectly. They are a great way to learn pattern alterations that you can then learn to apply to other patterns. The only drawback is that they tend to be very classic, traditional styles, not high-fashion ones.

PETITES AND PLUS-SIZED

Patterns are available that are designed for specific body types, where the proportions are different to the average. Check the pattern information and try these patterns if your measurements fit into their range.

RETRO VINTAGE PATTERNS

Several companies have re-issued vintage patterns from their own archives. They are a good way to get a vintage-style outfit in the right size.

VINTAGE PATTERNS

Buying vintage patterns is great fun. Making up vintage patterns can be less than fun. For a start, the sizing is different, the pattern notations are different, they are usually single-size rather than multi-size, and the instructions may be limited or even non-existent. Some pattern pieces might well be missing, too.

I really wouldn't recommend starting out in dressmaking with a vintage pattern, even if it does look easy. Modern patterns have a lot of instructions so you can learn techniques as you go. Vintage patterns may just say things like, 'Insert the zip' and give you no further instruction. This book will help, of course, but I can't possibly cover every eventuality in vintage patterns. I would suggest building a library of vintage patterns and start feeding them into your sewing diet as you grow in experience. If you are already a confident follower of patterns, then you will probably get on all right with most vintage patterns.

From the 1960s onwards the patterns are pretty similar to today's and are quite easy to deal with, although they may be single-size. Earlier patterns are usually unprinted, pre-cut tissue pieces with all the (limited) information marked on with punches and notches. Watch out for patterns with no seam allowances included.

Bear in mind what I said at the start of this section about knowing what suits you. I love 1950s dresses, but I know from the experience of trying on vintage ones that I don't have the waist for them and they look awful on me, so I collect these patterns just for fun.

Altering patterns

Altering patterns is a topic worthy of an entire book, of which many excellent examples exist. Style alterations are somewhat easier than fitting alterations. Fitting is best learned through a specialist book or through using patterns with in-built fitting variations (page 247). Having said this, there are some fairly simple alterations that can be done to a pattern. In all cases, make a toile (page 242) to check how your alteration works.

LENGTH
Length alterations are included in most patterns (page 245).

NECKLINES
Collarless necklines can be altered quite easily. To bring the neckline up, tape some paper onto the back of the tissue and redraw the revised neckline, then trim it to shape. To make the neckline deeper, just trim away the tissue. Use a French curve (page 281) to get a smooth line.

It is best not to change the neckline at the shoulders or they may become too wide or narrow. Make sure you change the back neckline to match the front if necessary. You will also need to change any lining or facing pattern pieces.

SLEEVES
It is usually possible to use different sleeves from another pattern if they are similar in the armhole area, ideally from the same garment type. Place the two sleeve patterns one on top of the other and compare the width and curve of the top. There may be a difference in the amount of gathering required to make the top of the sleeve fit into the armhole.

If the sleeves are very different, it may be better to make a composite sleeve, which works well if you want to change the cuff. Trace both sleeves and cut them out. Graft the bottom half of the sleeve you like onto the head (armhole section) of the original.

You can also make a long sleeve into a short sleeve by keeping the sleeve head intact and copying the rest of a short sleeve from another pattern. Always make a trial run in cheap fabric to see if it works.

CHANGING BUST, WAIST OR HIP WIDTH
This is easy using a multi-size pattern. Work out which size is best for each part of your body based on the measurements for the pattern. Re-draw a smooth line between the different sizes you need. Make sure you do this on all the necessary pattern pieces. Use a multi-size pattern to learn how much (or how little) you need to trim or add to a pattern to make it the right size for you.

You should be able to apply the same principle to a single-size pattern by adding or taking away a small amount on each seam. For instance, a skirt with two back pieces and one front piece has a total of three seams and six seam lines (two on each pattern piece). To reduce the waist by 3cm you will only need to remove 5mm on each seam line. A tiny adjustment on all pieces is usually all that is required.

If you don't have a multi-size pattern, it is much easier (in the long term) and more effective, to make a toile (page 242) and make the adjustments from that.

If you try the toile on inside out (assuming your body is fairly symmetrical) then you can pinch the seams in to fit and pin in place. If you think the pattern will be too small, then make a toile with extra-wide seam allowances to allow you to let it out only where necessary.

You can often compensate for a large bust and small ribcage by making darts under the bust, and can fit a curved lower back by adding darts between the bra line and waist.

For making minor adjustments in side seams etc. you can also do a fitting with the actual garment on inside out.

Experiment with a toile and you will find all sorts of ways of altering patterns to fit your unique figure. Try a specialist fitting book or an evening class if you have a figure that is hard to fit. It is possible for everyone, whatever shape, to have perfectly fitting clothes that look fabulous, but it does take time and effort to learn the skills required.

ADDITIONAL MEASUREMENTS
To make detailed fitting alterations, you will need more body measurements:

Back of neck to waist.

Waist to hip.

Arm length from shoulder bone to wrist.

Inside leg. You hold the end of the tape to your knicker line, and a friend reads the measurement at your anklebone.

Outside leg. From your waist to anklebone.

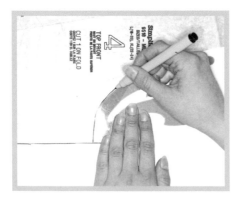

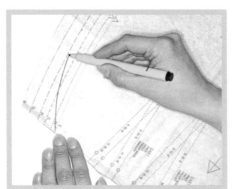

Crotch depth. If you find trousers too long or short in the body, this is an important one. Sit down and measure from your waist to the chair. This is sometimes called 'body rise', which is politer but less clear.

TIPS ON WAIST AND BUST MEASURING
If you are a bit lacking in waist, tie a string around your middle then move and bend until the string settles in one place. Establish this as your waist, keep the string in place and measure neck to waist, outside leg, crotch depth and waist to hip from this point.

When measuring or trying on a toile, make sure you have a well-fitting bra on. This is especially important if you have a large bust. Many women wear the wrong size bra and getting fitted properly will transform how your clothes fit. A bra should fit around your body, under your breasts, without cutting in or riding up your back. The wires should sit flat with the centre part flat against your breastbone. There should be no overhang in the cups or straps digging in.

Bust sizing in patterns is based on a B cup. If you are much larger or smaller, the pattern won't fit. Some patterns, such as fitted jackets, are made in different cup sizes, so try these or look for a personalised-fit pattern that includes directions for how to fit the pattern to your body.

Sew simple

Just because the fastenings do up doesn't mean that the garment fits. As you can see above, clothes and patterns are designed to have ease, so we can move and breathe and eat. If the fabric, seams, zips or buttons are under strain, then the garment doesn't fit. Read the fitting advice for dressmaking and apply the same rules to your shopping. And look all the more fabulous for it!

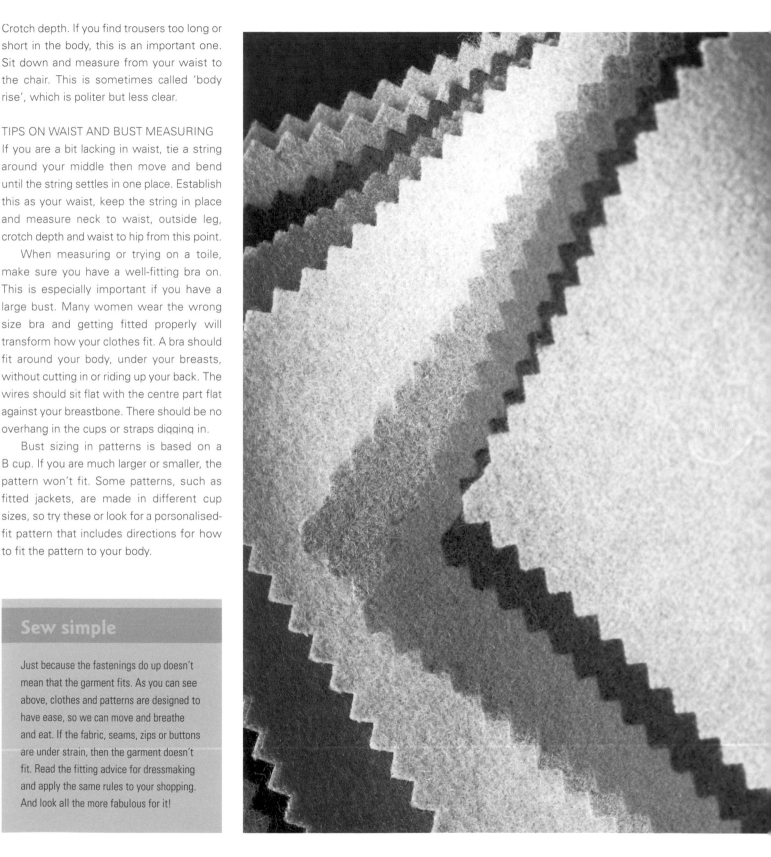

Pattern matching & placement

As mentioned on page 244, you will need extra fabric to match patterns and prints at seams, particularly at the centre front and centre back. It is also worth careful planning to make sure the prints are placed well on the garment.

A jacket will look very professional if you match the centre back seam and if the pattern is well matched on both lapels. One of the signs of a couture garment is excellent pattern matching on sleeves and curved seams, which will take a lot of time and fabric to achieve.

Large prints can be problematic for clothes, as you have to watch out for big splodges on your bottom or the flower-on-each-breast arrangement (unless that is your intention!). Try and arrange a large print so the main motifs are non-symmetrical on the body, perhaps left shoulder, right hip and left knee on a dress. Try not to have half a motif on an obvious seam as this will really stand out. It's usually not worth trying to match small prints, unless the garment has very noticeable seams at the front.

STRIPES AND CHECKS
Matching stripes and checks is tricky but worth doing – nothing looks smarter than neatly matched stripes on a seam. Striped fabrics look fabulous when they are bias-cut and the seams are matched to make neat chevrons. Allow lots of extra fabric to do this and follow the instructions on the right.

SINGLE-DIRECTION DESIGNS
When fabrics have a print or weave that is designed with a top and bottom, make sure all your pattern pieces are cut the same way up. Most fabric layouts include some pieces the wrong way up, to be economical with the fabric. Single-direction designs need to have the pieces cut out individually to ensure the design all runs the right way.

DIAGONAL PATTERNS
Diagonal fabrics are very hard to match unless the seams are all dead straight (which is unlikely!). Decide which is the most important seam to match (centre front or centre back) and do your best to match that seam and don't worry about the less visible seams.

LARGE PATTERNS
The simplest way to match patterns on garments is to select the most important piece of the pattern first and work out the best motif-placement on it. Lay the fabric out flat, print-side up, and move the pattern piece around until you find a pleasing arrangement, making sure you keep the grain line correct. Draw around the pattern piece, then trace the main motifs onto the pattern piece in pencil. You can then use this pattern piece to work out the motif-arrangement for the adjoining pattern pieces. Don't forget to allow for the seam allowances on the pattern pieces!

Sewing bias cut fabrics

The bias grain in fabric is the diagonal direction across the straight woven threads. See pages 16–17 for more information on this. Fabric cut on the bias has more drape, will cling to the body, and looks very attractive. The high point of fashionable bias-cut was the 1930s when Madeline Vionnet made it her speciality and created a trend for figure-hugging, ultra-feminine, bias-cut satin evening gowns. However, there is a reason why bias-cut clothes are the realm of the top designers – it is pretty difficult to get it right.

Any fabric can be cut on the bias, but very heavy ones won't necessarily drape very much. Very fine fabrics like chiffon and cut-out velvet (top centre leaf, page 286) are the most common fabrics used for bias cut skirts and dresses available in the shops. While these fabrics work beautifully in bias-cut, they are very hard to sew on the straight grain, and a real battle to sew on the bias.

Rather than starting with a frustrating disaster, learn to sew bias-cut clothes using light to medium-weight fabrics like cotton or linen that won't stretch out of shape so easily. Medium-weight wool is also a good choice. Choose a simple pattern like a sleeveless top, so you don't have fiddly bits of pattern or fitting to struggle with.

Follow the directions for sewing bias seams (page 47). Cut the pattern pieces with extra large seam allowance (up to 3cm) if you plan to stretch the bias out before you sew. Make sure you transfer all the markings onto the fabric before you remove the pattern piece, including the seam line, so you can sew accurately. Always test the fit as you go along, as it may shift around.

This dress, circa 1891, has the pattern of oranges matched in mirror-image to create a completely new pattern on the centre back. Careful cutting has created a consistent layout of motifs across the whole garment.

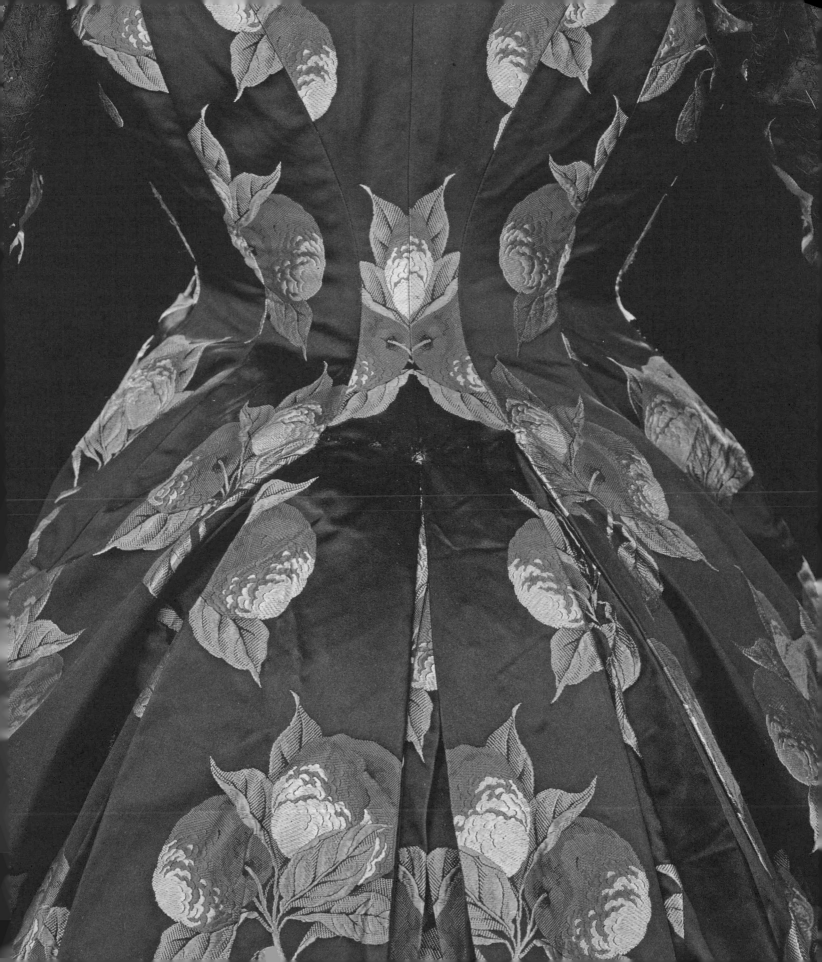

Dressmaking tips and tricks

As you do more dressmaking, you will find things you can adapt and change to personalise your clothes to your style and your preferred way of sewing.

Pockets

Get rid of side-seam pockets. Most basic trouser patterns include pockets in the side seams, which hang badly, cause wrinkles and look lumpy if you use them. I prefer to either put nice patch pockets on the back or to make front inset pockets, similar to jeans. Either copy one from existing trousers or find a pattern with this type of pockets.

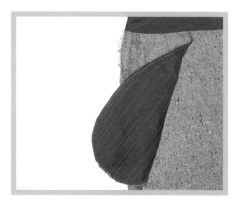

Patterns with pockets will include a pocket bag. This is the part of the pocket that you don't see from the outside and usually it would be made from a plain cotton with only the visible bit made in the main fabric. Look at jeans to see how they are made. I like to make the pocket bags from patterned cotton lawn, which is soft against the skin and looks nice from the inside.

Make the pocket bags with the printed side of the cotton lawn facing outwards and finish the seam allowances with French seams (page 40) and then they will look really special.

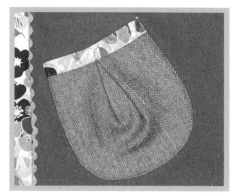

I like to make nice patch pockets rather than boring ones. Use interesting shapes and mix fabrics to make a fun pocket. Look at the pockets on the Pocket Handbag (page 118).

Elasticated casing

Elasticated trousers or skirts have a casing at the top – a fabric tunnel through which you thread the elastic.

In basic patterns, folding over the top edge of the fabric makes this. I prefer to cut off the casing allowance (leaving a seam allowance) and make a separate casing in contrasting fabric. This works well on thick or scratchy fabric, making the waistband comfortable against the skin.

Bra elastic is usually softer and more comfortable than standard cheap stuff. Use elastic as wide as you can for waists as narrow elastic digs in. Look at how shop-bought elastic waistbands are made – the elastic is sewn into the casing to stop it moving around. Insert the elastic into the casing as directed and then stretch and pin it in place and sew along the centre of the casing, through the elastic.

Another problem can be the side seam allowances catching on the elastic when you try and thread it. To stop this, press the seam allowances open (page 23) and stick them down with a snippet of fusible webbing tape (page 56).

Facings

Facings are the mini-linings used in sewing patterns around the neckline, armholes and other openings rather than full linings. They will help keep the shape of the garment and give a smart finished edge.

Make sure the raw edges of the facing are finished well. Double-fold bias binding (page 74) gives a smart finish for coats and jackets. Sewing close to the edge and pinking (page 37) will give a smooth finish and avoids a lumpy edge that will mark the fabric when you iron from the outside. You could also turn under a small single hem (page 52).

Use a nice fabric to make the facing, like a silk dupion inside a wool garment. It feels nicer against the skin and adds style to your sewing (although you are the only one who will see it!) For fine or sheer dress fabrics, make the facings from a co-ordinating colour of silk organza.

Tack the facings to all available seam allowances to stop them flapping about and getting caught up.

Make a one-piece facing by extending the facing pattern to join the armhole and neck facings into one piece, using the main pattern piece as a guide.

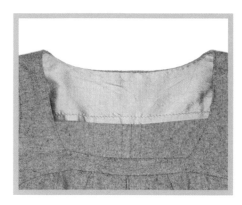

Sew around the armhole and neckline to stop the facing from turning out in the same way as for a faced hem (page 65, Step 8). You can also top stitch through all layers on the right side using pick stitch (page 28), or machine-sew close to the fold in a matching or contrasting thread. You could even turn this into a feature by using an embroidery stitch (page 196).

However, no matter how you make them, facings can flap around and get tangled when you put the garment on and can be very annoying. They can show through light fabrics or can leave a tide-line mark when you iron the outside of the garment. There are several things you can do to improve the situation. Try getting rid of the facings and make a full lining instead (see page 254).

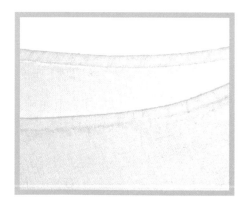

Alternatively, get rid of the facings and turn under the edges of the garment. Make a double hem and sew it in place by hand or machine (pages 52–53).

Another option is to bind the edges where there were facings. This works well on medium-weight fabrics, but not with very thick ones. I much prefer using bias binding on an armhole than a flappy facing.

You can make the your own binding from matching fabric (pages 72–75). Don't use ready-made binding unless its soft, or it will be annoyingly scratchy. Apply the binding using the single-fold technique (page 75).

Set a curve into the folded bias (page 73) and sew on the outside of the garment. Trim and clip the seam allowance (page 44) and turn the binding to the inside then slip stitch (page 29) it in place.

Dress shields

These funny things may seem like something left over from the 1950s, but they are brilliant in garments where sweat patches would show and for delicate fabrics that can get marked by sweat and deodorant. They are also good for dry-clean only garments, as you can take them out and wash them after each wear and so save on dry-cleaning.

Tack the shields inside dresses, jackets and tops and remove and wash them, or sew them inside jacket linings and unpick the seams to wash or change them.

Waistbands

I like to use a nice fabric for the insides of waistbands, particularly for wool skirts and trousers. It's a great way to use a small piece of special cotton lawn or silk.

Cut the waistband pattern in half lengthways, add 1cm seam allowances to both pieces and cut one piece in the outside fabric and one with the inside fabric. Sew along the long edge, press the seam allowance open (page 23) and proceed according to the pattern.

Lining

Linings are well worth the effort. A garment will look better, hang better, wear better and last longer with a lining. Linings will also make a garment warmer, of course, and a slippery fabric makes it easier to get on over other clothes.

In dresses, linings will help reduce transparency, make the dress more comfortable and it will skim your body for a flattering look. In coats and jackets a lining can get a lot of wear, so bear this in mind when choosing a fabric – a cheap one will wear out long before the main coat fabric.

The lining should be washable in the same way as the main fabric. Always pre-wash lining fabric to make sure it won't run or bleed onto the main fabric in the wash or in the rain.

Cheap synthetic lining fabric is one of my least favourite things. It's a pain to cut and sew as it slithers around everywhere, and it feels nasty on bare skin, doesn't breathe and can be inclined to static-cling. Going up a notch or two in price for a better quality of lining is advised.

Acetate is the cheapest, followed by polyester. Rayon is nicer to use, while Habotai silk makes a great lining. It is easy to pull on, keeps you warm or cool as required and makes you feel fabulous. For the amount you need for most garments, it might not be that expensive. Lightweight cotton can also be used in un-tailored garments and is nice for summer jackets and skirts, but it won't stop clothes creasing like a synthetic or silk lining. Heavier synthetic and silk satins are good for coats. See page 293 for advice on working with slippery fabrics.

Reversible linings

Collar-less jackets are ideal for turning into a reversible garment. The Vintage Jacket (page 264) can be reversible if you leave off the sleeves (or you could unpick them and swap them to the other side).

There is no reason why you should stick with plain linings. I like to use printed fabrics as linings. They cost a little more, but are so much more fun.

Interfacing

Interfacing is fabric used inside a garment to strengthen, stabilise and support the main fabric. There are different types and they are discussed in detail on page 292.

Each garment has different interfacing needs. For years I used iron-on interfacing of the appropriate type for the fabric, but now I prefer sew-in alternatives. Iron-on usually makes the fabric slightly stiffer, depending on the weight you use. If that is the effect you want, then great, but often it isn't good. Iron-on interfacing can also leave a bubbly effect on the front side of the fabric because it shrinks slightly when you iron it. Always test before you destroy the fabric!

For most purposes I recommend sew-in interfacing, and I prefer natural fibres to synthetics. Light cotton fabrics like poplin and lawn are great, and silk organza is fantastic for many fabrics, including sheers. Make sure the interfacing has the same washing directions as the fabric.

Iron-on interfacing

Thin, non-woven interfacing is hard to mark with chalk as it can tear. I use felt-tip pens, fading fabric markers or a very soft pencil. Thicker interfacing is usually fine with chalk.

To avoid the edges of the interfacing showing through on the right side, cut it with pinking shears for a softer edge.

If you have to join iron-on interfacing, place the edges close together but do not overlap them or you will get a ridge.

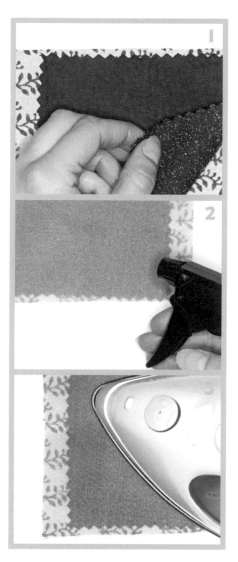

1 Place the fabric wrong side up and position the interfacing glue-side down.

2 Cover with a pressing cloth. Lightly spray the cloth with a little water.

3 Press for about 10 seconds or according to the manufacturer's instructions. Lift and replace the iron to make sure all the interfacing has been pressed. Leave the interfacing to cool before you move it. Then press the right side of the fabric and leave it to cool again.

Sew-in interfacing

This is available woven and non-woven, with woven being more expensive but better quality. For couture hems, cut the interfacing on the bias (page 17), but for interfacing whole garments, cut it on the same grain as the main fabric.

Sew along the edges of the interfacing using herringbone stitch (page 30) and catching just a few threads of the main fabric. Attach the interfacing securely in areas such as seam allowances and where it will show the least.

Depending on the pattern instructions and the thickness of the interfacing you may need to trim off the interfacing seam allowances before or after sewing (page 38).

To join sew-in interfacing, cut the pieces on the diagonal, overlap the edges and zigzag for a flat seam, preferably in an area that won't show through when the garment is ironed. If it might show through, then sew it together by hand with running stitch.

Designing

Although there are 20 innovative and exciting projects in this book, many of you reading this will find that the techniques pages spark off creative ideas for your own projects. You can easily adapt and develop ideas from the techniques and will find enough information to keep you going for some time.

Keep track of your ideas in a notebook or sketchbook if that helps. Unlike many designers, I don't often draw my ideas before I make them. I make notes of what pops up in my head and then go straight to fabric to experiment. So you don't need to have beautiful sketchbooks with your ideas all worked out, unless that is something you enjoy and are good at. Just do whatever works for you. You might want to stick in magazine clippings, colour samples, postcards or anything else that inspires you, from seedpods to fabric snippets.

When I am designing, I work in two ways. I love visiting museums and investigating historic dress and textiles. I photograph or sketch details I like and then make notes and the odd sketch about the design ideas they have sparked off. If I can't make it to a museum, I use costume books with detailed photographs for ideas. I then go straight to the fabric and start messing about with techniques and ideas until something suddenly clicks and the idea solidifies.

The other way I work is starting straight from the fabric. I just play around with a vague plan of a technique I want to try and fiddle, tweak, sew, cut, sew and cut again, until once more an idea works. Sometimes, quite often, they don't work, or what I've made isn't what I wanted. I put these bits aside and eventually come back to them, weeks, or even months, later. Several of the projects in this book were developed from samples that were lurking in boxes waiting for their moment to shine.

Coming up with original ideas isn't easy, but the best way to develop your design skills is by practice. I am a great believer in experimenting to develop ideas. By all means use other designers' work as inspiration, but try and tweak, change and build upon the ideas to create something new and unique. Challenge yourself to try something new, to combine and contrast ideas, inspirations and techniques. Try things like turning your design upside down, using completely different materials, changing the size or scale. Learn to assess your ideas, and decide how original they are, or if they are derived from someone else's. The secret of being a designer is to find your own voice, your own style, and then let that voice run wild!

Don't expect anything to happen fast. Do what I do – experiment with things, leave them to ferment and come back when they are ready. Don't rush it – the creative brain needs time. Sew, cut, drink tea, go for a walk in the woods, create, enjoy.

Customising and recycling

I am a great believer in recycling and re-use. We throw out a shocking amount of perfectly good clothes that could easily be transformed into something unique and wonderful.

Many of the decorative techniques in this book can be used to customise an existing garment or to add variety to something you are making from a pattern. You could even try a complete restyle on something that just isn't quite the right shape.

The Customised T-shirt (page 277) has been very simply decorated with fabric scraps. Start collecting little bits of fabric goodness like vintage buttons, lace and other treasures. Experiment and play around with items in your wardrobe and explore charity shops for things that would be just perfect for the project you have in mind.

Customising by sewing things on is incredibly easy. Gather ideas from magazines, try out techniques from this book and mix and match fabrics and trimmings. One of my favourite simple projects is adding buttons. The linen top below was ruined with a splodge of dinner staining the front, but a selection of colourful buttons have transformed it into a one-off piece and saved it from the scrap bag! I rather like this placement of a motif on the stomach, it's much more flattering than a design on the chest.

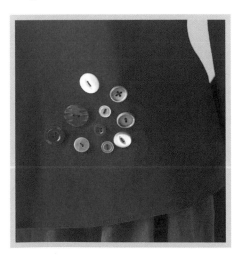

I tried a similar idea using Suffolk puffs (page 168), which are sewn onto the top above using the same technique as for the Silk Cuff (page 206).

If you have got the hang of dressmaking, you can always add decorative elements to your sewing projects. I often make several versions of favourite garments and like to ring the changes using decorations as well as different fabrics. Trims and edgings are easy to sew on, and various techniques are shown on pages 148–165. Try using the in-seam technique (page 153) to sew ric-rac into the side seams of a simple skirt pattern.

Embroidery stitches (pages 196–199) are a wonderful way to easily transform a garment. For the dress above right, I drew out the design on paper and traced it onto the fabric using a vanishing marker. The darker circles are made using fusible webbing (page 188) with fabric scraps and the rest is hand embroidered using a variety of co-ordinating threads.

The appliqué section in this book (pages 188–193) has lots of ideas that you could adapt for customising, like using fusible webbing for decorative appliqué (page 188),

or using 3-D appliqué shapes (page 190) on a skirt or jacket lapel. Machine embroidery (page 194) is great for flat areas like plain skirts or the backs of cotton shirts. Frills and ruffles (pages 130–133) are simple to add to skirt hems or even collars, while beads and sequins (pages 156–159) add a bit of quick and easy sparkle.

Whatever you do, make sure that your decorations are washable, or you will end up with a work of art that will only ever hang in your wardrobe.

The simplest embroidery detail I have ever done was to sew along the outside seams of a pair of black trousers in running stitch with white embroidery thread. It took just minutes but looked very smart!

Restyling a garment takes a bit of practice, but it is fantastically satisfying. It can easily go wrong, so try and experiment with cheap things from the charity shop before you cut into something special! At its simplest, you can restyle a garment by chopping off the sleeves and taking in the side seams for a more flattering fit.

Repairs and alterations

With this book in your hand, there is no excuse for clothes left languishing in your cupboard in need of turning up or a new zip. Most repairs and simple alterations can be made using techniques included in this book. A few other common repairs and alterations are shown here.

Hems

First, work out the way the hem was sewn in the first place, and match it to one of the techniques in the hems section (pages 52–67). Follow the steps to re-sew the hem in the same way.

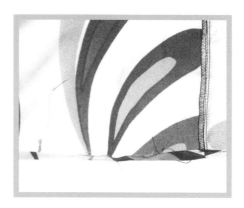

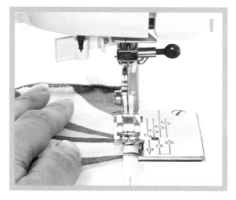

1 If the hem is machined, then re-sew on the machine using a double hem (page 52).

Shortening jeans

This method can be used on any trousers or skirts with decorative hems that you don't want to lose – you simply cut off the hem and re-sew it back on. This shortens the length by 3cm (as you are using two 1.5cm seam allowances). To make the length shorter still, cut off the hem and then remove any excess fabric, making sure you leave a 1.5cm seam allowance on the leg ends. If you need less reduction than 3cm, make the seam allowances smaller – remember that you will lose twice the seam allowance, no matter what that is.

1 Cut off the hem 1.5cm above the top of the hem. Remove any extra length from the trousers or skirt if required.

2 Place the cut off piece inside out, over the trouser leg end, raw edges together and pin. Using a zip foot, sew the pieces together right up against the edge of the hem.

Altering hems on trousers and skirts

To shorten a garment, put it on and ask someone else to mark the required finished length with pins. Measure a hem allowance below this mark; about 2.5cm for trousers and up to 4cm for skirts, depending on your chosen hemming technique. If the existing hem allowance is needed, then unpick it and press the crease out. Cut the excess fabric off and make a hem as required.

If there isn't enough existing fabric to lengthen a garment, then add a false hem. This can be an extra panel of fabric or a faced hem (page 64).

The decorative hem of the jeans is preserved.

Seams

Side seams usually burst because either the fabric or the stitching has torn.

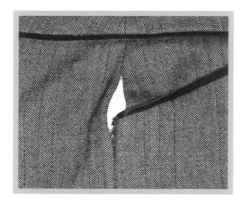

I If the fabric is intact, sew up the seam with backstitch (page 28) or by machine and finish the seams if required. Make sure you fasten the thread off securely (page 27).

If the fabric itself has torn, it needs to be reinforced and then the seam can be sewn up again.

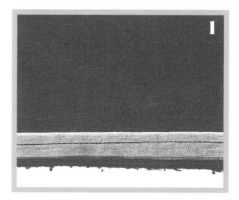

I Seam tape or the selvedge edges cut from thin fabric should be sewn along with the seam.

2 Iron-on interfacing can be used to strengthen damaged fabric.

Tears

There are various ways to repair a tear, depending on how large it is.

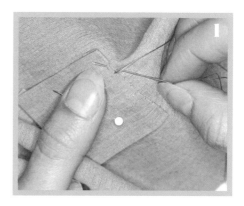

I Tears can be repaired with a patch. Cut the patch about 2cm bigger than the tear all around, then press under 1cm seam allowances. Pin the patch onto the front of the garment, covering the hole, then make tiny slip stitches (page 29) around the edge.

Finding matching fabric for patches can be tricky – if you turn up trousers, always keep the fabric scraps you cut off for patching, or try cutting a piece from facings or waistbands. Otherwise, go for something similar in colour and weight, or a complete contrast, in which case you could use a fun shape and make an appliqué (page 189).

To sew a tear by hand

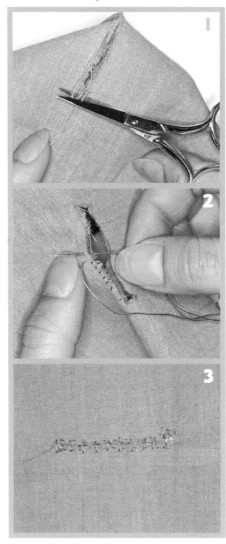

To machine darn a tear

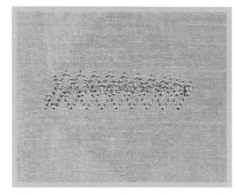

Using a matching thread will make the darned tear less visible on the front.

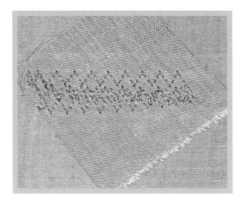

Place a piece of matching fabric or interfacing behind the tear. Overstitch the area several times using a 3-step zigzag or ordinary zigzag stitch (page 33).

Iron-on interfacing

Threadbare areas can be supported and stabilised using iron-on interfacing.

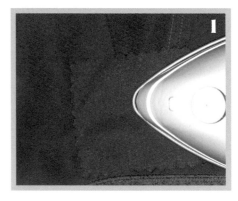

I First trim away any loose threads.

2 Overcast (page 29) the raw edges with a matching thread.

3 Sew the two edges together.

I Cut a piece of iron-on interfacing with pinking shears, so the edges won't show through on the right side. Iron this onto the back of the fabric with a piece of baking paper or a Teflon pressing cloth (page 284) underneath to make sure the glue doesn't come through the fabric onto the ironing board. The threadbare area can then be machine darned (left).

Other repairs

Consult wartime 'make-do-and-mend' books for interesting, if sometimes rather complex, repair ideas.

Replacing zips

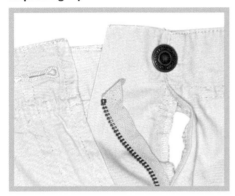

Zips in skirts and jackets can be replaced fairly easily, although fly-front trousers can be more tricky. The key is to look at the insertion method very carefully as you unpick the old zip. You will often need to unpick waistbands and remove top-stitching. I suggest making notes as you go, so you remember how to put the new one back and what to sew where, or take digital photos.

Take the broken zip to the shop and try to buy a new one as similar as possible. Shorten it if required (page 84). Follow the most suitable zip insertion instructions in the fastenings section (pages 84–89).

Hand-sewing is often easier as it can be awkward to get the zip under the machine.

Adjusting straps

Shoulder straps on lingerie and bras can be adjusted and moved quite easily. Unpick the stitching and move or shorten the strap. Get the placement absolutely correct by trying the item on and adjusting the strap while you wear it – you will need some help if it's the back you are adjusting!

If the fabric has torn, patch the damaged area with similar fabric before sewing the strap on. If the fabric has torn once, it may do so again, so it needs strengthening.

Replacing elastic waistbands

Elastic waistbands often need replacing. To get the correct length, take about 1m of elastic and put it around your waist. Stretch it to a comfortable length then mark on the elastic where you need to cut it.

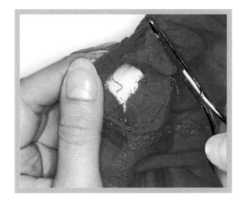

Unpick the stitching at each end of the casing and any additional stitching that holds the elastic in place. Use a safety pin to attach the end of the elastic to the end of the casing so you don't pull it right through. Use a large safety pin or bodkin (page 284) on the other end, and work it through the casing.

Overlap the two ends of the elastic, and use the safety pin to hold them in place – making sure the elastic isn't twisted. Sew a few vertical rows of zigzag stitching to hold the elastic firmly together. Sew up the casing, following the original stitching lines, making sure you have sewn through all the layers required.

If there was stitching through the middle of the elastic, use safety pins to stretch the elastic to the right length, and stretch it out as you sew.

Buttonholes

Fix torn buttonholes by overcasting (page 29) the raw edge and making a bar at the end. Alternatively, cover the torn area and existing stitching with new buttonhole stitches (page 32).

Altering size

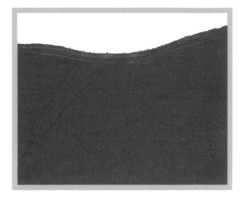

Dresses and tops can be taken in at the waist by sewing along the side seams. Test the fit with the garment on inside out, mark with pins, then draw a new sewing line with chalk. Follow the original stitching line then gradually move on to the new stitching line and back out again so the side seam is smooth. You may need to trim away the excess fabric and finish the seam (page 37).

You can also make waist and bust darts larger in the same way. Follow the instructions for darts (page 48) or use the existing garment darts as a guide.

Letting out a a skirt or dress is a little more complicated. A dress with darts at the waist is quite easy – just unpick the darts and re-make them smaller if required. Steam the fabric to get rid of stitching lines. Don't try this on velvets or other fancy fabrics as the original seam lines will always show.

The same can be done at the seams, if there is enough fabric. Unpick the seams and re-sew them closer to the edge of the fabric. Letting out 5mm on each side seam adds 2cm to the overall size, so a small adjustment is often enough.

Skirts and trousers with waistbands are harder to let out because the waistband will be too short for the newly expanded skirt. Unpick the waistband then unpick the darts, or adjust the side seams. Use the old waistband as a pattern and make a longer one from a different fabric, following the appropriate Circular Skirt steps (page 270).

You will need

Curtain fabric or similar heavy-weight fabric
Tape measure
Scissors
Iron
Curtain heading tape
Pins
Sewing machine
Sewing thread to match fabric
Scraps of lightweight fabric
Curtain weights
Hand-sewing needle

Cutting list

For each curtain, a panel of fabric the
correct height and width (page 228 and
pages 230–231), plus 5cm each side for
the side hems, 5cm for the top hem and
20cm for the bottom hem.

Techniques

Curtains, pages 228–233
Pressing and steaming, page 23
Blind hemming, page 66
Hem stitch, page 30
Curtain weights, page 229
Slip stitch, page 29

Quick curtains

These simple, unlined curtains are easy to make. The blind hemming technique and professional finishing make them look really smart.

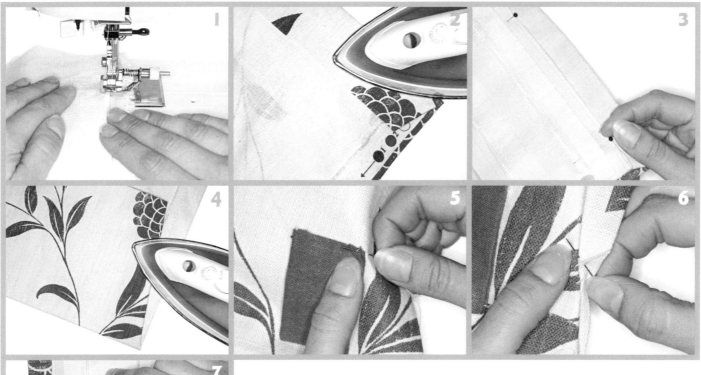

4 Mark the finished length of the curtain with pins (if you have measured correctly, this should be 20cm up from the raw edge). At this stage, measure the curtain from the top edge to the pins and check that the measurement is correct. Turn under the raw edge and press. Turn up the hem along the line of pins marking the correct length. Pin and press the hem fold. Fold under the side edges of the hem so that they slope in at a shallow angle, as shown here. The top of the hem should just touch the inner edge of the side seam.

5 Sew the hem using the blind hemming method or hem stitch it by hand. Make curtain weight bags from scraps of lightweight fabric and sew them to the hem.

6 Slip stitch along the folded-in hem edges, catching them to the side hems.

7 Pull up the heading tape and neatly pin the cords to the side hem.

1 Press under a 5cm hem down each side of the panel. Sew the hem using blind hemming. Press the sewn seams flat.

2 Turn under 5cm along the top edge, fold the corners in and press.

3 Apply the heading tape 2cm down from the fold.

You will need

Pattern pieces on page 297

Paper or newspaper

Pencil

Main fabric – 1.5m of 36-in wide vintage
    fabric or 1.2m of 118-cm wide fabric

Lining – 1.2m of organic cotton or other
    lightweight natural fabric

Scissors

Tailor's chalk or pencil

Tacking thread

Hand-sewing needle

Pins

Sewing thread to match fabrics

Iron

Clear plastic poppers

Techniques

Dressmaking, pages 242–255

Thread tracing, page 21

Darts, page 48

Sewing a seam, page 36

Sewing a curved seam, page 44

Clipping an inward curved seam, page 44

Notching a curved seam, page 45

Trimming seam allowances, page 38

Pressing and steaming, page 23

Slip stitch, page 29

Poppers, page 104

Vintage jacket

I based this jacket on a much-loved and now worn out vintage blouse. I've made several variations in special vintage fabrics; this one is a 1950s dress cotton.

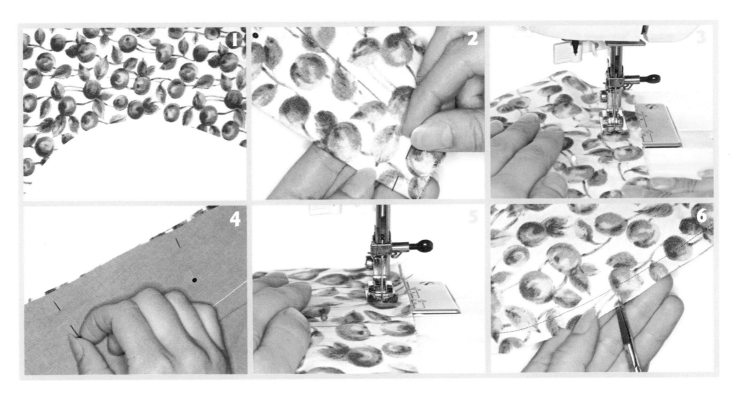

CUTTING OUT THE PATTERN PIECES

Enlarge then cut out each paper pattern piece. If the fabrics have a printed pattern, cut out all the pieces so that the pattern runs in the same direction on each. Cut out a set of all the pieces in the main fabric and a set in the lining fabric.

• Place centre back on a fold in the fabric so you don't have a seam up the back.

• Cut two front pieces, making sure you have a left and a right side. You can do this by folding the fabric right sides together and cutting out two pieces together.

• Cut two sleeve pieces, with the straight side on the fold in the fabric.

1 Transfer the pattern markings onto the main and lining fabrics. Mark the sleeve placement on the main fabric pieces by thread tracing over the chalk markings.

2 Make the darts in both front pieces of the lining and the main fabric.

3 Join the fronts to the back piece. Place the back piece right side up, then the front pieces right side down on top of it, matching the side seams and marks. Pin in place then sew using 1.5cm seam allowances. Clip the curved part of the seam and press the seam allowances open. Repeat the process with the lining pieces.

4 Lay the main fabric body flat on the table with the right side up. Place the lining on top, with the right side down. Match the markings and pin all around the edges

5 Using a 1.5cm seam allowance, sew all around the front edges, around the armholes, along the bottom hem and around the back of the neck. DO NOT sew up the shoulder seams.

6 Trim all the seam allowances to 5mm unless your fabric frays a lot, in which case trim to 1cm. As this jacket is fully lined, you won't need to finish the seams on the inside unless the fabric frays excessively. Clip and notch the curved seams.

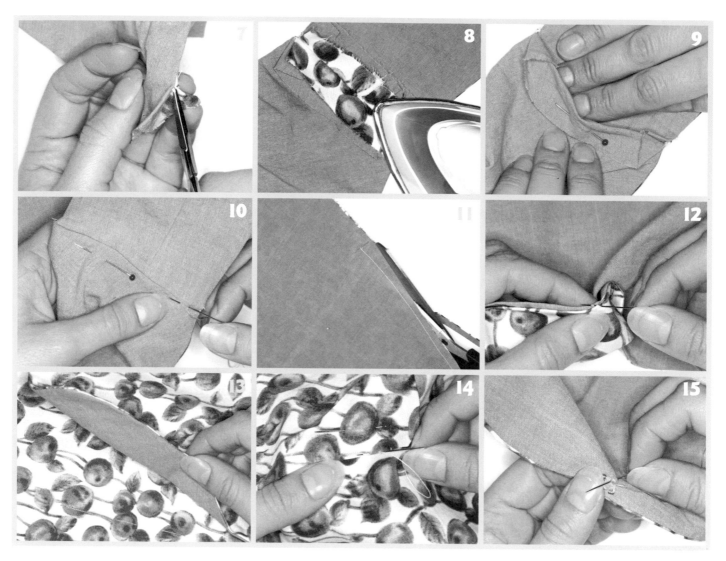

7 Turn the whole jacket the right way out through one of the open shoulder seams and press it. Next, sew up the shoulder seams. This is a bit fiddly, but worth it to get a really neat finish. Unpick the last 1.5cm of the side seam and fold and pin the lining seam allowances out of the way.

8 On the main fabric only, place the front and back shoulders together and sew the seams. Press the seam allowances open and tuck them under the lining.

9 Fold one side of the shoulder seam allowances flat and poke it under the other.

10 Fold the remaining seam allowance under and slip stitch it in place.

11 Make the sleeves by placing the main fabric and the lining pieces right sides together, matching the marks. Sew all around, using a 1.5cm seam allowance and leaving a gap as shown on the pattern. Trim, clip and notch the seam allowances, except across the gap. Turn the sleeves right side out through the gap.

12 Turn under the edges of the gap and slip stitch them closed. Press the sleeves.

13 Match the sleeve edges to the thread-traced markings on the main body. Tack the sleeves in position. Try on the jacket and adjust the sleeve placement if necessary.

14 Slip stitch the sleeves in place using a matching thread.

15 Try on the jacket and work out the placement of the poppers. You may want the jacket to wrap over or just to meet at the centre front. Sew on the poppers.

Sew different

This jacket is a loose fit, based on a medium size. It will fit a wide range of sizes, with more wrap-over for smaller sizes and less for larger sizes. If you are not sure if it will fit, try pinning the paper pattern onto yourself (pin through your clothes!) or make a toile (page 242). You only need to make the main body pieces, not the sleeves. If you make the pattern larger you might need more fabric than is specified in the materials list.

If you need to alter the size of the jacket, follow these instructions.

To make the back wider: place the edge of the pattern 1cm in from the fold. This adds 2cm across the back and bust.

To make the back smaller: trim 1cm off the centre back of the pattern and place this new edge on the fold. This takes out 2cm in the back and bust.

If further adjustment is necessary then add 5mm to each side seam, which will add 2cm to the whole bust measurement. Likewise, you can make it smaller by taking off 5mm.

You will need

For one pillowcase:

½m main fabric

½m backing fabric

¼m or fat quarter of contrast fabric

Tape measure

Tailor's chalk or pencil

Scissors

Sewing machine

Sewing threads

Pins

Iron

Techniques

Sewing a seam, page 36

Pressing and steaming, page 23

Single hem, page 52

Turning a corner, page 49

Zigzagging allowances together, page 37

Pieced pillowcase

I'm always frustrated by the boring range of pillowcases available in the shops. I don't like matching sets and prefer to make my own to contrast or co-ordinate with my bed linen. These are made from patchwork cotton, which is good quality and nice to sleep on, but it will need ironing. If you hate ironing, go for poly-cottons instead.

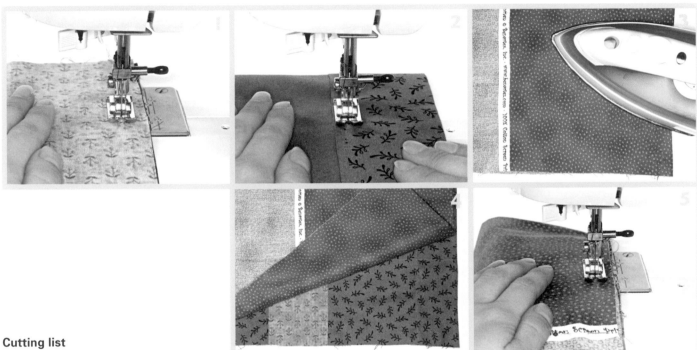

Cutting list

Pre-wash the fabrics before making up the pillowcase.

For the front panel

Main fabric (dark green)
50 x 23cm with selvedge edge along one long edge (A)
50 x 34cm (C)
50 x 18cm (E)
Contrast fabric (light green)
Two pieces each 50 x 10cm (B) and (D)

For the back panel

50 x 96cm with selvedge edge along one 50cm end

1 Mark the identifying letter for each piece on the back with chalk. To make the front panel, sew the long cut edge (not the selvedge) of piece A to a long edge of piece B then sew on C, then D and then E, so you have a striped panel about 76cm long. Press the seam allowances open.

2 Turn under a 6cm single hem along the selvedge end of piece A and sew in place, 1.5cm from the edge.

3 To make the back panel flap, mark 20cm from the selvedge and, wrong sides facing, turn over the fabric at the marked line. Press the fold.

4 Place the front panel face up with the hemmed edge to the right. Place the back panel on top of the front panel, right side down with the flap to the right and facing up. Pin the panels together.

5 Trim the edges if required and sew around the three raw edges, using a 1.5cm seam allowance and turning the corners neatly. Do not sew over the flap and hem end. Zigzag the seams and turn the pillowcase the right way out. Press the seams flat.

Circular skirt

A circular skirt is always a show-stopper and it's surprisingly easy to make your own made-to-measure pattern. There is a bit of maths, but just take it slowly and double-check all your measurements and it should go swimmingly. I made this skirt in a crisp organic cotton that gives it a full look, but you could try a floaty floral for a more romantic feel, or go for a real 1950s look and use vintage fabric.

The skirt is made from three pieces, one piece cut on a fold in the fabric to make the front, and two back pieces seamed together with a zip inserted. The pattern piece is a quarter circle, which makes a full-circle skirt.

You will need

Brown paper or newspaper
Tape measure
Calculator
Set square
Pencil
Paper
Dinner plate
Metre rule
Fabric
Scissors
Pins
Sewing machine
Sewing thread to match fabric
20cm zip
Small button (about 2cm)
Hand-sewing needle

Techniques

Dressmaking, pages 242–255
Stay stitching, page 34
Sewing a seam, page 36
Pressing and steaming, page 23
Ease stitching, page 34
Iron-on interfacing, page 255
Basic centred zip, page 85
Turning a corner, page 49
Outward corners and points, page 50
Slip stitch, page 29
Machine buttonhole, page 92
Curved hem, page 63

MAKING THE PATTERN

First, you need to make a personalised pattern on a large sheet of paper. You could use brown paper or sheets of newspaper taped together.

1 Make a note of your waist measurement. Decide on the length you would like the finished skirt, plus 5cm (L). This sample is 70cm long.

2 To make the waist the right size, you need the radius (R) of your waist measurement, so divide your waist measurement by 6.28. So a waist measurement of 70cm would have a radius of 11.146cm. Round the figure up or down to the nearest whole number, so in this case 11cm.

3 Following the diagram on the right, mark point 1 in the corner of the paper.

4 Use a set square or square edge to mark lines at right angles from this point.

5 Measure the distance R across to point 2 and the same to point 3.

6 Using the edge of a dinner plate, draw a smooth curve between points 2 and 3.

7 Using a metre rule, measure the distance L from point 2 and the same from point 3.

8 Mark the same distance L at several points, measuring down from the waist curve.

9 Join the hemline dots to make a smoothly curved line.

Cut out the shape and that's it, that's your own circular skirt pattern!

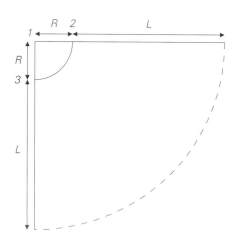

WORKING OUT THE AMOUNT OF FABRIC NEEDED

Once you have your pattern you will have to work out how much fabric you need – it will vary depending on your size and the length of the skirt.

1 Draw around the pattern piece to make a second one and mark one as the front and one as the back.

2 Draw on the markings as shown on the diagram with the zip mark 22cm from the waist edge.

3 Lay the pieces out as shown in the diagram below and measure the length and width the pieces take up. Fabric comes in several widths, so for narrow fabric you will need more length and for wide fabric you will need less. Work out your length requirement based on the most common fabric widths: 110cm, 140cm and 160cm. Remember, both pattern pieces need to be cut out on doubled fabric and the length you have worked out is for one layer of fabric, so you will need to double this to make all three panels for your skirt. As an estimate, you will need around 4 metres.

4 Lay out the pattern pieces and cut them out as shown, making sure the straight edges are on the straight grain and the front piece is cut on the fold.

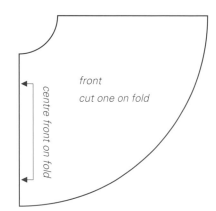

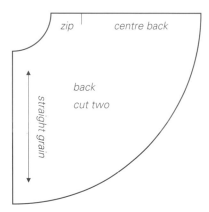

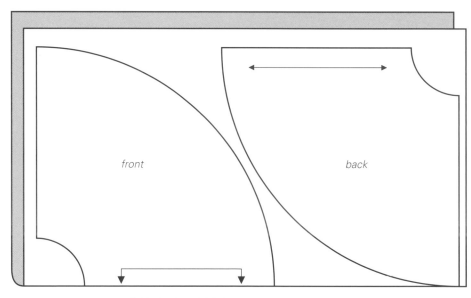

folded edge of fabric

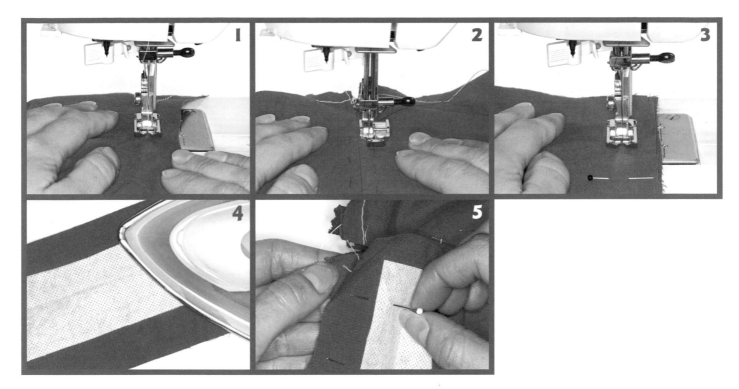

1 Cut out and immediately stay stitch the waist curves on all pieces.

2 Use 1.5cm seam allowances throughout unless otherwise stated. Sew up the back seam to the zip mark, leaving 22cm open at the top. Press the seam allowance open. Insert a centred 20cm zip in the back seam.

3 Sew up the side seams and press the seam allowances open. Try on the skirt and adjust the waist area if required by pulling up the stay stitching.

4 For the waistband, cut a strip of fabric 9cm wide by your waist measurement plus 6cm. Cut a piece of medium-weight interfacing 7cm wide by the same length, or use special waistband interfacing. Iron the interfacing to the wrong side of the waistband. Press the waistband in half along the length, then open it out and press under the seam allowance on one edge only.

5 Right sides together (so the interfacing faces up), pin one end of the raw edge of the waistband to the top of the skirt at the zip. Make sure that 1.5cm of the band protrudes across the zip. Pin the waistband around the skirt waist. You should have 4.5cm left at the other end to make the buttonhole in. If the waistband is too short you may need to ease the skirt waist slightly by pulling up the stay stitching threads to make it fit perfectly, and leaving 4.5cm of the waistband overlapping.

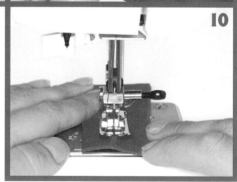

6 Sew the waistband to the skirt.

7 Trim the seam allowance and press it up towards the waistband. Don't trim the ends of the zip tape. Fold the waistband inside out and sew across the short end (the end you started pinning from in Step 5). This line of stitching should align with the teeth of the zip.

8 At the other end of the waistband, unfold the pressed-under edge. Sew across the short end, then turn the corner and sew along up to the zip, making a tab.

9 Clip the corners of the long and short tab ends of the waistband and turn it the right way out. Slip stitch the waistband to the seam allowance.

10 Make a buttonhole on the tab to fit your chosen button. Try on the skirt, work out where the button needs to be and sew it on. Hang the skirt on a clip hanger for 24 hours to let the fabric settle, then hem it.

Sew different

You can easily embellish this skirt with frills, ruffles or applique. You could wear the skirt with a 1950s net petticoat for a retro look, or make your own with frills or lace peeking out under the hem.

Customised T-shirt

I love customising clothes, transforming something boring from the back of the wardrobe or a charity shop into something special that you love and wear all the time.

You will need

Long-sleeved cotton T-shirt
Small scraps of felted wool, or other
    washable non-fray fabric, such as fleece
Scissors
Pins
Hand-sewing needle
Sewing thread to match the felt

Techniques

Felting, page 179
Hand-sewn appliqué, page 189
Felt appliqué, page 191
Slip stitch, page 29

1 Cut 17 leaf shapes from the felt.

2 Arrange six of the leaves in a flower pattern on the lower abdomen, or wherever you want, and pin them in place. Arrange nine leaves on the opposite shoulder, making some of them lie over the seams. Place one leaf on each cuff.

3 Using a tiny slip stitch and matching thread, sew the leaves in place. Be careful not to stretch the T-shirt fabric as you sew.

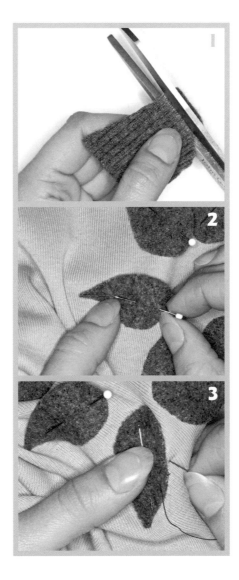

Sew different

Find leaf shapes in books about trees or use any other simple shape to make appliqué motifs. You could sew the motifs on using blanket stitch, or use other embroidery stitches to decorate the t-shirt.

You will need

Scraps of recycled wool felt in a range
   of co-ordinating colours
Scissors
Plain or velvet fabric
Matching or contrasting fabric
Pins
Hand-sewing needle
Tacking thread
Sewing thread to match each of
   the wool felt colours
Sewing thread to match the main
   cushion fabric
Sewing machine
Three buttons
40-cm square cushion pad

Pebble cushion

This cushion is fabulously textural and colourful – you can make it as zingy or as subtle as you like. It takes a while to sew on all the felt pebbles, so just do a few at a time.

Cutting list

43cm square of plain or velvet fabric. It is best to use something medium-weight and not too slippery or thin. The cushion shown is made from a piece of an old velvet curtain. Using the sewing machine, zigzag stitch around the edges of the square of velvet to prevent it fraying.

Two 43 x 28cm pieces of matching or contrasting fabric for the cushion back. Velvet is not recommended but furnishing cotton or linen would work well.

Techniques

Felting, page 179
Hand-sewn appliqué, page 189
Felt appliqué, page 191
Slip stitch, page 29
Button cushion, page 241

Sew simple

If you want to put some pebbles on top of larger ones, slip stitch them in position before tacking the whole pebble in place.

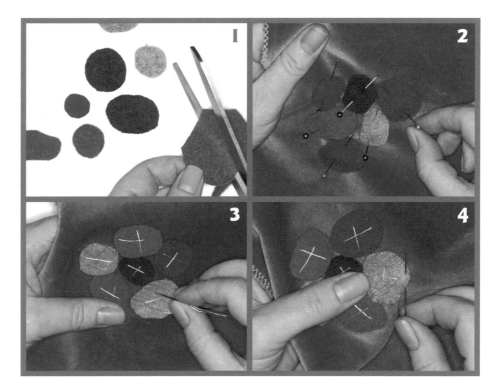

1 Cut out about 100 pebble shapes from the wool felt scraps, using the photographs as guides for shapes.

2 Starting in the centre of the square of velvet, lay the pebble shapes on the fabric, pinning each one in place as you go. Follow the main photograph or make up your own arrangement.

3 When you are happy with the arrangement of the pebbles, tack each one in place with a large cross. You can use the same thread for several pebbles as long as you don't pull it tight as you move from one pebble to the next.

4 Sew the central pebbles in place before you sew on the outer ones. Slip stitch each pebble in place using matching thread. Sew all the pebbles of one colour first so that you don't have to keep changing thread. Make up the button cushion.

Tools

On the following pages you will find detailed information on a range of sewing tools and equipment. You don't need to rush out and buy all of this, but do read through the pages and consider what you might find useful, now and in the future as you get more into sewing.

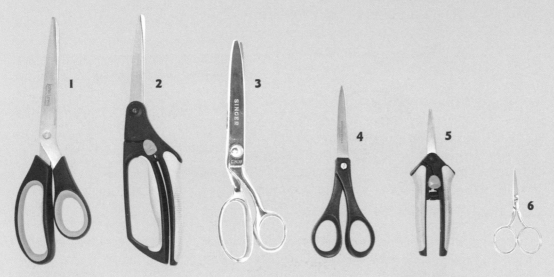

Cutting tools

1 Bent handle sewing shears are a must. The bent handles make it easy to cut fabric flat on the table. Drop-forged, all-metal ones are the best quality, but they are heavy.

2 Sprung shears are much kinder to your hands if you are doing a lot of cutting.

3 Pinking shears are scissors with zigzag teeth designed to leave a non-fraying cut. They are used for finishing seams and for decorative edging. Don't try and use fancy-edge paper scissors, they won't work on most fabrics.

4 Sometimes shears are too big and embroidery scissors too small, so a pair of basic, sharp scissors with pointed tips are very useful. Keep a separate pair for paper and paper-backed fusible webbing.

5 I like to use sprung snips for cutting little threads and making notches and clips.

6 A lot of the small sewing scissors on the market have quite chunky blades. I find these all-metal ones with fine, sharp tips the most useful type.

Invest in a set of scissor sharpeners, and use them regularly. Some sewing shops will offer a sharpening service. Wipe scissors clean of lint and any sticky residue from fusibles. Oil the joint with a drop or two of sewing machine oil if they start to creak a bit, but make sure to clean the excess oil off before you use them on precious fabric.

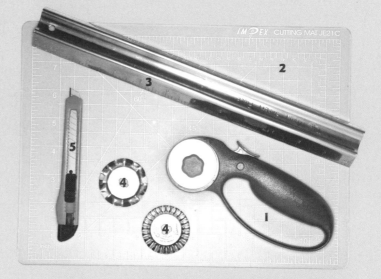

1 Rotary cutters are brilliant for cutting mainly straight lines – patchworkers use them all the time. Always use them with a self-healing cutting mat **2** and a safety ruler **3**. Replace the blades regularly and have them sharpened if you can. Look out for blades with pinked or fancy edges **4**. Follow the manufacturers instructions for safe use and for changing the blades.

5 An ordinary craft knife can be useful for ripping seams, sharpening chalk edges, cutting felt, leather and other thick materials.

For slash cutters, see pages 172–173.

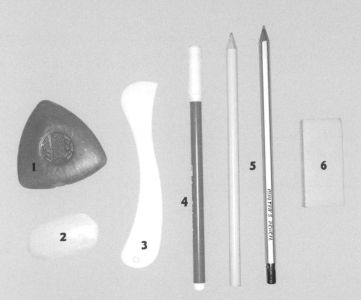

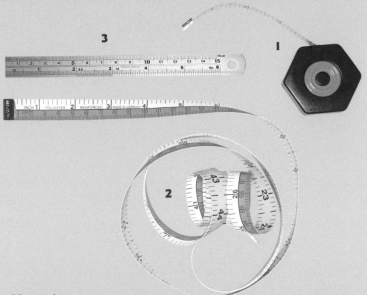

Fabric markers

1 Tailor's chalk comes in blocks, pencils and as a powder in a range of colours. **2** I like to use soap slivers for marking most fabrics (page 12). **3** A resin marker leaves a crease and a fine line and is designed for patchwork, but can be used in other places where a fold line needs to be marked. **4** Vanishing marker pens are very useful for temporary marking, but bear in mind that the marks don't last very long. For more permanent marking, try wash-out pens. To get rid of the marks without actually washing, try spritzing with water. **5** There are also water-soluble pencils available, and non-soluble marking pencils with strong, coloured lead for accurate marking on firm quilting fabrics, and an eraser **6** to remove the marks.

Measuring

1 A retractable plastic tape measure is fine for most things, but a wooden metre stick is very useful for measuring lengths of fabric. **2** A tape measure marked in centimetres and inches can be useful. A metal tape is good for measuring windows, but not much else in the sewing room. **3** A small metal ruler is useful for intricate work.

Dressmaker's carbon paper is used with a little spiked tracing wheel for transferring lines and markings from dress patterns. Place the paper coloured-side down on the back of the fabric. Put the pattern on top and use the tracing wheel to transfer the marks. Test your fabric to make sure the marks wash out.

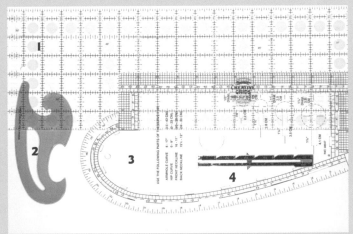

1 Clear plastic quilter's rulers are very useful and come in a range of sizes, but the markings are in inches only. They have non-slips pads on the underside, which makes them good for use with rotary cutters and for cutting lots of patchwork sections.

2 French curves are used for drawing in new necklines, armhole lines, etc. when adjusting patterns.

3 A set square or, even better, a combined set square and curve is very useful for pattern alterations.

4 A metal sewing gauge with a sliding marker is great for checking seam allowance widths and a host of other uses. It is one of my favourite tools.

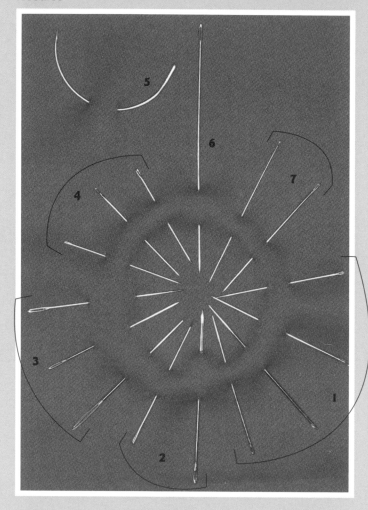

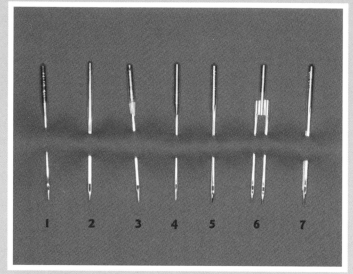

Hand-sewing needles come in a range of types and sizes.

1 For general sewing, use sharps, which normally come in packets of mixed sizes 5-10. The larger the number, the smaller the needle. Look for the best quality you can find as cheap needles may snag and bend. Throw out damaged needles safely – I use a film canister for damaged needles, pins and craft knife blades.

2 Leather needles have a chisel tip to help make the hole in the skin.

3 Embroidery or crewel needles have larger eyes that make them easier to thread, but don't use a too-big needle for the fabric as it will leave larger holes. A smaller needle will glide through the fabric.

4 Quilting needles are called betweens; they are shorter than general sewing needles and often very fine.

5 Curved needles are for upholstery.

6 Beading needles are long and fine to fit through tiny beads.

7 Straw or milliner's needles are very fine, but longer than betweens.

Machine needles come in many shapes and sizes. Like hand-sewing needles, you should use the right size for the thread and the fabric. The sizing system is rather odd as two systems are noted together.

1 The smallest size is 60/8 with the largest **2** being 110/18. 80 is a good general size for medium-weight fabrics. Fine fabrics need fine needles; usually 70 is good for silks, while 60 or 65 is best for really delicate fabrics like chiffon. Furnishing fabrics need 90 or 100, while really thick canvas and denim should have a strong 110 needle or a special jeans needle.

3 Ball-point needles are for stretch fabrics – the rounded tips don't cut through the fibres. They come in a range of sizes according to the fabric weight. Quilting needles are suitably fine and strong for the hard-work of a large quilt.

4 Leather machine needles have a chisel-tip, just like their hand-sewing counterparts.

5 There are lots of different needles for machine embroidery, including those for use with metallic threads. Check the needle type recommended for your chosen thread.

6 Twin needles are used for top stitching, certain decorative stitches (check your manual) and, with a special foot, for machine-made pin tucks.

7 Wing needles have blunt wings on either side that make a large hole as you sew. They are used for decorative effects on linen and similar fabrics.

Pins

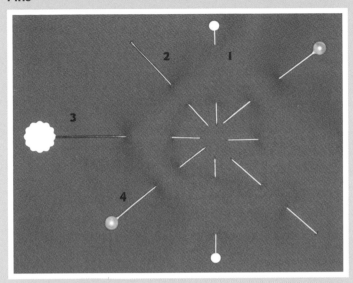

Beeswax

Waxing thread is explained on page 27. If you can't find beeswax in the sewing shop, try a DIY shop, as it is used for furniture polishing. Or make friends with a beekeeper. It doesn't need to be in a special container, just a lump kept clean in a box will do.

Needle grabbers

These amazing little rubber discs give you extra grip to pull needles through when sewing is hard work.

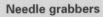

1 The best pins are long, glass-headed dressmaker's pins.
2 Long dressmaker's pins are okay too, but avoid standard, cheap pins, which are too short and thick.
3 Long, flat flower-head pins can be useful in fabrics like lace, but are too big for most sewing.
4 Decorative plastic-headed pins look very nice but aren't a lot of use. There is more about pins and pinning on pages 12 and 22.

Safety pins are useful for joining layers of quilts and for semi-permanent attaching before sewing. They vary in quality and cheap pins will be hard to get through fine fabrics and will cause damage. Small brass safety pins are my favourites for on-the-move sewing projects. Safety pins are also useful for threading cords and elastics. Pin through or knot on the elastic then feed the pin through the casing, making sure the pin is small enough to go through the casing.

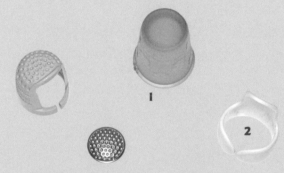

Stitch ripper

I prefer to use scissors to rip seams and open buttonholes, but many people use a stitch ripper for this. Longer-handled ones are slightly easier to use.

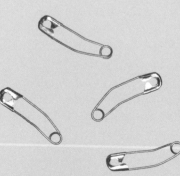

Quilter's curved safety pins are more expensive, but usually good quality and easier to get through thick quilt layers.

Thimbles

Thimbles are incredibly useful if you hand-sew a lot. They go on the middle finger of the sewing hand, to help you push the needle through the fabric.
Quilters use them a lot, so a patchwork shop is the place to look. I prefer plastic ones **1** or leather ones, but stick-on finger-pads come a close second. You may have to try a few before you find the right one, but persevere and enjoy the benefits.
2 A finger protector is what you need for the other hand if you stab yourself repeatedly.

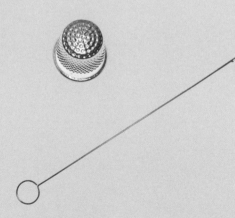

Loop turner

This gadget is for turning fabric tubes if you have forgotten to sew them with a cord inside.

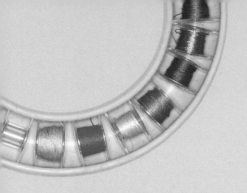

Bobbin holder

There are lots of different types of bobbin storage boxes. These plastic rings are very useful and portable.

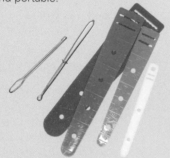

Bodkins and threaders

There are different sorts of plastic and metal giant needles for threading cords and elastics, rather than using a safety pin attached to the end.

Tweezers

Tweezers are useful for pulling out threads from ripped seams and for getting fluff and threads from the bobbin case. These sprung tweezers are designed for sewing rather than eyebrow plucking and they work well.

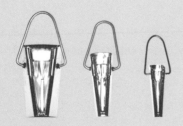

Bias tape maker

These are shown in action on page 72. They come in a range of sizes.

Pressing bars

These heat-proof plastic strips are designed for pressing narrow widths of bias tape. They can also be used for pressing and folding straight edges.

Dressmaker's dummy

A dummy is not cheap, but fantastic if you want to make clothes. They come in a small range of body-types so you should be able to find one suitable. Set the measurements to your smallest area, then dress it up in your underwear and pad it to match your shape. Quilt wadding and shoulder pads can be pinned on to add curves! An adjustable model can be changed to suit various people.

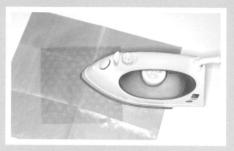

Teflon pressing cloth

This amazing cloth is non-stick and heat-proof, which makes it ideal for pressing anything with fusible webbing or interfacing that might otherwise stick to the iron.

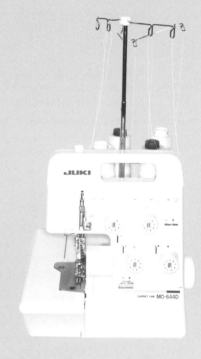

Overlocker

These special machines are designed for stretch fabrics, though can be used with most fabrics. They sew seams, overcast edges and trim the seam allowances in one go, which makes them ideal for dressmaking. This type of machine is used to make most shop-bought clothes, so take a look inside your garments to see how they work. Most have a stitch for the flat seams you see on T-shirt hems, and some have other stitches for different fabrics, such as sheers, to create frilled or decorative edges.

Sewing machine attachments

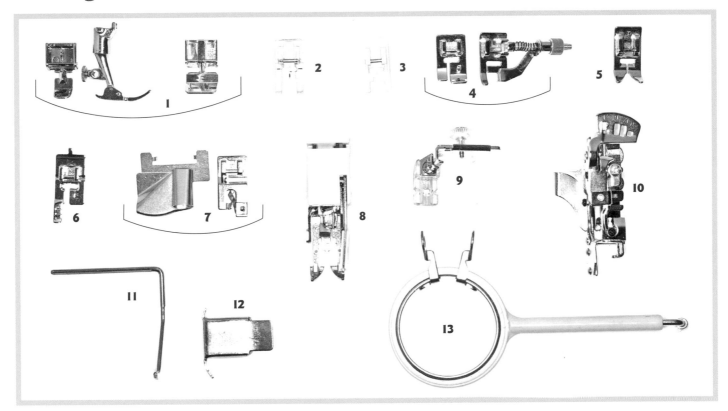

There are many feet and attachments available for modern machines. I have listed the most common ones here. To find out what is available for your machine, look on the manufacturer's website or ask for a catalogue. If you have a second-hand machine and unidentifiable feet, have a hunt on the Internet or ask your local shop for advice.

1 A zip foot is designed to allow you to get close to the zip teeth (page 84). If your zip foot is a narrow one then you can use it for sewing in any tight spots, but not for sewing zigzag stitch. Three types are shown here.

2 A clear view foot is designed for embroidery but I use one for all general sewing. They are invaluable when accuracy is vital.

3 A teflon-coated foot is for leather, vinyl and sticky fabrics, and anything that doesn't want to go under the foot properly.

4 Edge-guide feet can be for blind hemming or stitching in the ditch – anywhere where one side of the seam is thicker than the other, or where a line needs to be followed. Two types are shown here.

5 Zigzag foot. Depending on your machine, there may be no difference between a standard foot and a zigzag foot. Some standard feet only have a small needle hole so you will need the zigzag foot for any wide stitches. Sometimes zigzag feet have a channel on the underside to allow thick satin stitching to pass underneath.

6 A machine with auto buttonholing will have a special buttonhole foot. They are all different, so yours may not look anything like this.

7 Hemming and binding feet have attachments that roll and fold the fabric before it hits the needle, making rolled and folded hems with ease and sewing on bias binding in one step. I don't find them easy to use on floppy fabrics, but do try. Two types are shown here.

8 A walking foot is a clever contraption that has feed dogs in it, so the top layer of fabric is moved along just like the bottom layer. It stops the layers from shifting, which is essential when quilting or using velvet, which sticks to itself and doesn't feed properly.

9 Invisible zip feet are explained on page 89.

10 A ruffler foot is a frightening-looking contraption but is actually very easy to use. The ruffler foot works like the narrow knife pleat technique on page 133, and also makes very neat knife pleats. If you like pleats and ruffles, then buy one of these.

11 A guide bar attaches to the machine for use when quilting rows a set distance apart.

12 A magnetic seam guide fastens onto the machine and helps you keep a set distance from the edge.

13 This little hoop can be used for machine embroidery or darning.

Fabric guide

Fabric shopping can be overwhelming; there are so many different fibres, types, colours, textures and patterns available that it is hard to know where to start. Here is some information that will help make it easier to choose what fabric is best for the project you have in mind, and how to use it.

Silk is perfect for clothes, although heavy-weight silk fabric is available for curtains. Silk comes in many weights, from crisp organza and habotai **5**, which is good for linings. Silk dupion **6** comes in many colours and is often used for bridal wear. After pre-washing silk dupion can be used for most clothes. Silk/viscose mix velvet **7** is very soft, drapey and troublesome to sew. Light-weight silks **8** are available in patterns as well as lots of colours.

Thicker fabrics include silk tweed **9**, which is similar to wool but even more luxurious, and should always be dry-cleaned. Where possible, sew silk garments with silk thread, or a good quality cotton thread.

When sewing fine silks, use strips of tissue paper under the needle, and hold the fabric at slight tension to stop it snarling (page 58). Sew fine fabrics with a fine needle and a short stitch length. If creases are stubborn, iron the fabric while it is slightly damp.

Devoré velvet **10** is made with a silk base and synthetic pile. The pile is burnt away in a chemical process, leaving a fine base fabric. Treat it like habotai or chiffon.

Loose-weave fabrics **11** need to be handled with care. If interfacing is appropriate, interface the uncut fabric then cut out th pattern pieces. This will stop it stretching and reduce fraying. If fraying is a problem in any fabric, use an extra-large seam allowance and mark the seam line on it. Use a large needle and medium length stitch. A walking foot will help keep the threads together. Use thread tracing for markings if chalk or soap on the back doesn't work. Use bound seams (page 38) and bound hems (page 60).

Wool and silk

Wool is generally used for clothing and crafts, rather than for soft furnishings, though there are some hard-wearing upholstery wools. It comes in a range of weights, from fine wool crêpe, jersey and dress-weight **1**. These are all suitable for clothes, though they are not hard-wearing. To make wool more hard-wearing, it is often mixed with stronger fibres like nylon.

Wool suiting **2** is a better fabric for trousers and jackets, while wool tweed **3** can be very decorative, though it can get snagged easily. Wool fabrics should always be treated with care, as over-enthusiastic washing can felt or shrink it.

A lot of wool will be dry-clean only, though you can make it washable if you pre-wash it before cutting out (page 20). Knitted wool **4** fabrics should be interfaced with stretch interfacing and sewn with a stretch stitch, or on an overlocker. If the wool is scratchy, use a lining. If the fabric frays a lot, interface it before cutting out and finish the raw edges. Steaming will shape wool very effectively. Use silk machine thread or any good cotton or polyester thread.

Cotton and linen

Cotton and linen are hard-wearing, make good clothes and are mainly easy to sew. Cotton comes in a range of weights from sheer, crisp organdie **1**, traditionally used for christening gowns, to heavy canvas for tents and luggage. Liberty of London make high-quality printed cotton lawn **2**, perfect for clothes, while patchwork cotton **3** is heavier and best for crafts.

Batik **4** is a dye method often used on cotton or silk. Seersucker **5** has a crinkly texture and is traditionally used for summer clothes. Cottons can also be mixed with other fibres, including Lycra for stretch wovens **6**, which hold their shape well and can be used like normal woven fabrics.

Yarn can also be knitted to create jersey or T-shirting **7**, which should be sewn with a stretch stitch. Different weaving methods produce corduroy **8** and **9** and velvet **10**, which is good for curtains.

Cotton moleskin **11** is a slightly furry fabric suitable for tailored clothes. Ticking **12** is traditional fabric used for mattresses and is suitable for soft furnishings. Denim **13** is a hard-wearing fabric, usually made from cotton and dyed with natural indigo. It should be sewn with a special jeans needle and strong thread.

Linen, made from the processed stems of the flax or linseed plant, is available in many different weights from fine handkerchief **14**, medium-weight **15** to upholstery weight **16**. It hangs particularly well when cut on the bias. Linen creases readily and is best ironed slightly damp. For clothes, linings can reduce the creasing. Linen will shrink on the first wash. Because it frays so much, use a bound seam (page 38), extra-large seam allowances, or finish the raw edges as soon as the fabric is cut.

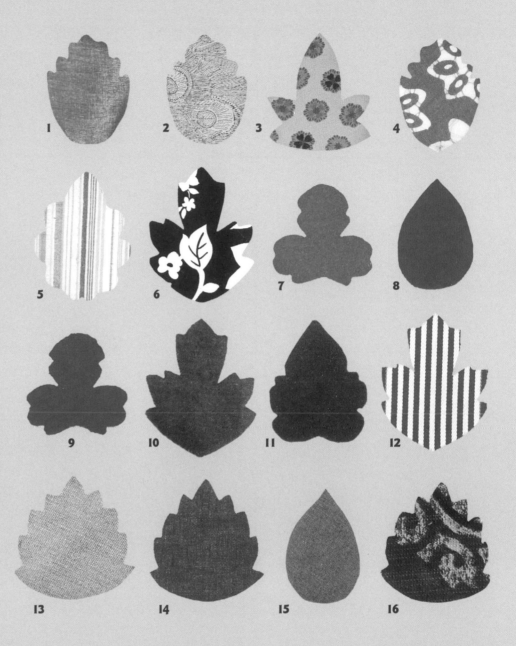

Eco fabrics

Hemp **1** is a plant fibre that is very similar to linen, though it creases less. It will soften with each wash. It requires far less water to grow than conventional cotton or linen, and is resistant to pest and disease.

Organic cotton **2** is available in a range of weights, mostly suitable for clothing, plus corduroy **3**, denim and jersey. It is often produced under fair trade conditions with less water and chemicals than in conventional production.

There are lots of fibre blends available, such as hemp mixed with silk **4** and sustainable bamboo or soya fibre **5** that are silky in texture and naturally breathable. Printed cottons with low-impact dyes **6** are also available and some producers use natural fabric dyes.

Peace silk **7** is produced from silkworms that complete their natural life-cycle, rather than being killed to wind unbroken lengths of silk from their cocoons. It is usually a natural golden colour rather than bleached white.

Organic wool is steadily becoming more available, and with it the guarantee that the sheep have been ethically farmed and the wool has no chemical treatments.

Recycled and vintage

Almost any sort of fabric can be found second-hand or vintage. Recycled fabrics include curtains, bedding and clothes.

Bed linen **1** can be cut up for large pieces of fabric. It is usually made from cotton or poly-cotton, so is quite durable and suitable for clothing or crafts. Wool blankets **2** can be felted (page 179) and dyed and used for crafts projects.

Old shirts **3** or other clothes are good for prints and nice fabrics in small quantities, while old silk dupion wedding dresses **4** are a particular favourite of mine because they yield so much fabric. Wool knitwear **5** is excellent for felting (page 179). Silk saris **6** are also a great source of yards of embroidered and decorative fabric, which I like to use for linings for special garments.

Curtains are a great source of large pieces of fabric and are a good way of getting 1950s and 60s fabrics like linen **7**, cotton velvet or barkcloth **8**, which has a textured weave. Other vintage fabrics are usually found in lengths or pieces, and can include printed cottons **9** and rayon, shiny satins (often from bedspreads), taffeta **10** and even lace and embroidered net **11**.

Heavy-weight

Most heavy-weight fabrics are designed for hard-wearing upholstery or curtains and are unsuitable for clothes – the exception being denim. Use that as an example of the type of garment you can make with heavy fabrics; they won't drape or hang, so only really work for very structured clothes. They are, of course, perfect for cushions.

Furnishing fabrics can be made of all sorts of fibres including linen, cotton **1** and synthetics, as well as many mixes, and are woven so that they won't stretch. They can be velvet **2** – either all over, or a velvet pattern on a plain background **3**. Chenille **4** is similar to velvet with a shorter pile.

Decorative weaves, like damask, can be cotton **5**, silk or synthetics **6**, or include metallic threads **7** (always change the needle after sewing metallics). Embroidered fabrics **8** are often expensive but look stunning. Medium-weight fabrics designed for cushions and crafts are similar to patchwork cottons and are usually printed **9**.

Sew the fabric with the appropriate thread depending on the fibre content (page 19), but make sure it is a good quality thread as curtain seams hold a lot of weight. Use a large needle and large stitches when the fabric is very thick. Most furnishing fabrics are dry-clean only, though you can try pre-washing (page 20). Press heavily-textured fabrics over a folded towel so the surface isn't crushed.

1

2

3

4

5

6

7

8

9

10

11

12

Synthetics and others

There are hundreds of different types of synthetic fabrics. Synthetic lace **1**, net **2** and tulle are best sewn with polyester thread with a narrow, short zigzag stitch, or very short straight stitch. Use large, flat-headed pins and thread tracing for markings (page 21). For fine lace and tulle, sew the fabric sandwiched between layers of tissue. Use a pressing cloth as these fabrics melt.

Very fine fabrics like chiffon **3**, either in polyester or silk, should be sewn in a similar way to lace and net. You may need to hold the fabric in slight tension (see page 15). Use a fine needle and cotton thread and don't reverse to fasten off. Chiffon is hard to sew - don't try a major project until you have succeeded with a smaller one. For cutting out, use old sheets or tissue paper as an under layer, place the fabric in a single layer, pin and cut through both layers, then discard the under layer. This stops the chiffon from sliding and stretching. French seams (page 40) are traditionally used for sheer fabrics and hand-rolled hems (page 58) are useful.

Polyester and other synthetic fabrics **4**, **5** and **6** are similarly hard to cut and sew. Follow the directions for chiffon. Hand-sewn hems are easier to handle than machine-sewn ones, which can twist and buckle. Fake fur **7** should be cut with a nap layout (page 244). Trim away the pile on the seam allowances to reduce bulk. Use soap slivers to mark the woven underside. Don't use iron-on interfacing and use a walking foot or reduce the presser foot pressure.

Leather **8**, fake suede **9** and vinyl fabrics **10** are best sewn with a Teflon-coated presser foot. Use fabric markers on the reverse side and be aware that stitch holes are permanent. Fake suede and fine real skin can be machine hemmed or use glued hems (page 57). Use polyester thread for all of these fabrics, and large needles if the fabric is thick. Leather is best sewn with a leather needle with medium-large stitches and use paperclips or mini-pegs to hold seams together. Store leather rolled or completely flat as creases are hard to remove. It can be dry-pressed on medium heat. Fake leather and suede should be pressed on low to medium heat with a pressing cloth.

Fleece **11** and craft felt **12** are usually all synthetic and neither fray. Fleece is stretchy, so use a stretch stitch and polyester thread. It can be backed with iron-on interfacing, which makes it easier to use. Craft felt is usually synthetic, non-colour-fast and not suitable for garments; try wool felt or boiled wool instead. Use soap for marking and iron-on interfacing to stiffen felt.

Interfacing, wadding and stuffing

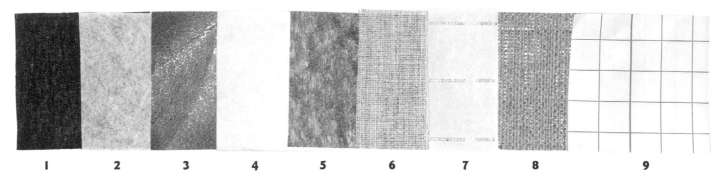

| 1 | 2 | 3 | 4 | 5 | 6 | 7 | 8 | 9 |

Interfacing

Interfacing is used on clothes to stabilise, strengthen and support fabrics. It is most commonly used on collars and lapels, the fronts of tailored jackets, on waistbands, around buttonholes and sometimes in bodices. In crafts it is used for strengthening and sometimes stiffening, for example in handbags. Special interfacing for waistbands and for pelmets is also available.

Interfacing can be iron-on or sew-in, light-, medium-, or heavy-weight (and variations), black, white, charcoal and skin colour, woven or non-woven, stretch or tricot (for jersey), reinforced with lines of stitching or made of animal fibre, called hair canvas.

1 Medium-weight woven iron-on

2 Medium-weight non-woven iron-on

3 Heavy-weight non-woven iron-on

4 Heavy-weight non-woven sew-in

5 Lightweight non-woven sew-in

6 Hair canvas

7 Waistband interfacing

8 Buckram

9 Stick-on pelmet interfacing

On the whole, it's best to obey the rules and use interfacing where it is recommended in a pattern. Though those of you with plenty of experience of dressmaking will know that there are certain fabrics and certain situations where you can do without interfacing. What I suggest is trying different types of interfacing and finding what works best for you, your preferred types of clothes and the kinds of fabrics you like to use.

If the pattern is for a soft fabric that needs interfacing to hold its shape, and you use a heavier fabric, you may be able to do without interfacing. I never interface facings, but then, I don't tend to use facings much anyway (pages 252–253).

Years of sewing have taught me that I don't like the way cheap, non-woven iron-on interfacing affects the hand of the fabric. It is the easy option, but not always the best, as it can leave bubbles and creases on the right side. It is usually okay for handbags and craft projects, and essential for appliqué (page 189), but for clothes I think sew-in is better. I'm willing to give woven iron-on a chance, as that seems to perform much better and can be cut on the bias. I used this for the couture hem technique (page 54). There is more about applying interfacing on page 255.

To use sew-in interfacing, cut the pattern piece without seam allowances and herringbone stitch (page 30) the interfacing into the seam allowances, catching just one or two threads of the main fabric. Then sew the pattern piece as if it was one piece of fabric. The same applies to traditional interfacings like silk organza or cotton lawn, except with these fine fabrics you can cut them to the same size as the pattern piece then sew them as one fabric and layer the seam allowances. Cotton or wool flannel can be used where a heavier interfacing is needed, or try recycling wool blankets, fleece jackets and cotton bedsheets. Hair canvas is a specialist interfacing for tailored jackets, but it can be used in place of heavy-weight interfacing for bags and craft projects or, of course, tailoring, should you wish to try it.

Super-firm interfacing for pelmets would also be useful for bags or for serious stiffening. A self-stick plastic version is also available, but it is non-washable. Traditionally, pelmets were made with buckram, which is hessian sacking fabric, stiffened with glue. This is still available in some places and is certainly interesting for its sculptural potential.

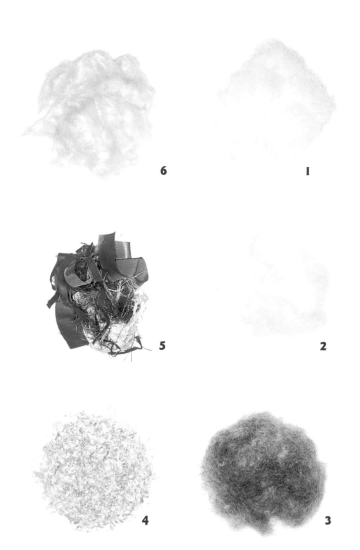

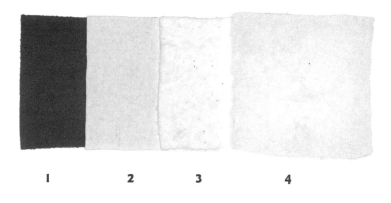

Wadding

Wadding is used to make quilts; either bed quilts, quilted fabric to be cut up to make clothing or for smaller projects like the Quilted Placemats (page 216).

Quilt wadding comes in polyester **4**, cotton **3**, organic cotton and, occasionally, wool. Polyester is cheaper, easily washable, thicker and easier to buy, but cotton is natural and breathable. Both have their pros and cons. Try each type on a small test quilt and see what works for you. There is more about wadding on pages 180–181.

You could try alternatives to conventional wadding, such as polar fleece **1**, wool **2**, or cotton flannel or recycled blankets. All of these will give a different result and feel.

Stuffing

Stuffing is used for pincushions, stuffed toys, cushions and in trapunto quilting (page 186).

Polyester stuffing **1** is cheap, washable, usually hypo-allergenic and is fine for most purposes. I prefer to use wool for anything non-washable. I like merino wool tops **2** (sold for spinning and feltmaking) for trapunto quilting and for small projects. Coarser wool **3** sold as stuffing is good for larger projects. Sawdust **4** is fine for pincushions and tailor's hams, as long as the fabric is a close weave. You can also use sand, but line the pincushion with calico first. Tiny fabric scraps **5** and thread ends can be saved up for stuffing.

Be aware of fire safety precautions if you sell or give away anything with stuffing. Polyester is the best bet in this case, particularly for children. Kapok **6** is a natural fibre, similar to cotton, and was traditionally used to stuff toys. It flies around all over the place and gets up your nose, in your eyes and lungs. I don't recommend it for anything bigger than a pincushion!

Sew different

A quilted fabric can be made by making a quilt sandwich (page 181) and sewing it by machine. The fabric can then be used like any other fabric to make clothes or crafts with. Machine quilting can follow formal, traditional patterns or be in very contemporary, swirling freehand designs.

Templates

Further designs for American smocking, page 177

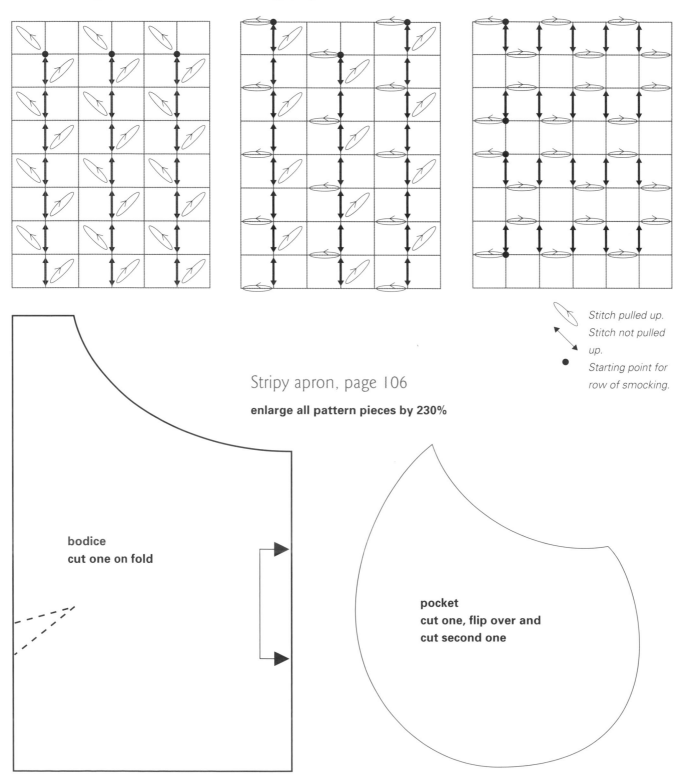

Stitch pulled up.

Stitch not pulled up.

● *Starting point for row of smocking.*

Stripy apron, page 106

enlarge all pattern pieces by 230%

**bodice
cut one on fold**

**pocket
cut one, flip over and
cut second one**

Pocket handbag, page 118 **enlarge all pattern pieces by 166%**

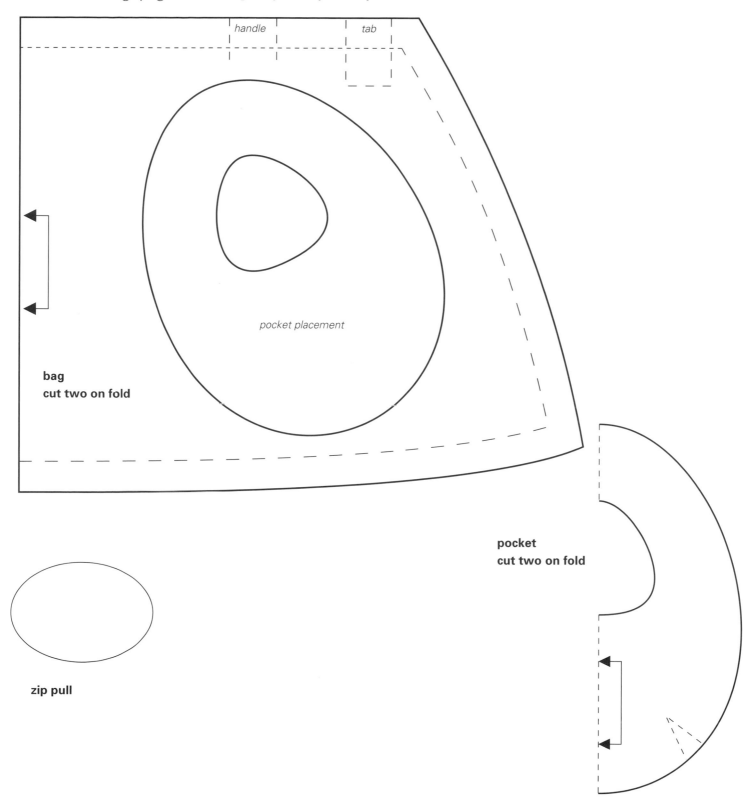

handle

tab

pocket placement

**bag
cut two on fold**

**pocket
cut two on fold**

zip pull

enlarge all pattern pieces by 150%

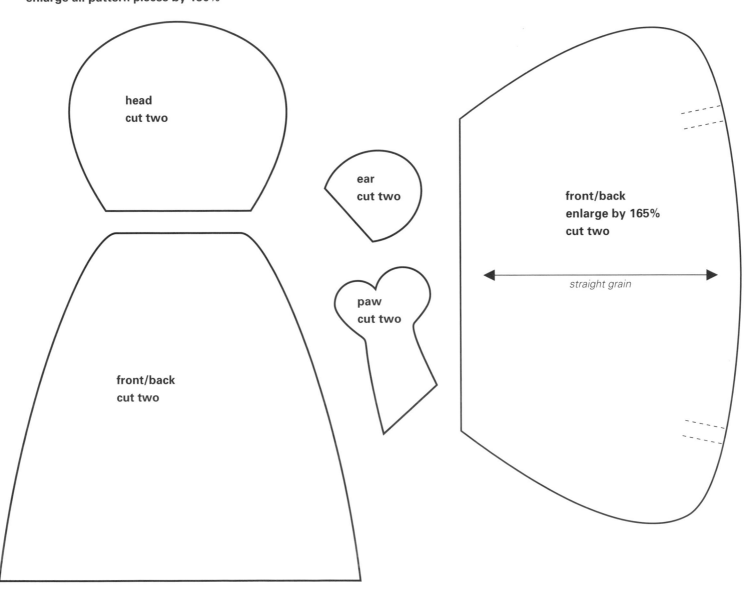

**head
cut two**

**ear
cut two**

**front/back
enlarge by 165%
cut two**

straight grain

**paw
cut two**

**front/back
cut two**

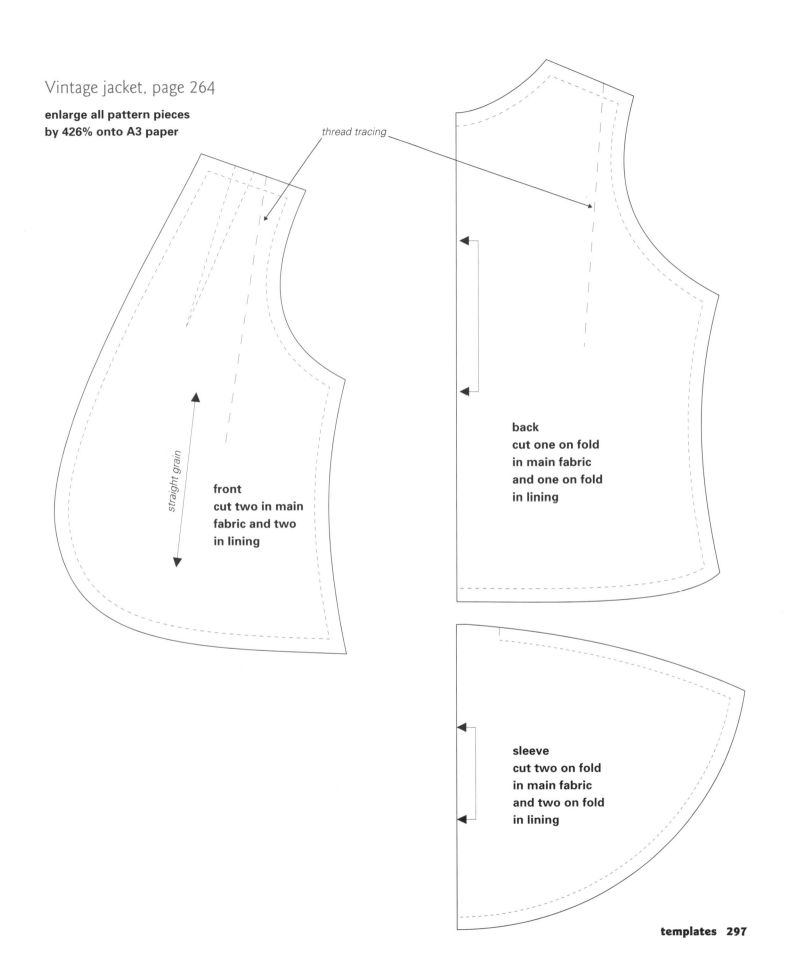

Vintage jacket, page 264

enlarge all pattern pieces by 426% onto A3 paper

thread tracing

straight grain

**front
cut two in main
fabric and two
in lining**

**back
cut one on fold
in main fabric
and one on fold
in lining**

**sleeve
cut two on fold
in main fabric
and two on fold
in lining**

Glossary

Alpaca Fabric made from the alpaca sheep.

Armscye The armhole line.

Bagged-out lining A lining that is sewn to the main fabric around the hem.

Barkcloth A crinkle-weave fabric, usually cotton. Popular in the 1950s.

Basting US term for tacking.

Bias The diagonal grain of the fabric.

Block A basic pattern piece of standard size that is used as the basis of a dress pattern.

Bodice The upper part of a garment, covering the chest and abdomen.

Bodkin A large needle, usually blunt, for threading cords and elastic.

Bolt A full roll of fabric.

Boning Stiff plastic strip used to shape strapless dresses.

Bouclé A loopy, loose-weave fabric.

Brocade A type of weave that produces an all-over pattern, usually a fairly heavy weight.

Brushed Fabric that has been treated with stiff brushes to raise a fluffy surface.

Buckram Stiffened hessian fabric for pelmets.

Bust point The position on a pattern or garment that should fit right on the nipple.

Buttonstand The area of a garment that has the buttons, often two layers of fabric.

Calico In the UK this means a cheap, unbleached cotton fabric. In the US it is usually a printed lightweight cotton.

Cashmere Yarn and cloth made from the wool of the Kashmir goat.

Casing A hem or channel with an opening for threading elastic or a drawstring.

Chambray A light fabric, usually cotton, often with blue/white warps and wefts.

Chenille Furry yarn and fabric woven from it.

Chiffon A very light, thin, transparent fabric, traditionally silk, now often synthetic.

Chintz Cotton with a shiny, glazed surface. Used to refer to printed floral fabric, but chintz generally refers to the glazed surface.

Colourfast A fabric dyed with a colour that will not run in the wash.

Cotton Fabric or yarn from the cotton plant.

Couture French term that means 'sewing', but usually refers to high-end, made-to-measure designer fashion.

Crêpe A fabric woven with very tightly spun fibres that crinkle up slightly, giving the fabric a slightly rough texture. Usually wool or silk.

Cross-grain The threads in the fabric that run from selvedge to selvedge.

Damask A brocade weave with only one colour where the pattern appears shiny on a matt surface. Usually cotton or linen.

Devoré A type of patterned fabric where the design is in raised velvet or satin with a sheer background. Also called burn-out.

Drape How the fabric hangs.

Dressform A dressmaker's dummy or adjustable mannequin.

Duchess satin A heavy-weight satin, usually silk or polyester.

Dupion(ni) A type of silk, often woven by hand, with small slubs or lumps on the yarn. Sometimes called raw silk. Shantung is similar, but lighter.

Ease Extra space allowed in clothes so you can breath and move.

Facings Small linings within specific sections of a garment.

Fashion fabric The main fabric in a project (usually dressmaking), used to distinguish between linings and interfacing.

Feed dogs The teeth under the sewing machine needle that grab and move the fabric backwards as you sew.

Felt Non-woven fabric made by compacting fibres. Traditionally made of wool or animal fibres; craft felt is usually synthetic.

Flannel Brushed cotton or wool fabric.

Flax The plant that produces linen.

Fleece Either the shorn wool of a sheep or other animal, or a warm, fluffy cloth created from synthetic or natural fibres.

Free arm Most machines have a removable plate so you can easily place sleeves and other tubular pieces over the free arm to sew around them.

French curve A type of curved ruler.

Gaberdine A tight-woven worsted fabric with a slight twill weave.

Gather To draw up the fabric by the use of pulling up stitches.

Grading Trimming seam allowances.

Grain The direction of threads in fabric.

Gusset A shaped piece of fabric sewn into a seam to give more movement, often used in underarms.

Ham A ham-shaped, firm stuffed cushion for pressing curves.

Hemp Yarn and cloth made from the fibres of the hemp plant.

Herringbone A weave that produces a zigzag effect on the fabric surface, or a type of hand-sewing stitch.

Horsehair A stiff braid or fabric made from horsehair, used to shape hems or garments.

Interfacing A special fabric used to support or stiffen the fashion fabric.

Interlining A fabric used for stiffening, supporting or adding opaqueness or warmth between fashion fabric and lining fabric.

Jacquard A type of weaving that produces brocade-style weave on a mechanised loom.

Jersey A knitted fabric, often T-shirt or sweatshirt material, often cotton.

Lamé A fabric woven with flat metal threads, often now synthetic but originally silk.

Lawn A fine, tightly-woven cotton cloth, either plain or printed.

Layering Trimming the seam allowances.

Linen Yarn and fabric from the flax plant.

Lining The inside layer of fabric in a garment, which helps keep the garment in shape, makes it more comfortable and hard-wearing.

Markings Symbols used for directions in patterns.

Merino Soft wool from the merino sheep.

Microfibre Extremely fine synthetic yarns that are often silky in feel.

Mohair Yarn and cloth made from the spun hair of the angora goat.

Moiré Fabric with intentional look of water staining, sometimes called watered (silk).

Muslin In the UK this is a cheap, loose-weave cotton fabric. In the US it is a toile.

Nap The pile or long fibres on cloth that run in one direction.

Notch A mark on a paper pattern that helps with garment construction.

Notions US term for haberdashery.

Organdie Usually cotton in a tight weave, transparent and stiff.

Organza Silk or synthetic woven fabric that is transparent and slightly stiff.

Overcasting A hand or machine stitch that finishes a raw fabric edge.

Peplum A flared or frilled extension to a bodice over the hips.

Pile A raised surface, like fur, found on velvet.

Pinking Cutting fabric with pinking shears.

Piping Fabric-covered cord inserted into a seam as decorative trim.

Piqué Medium-weight knit or woven fabric with raised design.

Placket The part of a garment where the fastenings are attached.

Poplin Slightly-ribbed cotton fabric.

Princess seam A seam curved over the bust.

Rayon An early manufactured fibre, made from wood pulp.

Remnant Short lengths of fabric left at the end of the roll and sold cheaply in shops.

Revers The turn-back pieces of a collar on jacket, where the wrong side shows.

Satin A type of weave with a smooth surface on the right side.

Seam allowance The amount of fabric between where you sew and the raw edge.

Self-fabric The same fabric as the garment.

Selvedge The finished, woven edge of the fabric that doesn't unravel.

Serger American term for overlocker.

Silk Fabric or yarn produced from the cocoons of silkworms.

Sizing/size A finishing treatment on fabric to stop it creasing when in the shop. Needs washing out before use.

Sleeve roll A firm, sausage-shaped cushion for pressing sleeve and trouser seams.

Sloper US term for Block.

Stabiliser A non-woven fabric used behind the main fabric in machine embroidery.

Stay stitching Stitching to keep a curved or bias edge from stretching.

Stay tape Straight-woven ribbon used to stablise seams that might otherwise stretch.

Stitch in the ditch A line of stitching running over or right next to a stitched seam.

Tab Extension of fabric, usually for fastenings.

Tafetta A crisp, plain-weave fabric, traditionally silk, now usually synthetic.

Tailor's tacks Loose stitches through layers of fabric, cut to leave bits of thread as semi-permanent markings.

Tapestry needle A thick, large-eye needle.

Thread count The way of measuring the number of warp and weft threads in a cloth. A high thread count means a fine weave.

Ticking Cotton fabric for mattresses.

Toile A rough garment made to test the fit.

Top stitching A line of decorative stitching visible on the right side of the garment.

True bias 45° diagonal across the fabric grain.

Tulle Finely-woven net fabric, either synthetic or silk. Softer and more drapey than nylon net.

Tweed Usually a wool fabric, medium-heavy weight used for coats. Often has flecks of other colours in the yarn.

Twill A weave, often with diagonal lines on the right side, includes satin and denim.

Velvet Fabric woven with a pile. Can be cotton, silk or synthetic.

Viscose A type of rayon.

Voile Lightweight, crisp fabric.

Warp The lengthwise threads when weaving fabric.

Weft The crosswise threads when weaving fabric.

Whale The ridged parts of corduroy.

Worsted A yarn and fabric made from wool.

Yardage The amount of fabric needed for a garment or project.

Yoke The shoulder area in a garment, often cut in a separate piece.

Reading

Books

Betzina, S. *More Fabric Savvy*, Taunton Press, 2004.

Betzina, S. *Fast Fit: Easy Pattern Alterations for Every Figure*, Taunton Press, 2004.

Cargill, K. *The Curtain Bible: Simple and Stylish Designs for Contemporary Curtains and Blinds*, Quadrille, 2003.

Conlon, J. *Fine Embellishment Techniques: Classic Details for Today's Clothing*, Taunton Press, 2001.

Guerrier, K. *The Encyclopedia of Quilting and Patchwork Techniques*, Search Press, 2001.

Holman, G. *Bias-Cut Dressmaking*, Batsford, 2001.

Mullin, W. & Hartman, E. *Sew U Home Stretch*, Little, Brown & Company, 2008.

Mullin, W. & Hartman, E. *Sew U: The Built by Wendy Guide to Making Your Own Wardrobe*, Little, Brown & Company, 2007.

Reader's Digest New Complete Guide to Sewing: Step by Step Techniques for Making Clothes and Home Accessories, Reader's Digest, 2003

Thomas, M & Eaton, J (ed). *Mary Thomas' Dictionary of Embroidery Stitches*, Caxton, 2001.

Vogue Sewing Revised and Updated, Sixth and Spring Books, 2006.

Wolff, C. *The Art of Manipulating Fabric*, Krause Publications, 1996.

Ordoonez, M. *Your Vintage Keepsake: A Csa Guide to Costume Storage and Display*, Tech University Press, 2001.

Magazines

Selvedge (www.selvedge.org)

Threads (www.taunton.com/threads)

Sew Today (www.sewdirect.com)

Suppliers

Broadwick Silks
www.thesilksociety.com
Specialist silk supplier.

Whaleys of Bradford
www.whaleys.bradford.ltd.uk
UK-made fabrics, mainly wool.

Cloth House
www.clothhouse.com
The finest fabric shops in the UK.

Stef Francis
www.stef-francis.co.uk
Hand-dyed threads and fabrics.

VV Rouleaux
www.vvrouleaux.com
Luxury ribbon and trimming specialists.

Klein's
www.kleins.co.uk
Professional haberdashery and tools.

MacCulloch and Wallis
http://www.macculloch-wallis.co.uk/
Specialist fabrics, tailoring and haberdashery.

Cheap Fabrics
www.cheapfabrics.co.uk
Just what it says – cheap fabrics online.

Rag Rescue
www.ragrescue.co.uk
Vintage fabrics and trimmings in small pieces.

Wingham Wool Work
www.winghamwoolwork.co.uk
Yarn, wool tops and wool stuffing.

Liberty
www.liberty.co.uk
Fine quality printed cotton lawn and retailer of Rowan and other patchwork fabrics.

Hemp Fabric UK
http://www.hempfabric.co.uk/
Organic hemp and other fabrics.

Cotton Patch
www.cottonpatch.co.uk
Patchwork supplies, tools and fabrics.

Organic Cotton
www.organiccotton.biz
Fair-trade organic cottons in a wide range of different colours.

Harlands Organic Furnishings
www.organic-furnishings.co.uk
Specialist suppliers of organic fabrics, mainly for soft furnishings.

U Handbag
www.u-handbag.com
Bag handles, fastenings and other supplies.

Clothkits
www.clothkits.co.uk
Pre-printed clothes kits ready to cut and sew.

Morplan
www.morplan.com
Equipment and supplies for fashion design.

John Lewis
www.johnlewis.com
Nationwide department store, often with fabric and sewing sections.

Online resources
www.schoolofsewing.co.uk
www.englishcouture.co.uk
Specialist sewing schools.

www.BurdaStyle.com
A dressmaking community with free patterns, project sharing, resources and columns.

www.taunton.com/threads
Extensive sewing resources and forum.

www.patternreview.com
Thousands of reviews of sewing patterns.

www.decadesofstyle.com
Re-issued patterns from the 1910s–1950s.

www.voguepatterns.com
www.mccall.com
Current sewing patterns.

www.craftzine.com
Craft resources, forums and information.

www.etsy.com
Online shop for independent makers. Also good for buying supplies.

www.marthastewart.com/crafts
Wide range of craft projects.

www.embroiderersguild.org.uk
The Embroiderers' Guild.

www.textilearts.net
Textile arts in the UK and beyond.

www.thetextiledirectory.com
Website to accompany a great book of textile resources in the UK.

www.twistedthread.com
Organisers of fabric and sewing events.

www.quiltersguild.org.uk
The Quilters Guild.

The Victoria and Albert Museum (V&A)
www.vam.ac.uk
An extensive collection of textiles and fashion, and lots of online resources.

Blogs
These are just a few blogs – there are thousands out there to explore.

A Dress A Day
www.dressaday.com/dressaday.html

Erica B's DIY Style
www.ericabunker.com

Ruth Singer
http://mantua-maker.blogspot.com/

Whip Up
http://whipup.net/

Index

Acknowledgements

I am hugely grateful to my editor, Kate Haxell, for her ability to organise my chaos into this beautifully presented book. I must also thank Muna Reyal for needing to learn to sew so much that she commissioned this book – I hope she actually uses it! Likewise my agent, Sophie Gorrell Barnes, who brought myself and Muna together to create this book and who shared the enthusiasm and excitement of its early stages. Thanks also to both photographers, Jan Baldwin and Dominic Harris, who have created stunning work that I am delighted with, and to Louise Leffler for the great book design.

My family are always wonderfully supportive of my wild adventures in fabric and I would not have made it to the end of this book without the support of Mog Singer and Gillian Spraggs. I would not have made it even to the start of this book without Penny Eaton, who taught me to sew in the first place, for which I am eternally grateful.

Over the years I have been inspired and educated by many sewing writers, tutors and designers, and acknowledge my debt to all who have sewn before me. I never expected to be writing about sewing and made a tentative start to writing about my own work on my blog two years ago, inspired then and now by Erin's marvellous blog, A Dress a Day. I want to thank all my blog readers for their encouragement and positive feedback during the writing of this book, and other blog writers in the amazing online craft community who have provided ample fabric-based distraction in the name of research.

Students are an essential part of my workforce and I have to thank Zoe Murphy, Amy Thackeray, Christina Agbenorhevi and Jolene Huber for their help with aspects of this book. Thanks also to everyone else who helped and supported along the way, including many long-suffering friends who have been sorely neglected during the making process.

Many thanks are owed to Rowan Fabrics for Amy Butler and Kaffe Fassett fabrics used in some of the samples and projects.

Ruth Singer is an accomplished textile designer-maker who creates bespoke and limited-edition textiles for interiors using organic and vintage fabrics. She is a skilled textile historian and uses traditional hand-sewing skills like pleating, quilting and appliqué to create unusual textures and sculptural effects. Ruth has shown her work at exhibitions including the Crafts Council's 'Origin' show and at New York Design Week. Her work has also appeared in publications including the *Guardian* and *Elle Decoration*.